J. Randy Taraborrelli bega[...] age of seventeen. Formerly editor-in-chief and publisher of *Soul* magazine, he was most renowned for his three-part authorized biography of Diana Ross entitled *Diana: The Untold Story*, which appeared in the magazine. This spawned the book *Diana* and he has also published a second book, *Motown – Hot Wax, City Cool and Solid Gold. Cher* is his third book and he is presently touring the USA for his fourth book – a biography of Carol Burnett. J. Randy Taraborrelli lives in Los Angeles, California.

J. Randy Taraborrelli

CHER

Pan Books
in association with Sidgwick & Jackson

First published in Great Britain 1989 by Sidgwick & Jackson Ltd
This edition published 1990 by Pan Books Ltd,
Cavaye Place, London SW10 9PG
in association with Sidgwick & Jackson Ltd

9 8 7 6 5 4 3

© J. Randy Taraborrelli 1986 & 1989

ISBN 0 330 31483 1

Printed in England by Clays Ltd, St Ives plc

For my sister, Roz

contents

'I was this kid who came from no place. Not particularly attractive, not particularly talented. But I had . . . something.'

– Cher

It's difficult to reconcile Cher's past with her Academy Award-winning present. The days when she co-starred in two TV series with Sonny Bono, and starred in one of her own – back when she was, to use her own words, 'queen of a mediocre medium' – seem light years ago. But, oh, the memories . . . .

Back in the mid-seventies, Cher was a regal recording and television star who sang of 'gypsies, tramps and thieves', of 'dark ladies' and 'half-breeds'. With great flair, she paraded about in skimpy, bugle-beaded, sequinned Bob Mackie gowns that were always short on fabric and propriety and long on skin and scandal; no one on television ever wore so little and had so much made of it. 'But it was all a joke,' Bob Mackie now explains. 'How could anyone take it seriously – a woman walking sexily down a long ramp wearing a low-cut gown with her bellybutton showing, wrapped in an expensive fur and singing "He Ain't Heavy (He's My Brother)"? Cher and I never took it as seriously as everyone else did.'

When Mackie sang the praises of her armpits ('She has the most beautiful armpits in the world. As much as anything else, I designed for them'), it didn't seem like Cher had much more than that on the ball, as if it was easy being a television star. It wasn't. 'She spent a lot of time throwing up because of nerves,' says a former associate.

When she became a media star, Cher also became the heroine of a sensational – and ridiculous – real-life soap opera. After she and Sonny separated, she claimed that he had held her in 'slavery' all those years they had been together and that in doing so he had somehow violated the Thirteenth Amendment of the United States Constitution. It was said that her then-boyfriend, record industry tycoon David Geffen, encouraged her to make such an outrageous accusation. 'If things were so tough,' Bono says today, 'why wait until you're at the epitome of success and know you can go it alone before finally leaving. I'm suspicious of that. I really am.'

Cher was naive and afraid; Geffen took her under his protective wing. She certainly had a lot to learn: she was twenty-seven and still didn't know how to write a cheque. When she and Geffen threatened to move into the Bono mansion *with* Cher's estranged husband and his new live-in girlfriend, Sonny took the hint and moved out.

Geffen was soon banished from Cher's life and became just another footnote in her romantic history. Three days after her divorce from Sonny, she married Gregg Allman, a scruffy rock and roll musician and leader of The Allman Brothers band, in Las Vegas. On their first date, Gregg passed out over a plate of Chinese food. 'Isn't this sweet? He's so tired,' Cher said innocently. But Gregg turned out to be a junkie, a heroin addict like her father. They separated. They got back together. She filed for divorce. They got back together again. 'Being married to Gregory was like going to Disneyland on acid,' Cher said later. 'You knew you had a good time but you couldn't remember what you did.'

When Cher found out she was pregnant with his child, she was confused and kept the news to herself; could she bring a baby into this circus of a marriage? On what she remembers as one of the worst days of her life, her press agent rang at six o'clock in the morning – just in time for morning sickness.

'Cher, do you know Gregory's divorcing you?' he asked, not realizing that he was actually breaking the news to her that she would probably be a single mother.

'No,' she said, without missing a beat. 'Hum a few bars, will ya?'

That's the kind of humour that gets her through the tough days.

Cher got back with Gregg again and then promptly starred with her ex-husband Bono in a prime-time television variety series. America tuned in: Sonny and Cher joked about her pregnancy and yucked it up about 'that other guy' to whom she was now married. As Cher became an oversized cartoon figure (gossip magazines and tabloids printed such scandalous headlines as 'Cher Says "God Forgive Me for What I've Done!"' and 'Please Sonny, Don't Take My Child!'), an incredulous public lapped it all up; here was a woman whose life made absolutely no sense whatsoever and she wasn't even ashamed.

At night, the pregnant Cher would go home after spending a long day at the television studio with her ex-husband Bono, 'the dictator'. She would put their blond-locked daughter named Chastity to bed and then throw her drugged-out husband into a running shower where, like a cranky baby, he would sleep noisily in a corner. Disgusted and alone, Cher would also retire to a restless sleep.

Such was the life of this television icon.

'You can take everything I know about men and put it on the head of a pin, and still have room left for The Lord's Prayer ...'
— **Cher**

One wonders if Cher will ever work her way through the hostility she still feels toward Sonny Bono. In recent years, she's been damning him, calling him 'a slave master'. Part of her therapy seems to be to hang on to years of anger and then vent it all twice a year in television interviews. But Cher's intimates know that when she's damning Sonny, she's really working on forgiving herself.

Cher is still embarrassed because she believes she was manipulated by the man she loved. She naively allowed herself to enter into a contract with Sonny Bono that outlined her role as a hired hand and *employee* of Cher Enterprises, entitled to vacation time she probably never got. And no sick days. Now she believes Sonny only loved her for the first couple of years of their relationship, and after that he loved a money-making machine he had created called 'Sonny and Cher'. Did he mastermind her career for her because he believed it was what she really wanted, or was he just trying to build himself a dynasty? In Cher's mind, this important question remains unanswered.

Cher's nagging fear – as irrational as it may seem, considering her present success – is that everything she has achieved today and will ever achieve in the future is somehow intrinsically tied to what *he* was in her past. She won't openly admit to this, but the fear is there. All she will say is, 'He does have that prestigious place in my life, and I have to work it out if it takes all my life.'

He was twelve years her senior and found her in 1962 when she was Cherilyn Sarkisian, a spoiled, smart-mouthed sixteen-year-old brat who had run away from home and was just recovering from a bout of hepatitis. In her own words, 'I didn't know my ass from first base.'

She'd had an unusual life despite her tender years. She'd already made love to Warren Beatty, and she did so just because her mother and girlfriends thought he was handsome. The fact that he was making $150,000 a picture was pretty impressive, too. She tracked him down and Beatty added her to his list of sexual conquests in 1962, the year the Hollywood Press Association gave him its Sour Apple Award for being unco-operative and rude, the year he was on the rebound from having been dumped by both Joan Collins and Natalie Wood. To him, Cherilyn was just another teenager passing in the night; he treated her dispassionately. 'And *what* a disappointment *he* was,' she told everyone.

Sonny was able to cut through her rebellious bravado like a shark through jellyfish. Underneath it all, he found a shy, awkward child, a high school dropout who felt inadequate. She was dyslexic but didn't know it at the time. Her childhood was dotted with periods of deprivation, poverty and an unsettled home life: her father was a convict and a heroin addict whom her mother would marry three times.

Bono craved success, recognition and respect from a cutthroat record industry. Cher ached for financial security and Tony Curtis's mansion. She had all of that and more after 'I Got You Babe' became Sonny and Cher's signature song and gimmick in 1965. They wore outrageous clothing, snubbed The Establishment and represented the so-called Love Generation. They acted as if they were married – they weren't. Sonny acted like a teenager – he wasn't; by 1965 he was thirty.

There were more hit songs ('The Beat Goes On' and 'Bang, Bang (My Baby Shot Me Down)', two flop movies (*Good Times* and *Chastity*) and, by the end of the decade, Sonny was an egomaniac, Cher was a puppet, and together they owed the government $190,000. To pay the bills, husband radically recreated his wife into a television star, the Cherokee Indian with deadpan manner and sarcastic wit. 'The Sonny and Cher Comedy Hour', on CBS, became a highly rated Seventies' phenomenon.

Cher turned her entire life over to this shrewd man, and he in turn made her a star. 'He controlled the whole situation,' she has said. 'He booked the gigs and managed every phase of the work. To me, it was all too much hassle . . . a pain in the ass.'

Today, Sonny Bono is mayor of Palm Springs, California, and Cher is . . . well, Cher. Sonny doesn't like talking about his ex-wife. 'Talking about Cher is a no-win situation,' he explains. 'We're not two friends who validate each other or help each other . . . and I don't feel that comes from my end. She recently did an interview for her perfume line and somehow attached it to "Sonny would never let me wear perfume" or some victim point of view, which I think is more an angle of how to be interesting than a way of being open. I just wish she wouldn't talk about me, period.'

But Cher keeps hammering away.

'He was this Sicilian dictator husband. I could say *nothing*. I got *suicidal*,' she told *Cosmopolitan*.

'I felt like a slave who was being set free,' she said of leaving Sonny in an interview with Barbara Walters.

'If I ever get over living with him, it will be a miracle,' she told *Rolling Stone*.

Maybe, in her estimation, Sonny was a lousy husband, but then again, Cher has to admit today that 'I know more about acting than I do about relationships, and I don't know anything about relationships.' In his defence, Sonny Bono was a brilliant career strategist who gave Cher the one thing he says she begged him for: not a happy marriage, not a cosy home life, but F-A-M-E. Unfortunately, fame for fame's sake can be a rather empty experience. In 1975, Cher picked up a copy of *Time* magazine with her picture on the cover, read it and then tossed it into the trash after deciding, 'What a bunch of shit! This story is about someone who has nothing.'

> 'I kept thinking, I must be Dinah Shore. I'm not really very talented, but people like me anyway. There are some people who are respected because their talent is so mammoth. That's a luxury.'
> – Cher

Can a girl from the wrong side of the tracks who got off to a bad start have a career in Hollywood as a serious actress? Cher decided that she would never know the answer to that question unless she finally got serious about it and started to *act*. 'I mean, you can call yourself a brain surgeon but unless you're doing surgery, it doesn't mean shit.'

In 1982, she decided to accept the challenge of a respectable acting career and promised that she'd never again violate her talent by making a 'fool' of herself in Las Vegas for $350,000 a week. She took a $345,000-a-week cut in pay and appeared on Broadway in *Come Back to the Five and Dime, Jimmy Dean, Jimmy Dean* and then in the low-budget film version of that play. 'I'm an actress now,' she proclaimed after getting decent reviews for her work. 'A serious actress.' It was a mad and sudden turnaround, a dash toward integrity, a 'serious' bill of goods being sold by a girl who was primarily known for her bellybutton. But nobody was buying.

In November 1983, she and some friends decided to sneak into a Los Angeles movie theatre to see the audience's reaction to a 'trailer' – a film advertisement shown prior to the main feature – for her first major film, *Silkwood*. Cher had said that she believed that her work in the film, her portrayal of confused, lonely lesbian Dolly Pelliker, was her most assured to date; she was proud of herself.

Meryl Streep and Kurt Russell appeared on the screen with accompanying introductions and brouhaha. The audience applauded graciously, acknowledging the artistry of both actors – Streep's probably more so than Russell's – because these stars registered as *serious* in the minds of the young crowd.

With great ceremony, the voice-over added, '. . . and co-starring Cher!'

'Oh, *sure! Cher!* She'll be just *great* with Meryl Streep,' someone snickered. The entire theatre erupted into laughter as the humiliated butt of their jokes sank deep into her seat.

Despite the prevailing cynicism, Cher acquitted herself magnificently in *Silkwood*, revealing great range and ability in a performance that, much to her amazement and that of her harsher critics, garnered an Academy Award nomination. In her next movie, *Mask*, she won accolades for her performance as a boozing but compassionate mother, Rusty Dennis. Today, she insists flatly that 'I will never be better than I was as Rusty Dennis.' It wasn't an easy working experience, though, and she grew to despise *Mask* producer Peter Bogdanovich, a man she calls 'a pig'. The two battled constantly. Last year, Cher said that at the root of the professional differences was, in her opinion, the fact that he 'likes women who are real subservient, who look at him and think he's the greatest thing that ever happened'. Ultimately, Cher claims, the producer was miffed because she wouldn't go to bed with him.

In his defence, Peter Bogdanovich says, 'I'm just another guy she can kick around in the media, like Sonny, and get laughs with. I think she's a troubled woman. I think she's been unhappy, been hurt, been through the mill. There's a huge difference between people's private lives and public personas.'

Undaunted by her experiences with *Mask*, Cher churned out three more films in eighteen exhausting months. She was the lusty Alexandra Medford, one of Jack Nicholson's trio of lovers in *The Witches of Eastwick*. She didn't think she'd get the part; on her fortieth birthday she got a call from the producer, George Miller, who told her that Jack Nicholson didn't want to work with her because she was unattractive. Now she believes that was a lie but then, as Chastity and her friends sang 'Happy Birthday' over the candlelit cake, she cried. Eventually, she did the movie and now she wishes she hadn't.

She played a tough but sensitive over-worked public defender named Kathleen Riley in *Suspect* with Dennis Quaid. She's not completely happy wih that film and neither were the critics.

And then came *Moonstruck*, and the Academy Award for Best Actress. Whoever would have believed that Cher would one day win an Oscar? Even in her most golden slumbers, she probably never imagined herself at a podium brandishing that gold statuette in front of a cheering audience of her peers. Certainly with her portrayal of New Yorker Loretta Castorini, the love-struck Italian book-keeper, Cher proved that she can act and that she's a resounding success in her new profession.

But the road ahead could still be paved with uncertainty and only time will tell if Cher will continue to challenge herself and sustain a career as an actress. If she continues to handle it all with the heart and intelligence she's demonstrated in the last five years, it would seem that her chances of longevity in Hollywood are good. The fact that she hasn't demanded a 'star-turn' in any of her films speaks volumes about her seriousness as an actress. She doesn't feel compelled to be the centre of attention; she doesn't have to be the focus of every scene. She's satisfied with being part of a superb ensemble, confident and secure enough in her ability to offer co-stars a chance to shine, a chance to make a good movie. Unlike many of her peers in Hollywood, Cher seems to understand that great stars don't always make good movies – but good movies usually make great stars.

'You must be confusing me with someone who gives a shit.'
– Cher (a line from *Mask* she added to the script herself)

Today, in her continuing quest to secure her identity as a serious film star, Cher knows what's expected of her but continues to send out signals that are decidedly mixed. She wants to be 'a serious actress' but she appears in music videos wearing sleazy sado-masochistic-looking leathery outfits that do nothing for her credibility. In form-fitting leotards and outrageous hairstyles, she continues to do seductive Jack LaLanne Health Spa commercials in which she warns America, 'You *promised* to shape up.' She does exotic advertisements for her perfume, Uninhibited, in which she wonders when she'll be too old to wear a motorcycle jacket.

One of her directors thinks she's a schizophrenic. 'Anyone who could be a personality and wear those clothes and who is also a serious actress has to be a schizophrenic,' observes Peter Yates, who directed her in *Suspect*.

When her good-looking twenty-four-year-old Italian boyfriend Robert Camilletti was arrested for attempting to run down a snooping *paparazzo* with her Ferrari, she went down to the police station and personally posted bail. There she sat, stewing in her solitude in a Los Angeles station house, waiting for her hot-headed mate to be released from the pokey. Photographers swarmed all over her but she ignored them, acting as if they didn't even exist. Academy Award winners just don't do these kind of things.

'But I do whatever I want with my life and I don't give a shit who knows it or who cares,' she declares. 'As long as I'm happy doing it, everybody can just kiss my ass. . . .'

That doesn't leave much room for interpretation – or does it?

Sonny Bono said in November 1988 that, in his opinion, Cher is the shrewdest media manipulator in Hollywood. 'She can shoot off her mouth, do it effectively and even be offensive but still create a curiosity,' he says. 'And the media loves it because she's Peck's bad girl.'

An interesting analysis, but not the total picture. Cher is as insecure as she is smart. When she tells her public to become 'affectionate' with her 'buttocks', she's really exercising an old adage: when in doubt, *shout*. She's a woman who desperately wants to do a lot with her time on this earth but is constantly afraid of how she is being perceived by her public. Regardless of what she says to the contrary – her personality is definitely duplicitous – she does 'give a shit', so much so that it hurts.

Rather than allow herself to be discouraged by rejection and criticism, Cher always comes out fighting and swearing like a teenager in a bar on a Friday night. She talks a good game, blows off steam, kicks sand in peoples' faces, but inside she's just a frightened child who, as capricious and superficial as it might sound, just wants to do what she wants to do when she wants to do it. In other words, there's still a lot of leftover insolence from those days when she was a teenager who wanted to dance the night away with her live-in mate Sonny at the Whiskey-A-Go-Go on Sunset Strip in Hollywood. But Sonny was an adult who had to work the next day; he was anxious to sleep. So she'd tell him to go to hell and then storm out alone and find someone else – somebody like Warren Beatty – to have a good time with, just to prove the point that 'nobody tells me what to do and when the hell to do it'.

Twenty-five years later, she's in Hamburg, Germany. It's one o'clock in the morning. She and some male friends venture into the red-light district and come across a sign prohibiting men under eighteen and women of all ages. So Cher stuffs her hair under a cap and pencils in a moustache and five o'clock shadow. She and her friends stroll through the off-limits area and get front-row seats at a steamy sex show – because 'nobody tells me what to do and when the hell to do it'. She likes her life – the fact that she gets to have it all her own way – but understands that it's not for everyone. 'If everyone was like me, if everyone did what they wanted, who would there be to work the tollbooths?'

> 'In this business it takes time to be really good – and by that time, you're obsolete.'
>
> – Cher

Most celebrities have one career and are remembered for it, or one facet of it: Lucille Ball is best known for 'I Love Lucy'; Diana Ross will probably always be thought of as a recording artist, not an actress; Carol Burnett and Mary Tyler Moore are best remembered for their television series in the Seventies. But Cher has had many cycles of success, each career even more interesting than the one preceding it. She is what they call in Hollywood 'a survivor'. It's as if she keeps rising like a phoenix from the ashes of whatever happened to be her last commercial reincarnation. She was a successful recording artist in the Sixties, a popular if not beleaguered television star in the Seventies and now, in the Eighties, a powerful movie star.

'Listen, if Cher had been on the Titanic,' Joan Rivers has quipped, 'they'd have cleaned off the ice and kept on sailing.'

Her obvious talent notwithstanding, maybe the reason for Cher's longevity is that she has always responded to show business's basic premise just to be entertaining – just to be famous. Isn't it fascinating that, today, our perception of Cher isn't as frivolous as it was, say, in the Seventies when we wondered how low-cut her next gown would be? It seems that we've accepted 'the kid who came from no place' for what she is, and that now we respect her and even like her for it as well.

How satisfying it must be for her to know that she hasn't really changed at all . . . that, indeed, *we* have.

J. Randy Taraborrelli

June 1989

part one

THE PUPPET

'I was chicken and poor, which isn't hip because you haven't got clothes and all that stuff. So I developed SMB – Smart Mouth Bitch. Which meant, "Don't screw with me because I may not have clothes or what everyone else has, but I can cut you to ribbons." When I met Sonny, I had that reputation. I gave him the finger. . . .'

– Cher

In 1962, Southern California was a hotbed of fresh and exciting music. The first so-called 'beach party' movies were drawing hordes of young people into local theatres, where they could escape to teen paradises. Annette Funicello and Frankie Avalon became new teen idols as they surfed and partied on the sand with their irresponsible friends, none of whom ever seemed to have parents or other authority figures.

The period's carefree abandon was reflected in the record charts: Joey Dee and the Starlighters were dancing 'The Peppermint Twist'; Gene Chandler proclaimed himself the 'Duke of Earl'; Shelley Fabares swooned over 'Johnny Angel'; Little Eva popped her fingers to 'The Locomotion'; and Bobby 'Boris' Pickett and the Crypt-Kickers demonstrated that poor diction could sell too with 'The Monster Mash'.

Philadelphia was once the music capital, thanks to Dick Clark's 'American Bandstand', but now Fifties teen stars packed up their hero sandwiches and migrated to Los Angeles in search of their futures. This was an awkward period in popular music, after Elvis Presley's salad days and before the Beatles ushered in the next big rock movement. In Detroit, Berry Gordy was beginning to experiment with something he would call 'The Sound of Motown'.

Los Angeles had a sound of its own. The City of Angels had become a bastion of hard-driving rhythm-and-blues music with legendary forces recording for Southern California record companies: Fats Domino and T-Bone Walker at Imperial; The Five Keys and Shirley and Lee at Aladdin; Etta James and The Cadets at Modern; and Larry Williams, Little Richard, and Don and Dewey at Specialty. It seemed as if record companies were rooting themselves all over the city. Sunset Strip was dotted with young, aggressive, record tycoon 'wanna be's' like Herb Alpert, Lou Adler, Frank Zapa, Phil Spector, Doris Day's son Terry Melcher, and a little storm of ambition named Sonny Bono.

Salvatore Philip Bono was born in Detroit, Michigan, on 16 February 1935, the youngest of three children (he has two older sisters) born to Santo and Jean Bono. His mother called him Sonny and the name stuck.

He was about as full of himself as it was possible to be, or at least that was the impression he gave to his little clique of show business friends and associates. Few knew that inside that brash interior beat the heart of a very insecure man. He was a pint-sized *paisano* struggling for recognition in a stifling record industry that seemed filled with giants. His friends would later recall that he was constantly nagged by feelings of self-doubt and inadequacy. He wanted desperately to believe that he had natural ability as a songwriter and producer. Long nights were spent at the piano, searching in his mind for original melodies. But somehow the *magic*, or whatever it's called that happens when a natural artist settles his mind on his craft and sees inspired results, never seemed to be there.

He could be a great mongrel, though. Borrowing a little of this riff, and a lot of that one, he could compose a song that seemed respectable to the uninitiated, even though he knew in the far corners of his soul that his art was not the result of any real invention. It pained him, but it didn't dissuade him, because he was a fighter, a hot-blooded, strong-minded Italian.

In 1942, with World War II raging, Santo Bono packed up and left Detroit with his family, and moved to Los Angeles in pursuit of work. Food and clothing were rationed, times were desperate, but at least on the shores of sunny California Bono could find employment as a factory line worker – the kind of job for which nearly every man in Detroit was skilled but few could secure, because there were just so many jobs to go around. His wife would help make ends meet with her work as a beautician. But the marriage was not able to endure these difficult times, and the Bonos were soon divorced.

Sonny went to high school in Inglewood, California. He was a poor student, never able to concentrate on his work, always dreaming about what he would do with his life after he finished with his education. His father wanted Sonny to be respectable, to have a trade he could earn a living at, but Sonny wanted to write songs. He wasn't certain he was any good at it, but still, it's what he wanted.

Juvenile delinquency was becoming a major civic concern, and so when Sonny announced to his parents that he was quitting school in the eleventh grade, they were furious. 'Is *this* how we raised you?'

They considered him a fine candidate for a job as a street cleaner. He became a delivery boy for a grocery store instead.

He fell in love and on 10 November 1954, he got married. His wife, Donna Rankin, was eighteen years old, a year younger than he was. In 1958, they had a daughter, Christy.

But by 1955, Sonny Bono's life was a series of odd jobs and disappointments. His talent as a songwriter was unrefined. By July of that year, the country was swept away by a force that pop music purists called 'the greatest evil of all time' – rock and roll.

Bill Haley, a cherub-faced singer and guitarist from Bono's home state of Michigan, wasn't the first rock-and-roll star, but he was the one responsible for bringing this musical genre into America's consciousness. His July 1955 hit record, '(We're Gonna) Rock Around the Clock', became an anthem for youngsters everywhere.

The next couple of months would be confusing ones in popular music, with Mitch Miller and Pat Boone sharing chart action with The Platters and The Four Aces. Soon, though, rock and roll's strength would be overwhelming, and that music would become the dominating force in entertainment.

Sonny Bono watched and listened as all of this unfolded. *Look* magazine reported that the phenomenon 'has dragged music to new lows in tastes', and that Elvis Presley, the duly appointed 'king', was 'as vulgar as they come'. A *New York World-Telegram* columnist insisted that this new music was 'contrived by corrupt, indecent men'. *Variety* agreed wholeheartedly, adding that 'the lyrics to rock-and-roll songs are nothing more than obscene phrases set to music'.

'It's just a fad,' conventionalists agreed. By the late Sixties, this 'fad' would be generating $2.5 billion a year.

To support his young wife, Bono worked as a waiter, and then as a butcher's assistant, and finally as a truck driver. He was quickly becoming bored by his pattern of nonproductivity; he wanted to make money, and he wanted to make a lot of it. He may not have had an education, but he did have strong instincts and great street sense. There's an astounding demand for rock and roll, he reasoned, and with a serious investment of both time and money, he could probably make a living as a songwriter, producer – hell, maybe even a singer. 'There's no mystery to making money off this thing,' he said enterprisingly to his friends. 'There's a market out there; all ya gotta do is fill its needs.'

Specialty Records had its offices on Sunset Boulevard in Hollywood. Harold Battiste, a black man and former schoolteacher turned jazz musician, had recently arrived in town from New Orleans. He was hired as an artist relations consultant for Specialty, a record label best known for its rhythm-and-blues line-up.

Producer and writer Bumps Blackwell envisioned the lead singer of one of the company's acts, The Soul Stirrers, as a solo artist. He and Battiste booked a recording date for the young Mississippi-born vocalist. When Specialty's owner Art Rupe attended the session, he was furious at what he heard Blackwell producing. The thin, handsome black singer was crooning to a lush, melodic track. His voice was elegant, tender. But Rupe believed that blacks had to sing, or 'holler' as he called it, like Little Richard if they were to make money for his label. 'If he can't sing like Little Richard, he's off the label,' Rupe told Battiste and Blackwell.

Bumps Blackwell was disgusted by Rupe's narrow-minded philosophy. He took the singer to Keen Records, another local label. That's where Sam Cooke became a recording sensation with 'You Send Me', which, released in September 1957, hit number one by December. The record knocked Elvis Presley's 'Jailhouse Rock' off the top of the charts, sold a million copies, and embarrassed Art Rupe more than a little.

Rupe instructed Battiste to 'do *something*' to, as Harold put it, 'save face for Specialty' by creating a new image for the label, one that would be youthful and exciting and would bolster its roster of artists. Battiste had been impressed by the young trucker Bono, who stopped by the company from time to time on his way to work, pedalling 'his non-songs'. He wasn't as interested in Sonny's musical prowess as he was in his driven sense of determination and magnetic charisma.

'He was charming as hell,' said Harold Battiste with a grin. 'His personality was contagious. I knew that if he could make me believe his songs were great – and they really weren't, though they weren't terrible – he could sell a recording artist to a disc jockey, because Sonny had style. Man, the cat had *boundless* energy and ambition to *be* somebody . . . *anybody*, as long as it was a person who'd be respected.'

Sonny Bono was twenty-one years old when Battiste hired him as his partner in the artist relations and promotional division of Specialty. The first order of business: dig into the recording vaults to see what else Sam Cooke might have waxed for the label, material that Art Rupe still owned, and then issue it to an eager Cooke audience to cash in on the singer's growing popularity. They released 'I'll Keep Coming Back to You' by Cooke, and it sold a million copies. Art Rupe was pleased. Sonny Bono was in.

His job would be to screen song material submitted to the label and determine which song would be best suited to the company's artists, a little-known lot (with the exception of Little Richard). He would also write as much material as he could convince Battiste was strong and commercial. The next few years would be a whirlwind of record releases and writing/producing credits for Bono; a body of work that, many rock historians maintain, deserves further examination.

Much to his wife's chagrin, Sonny invested the money he made at Specialty back into the company, and into record labels he'd started in hopes of competing nose-to-nose with 'the big dogs'. Working triple duty for Specialty, and for his own little companies – with names like Go Records and Name Records – Sonny Bono became a recording artist (using pseudonyms like Ronny Sommers and Don Christy – taking the first part of his wife Donna's name, and his daughter's). He stole every one of Steve Lawrence's mellow nuances and coloured his work with them for compositions like the ill-fated 'I'll Always Be Grateful' and 'As Long as You Love Me'.

He wrote seven songs for single release by Specialty artists, none of which was immediately successful (one, 'She Said Yeah', recorded by Larry Williams, was later recorded by The Rolling Stones; another, 'Ko Ko Joe', by Don and Dewey, would find greater fortune when recorded by The Righteous Brothers in 1963). Undaunted by his inability to strike pay dirt on the pop charts, Bono continued to write and produce for artists with names like The Marathons, The Pearlettes, and Prince Carter. No luck.

'Sonny was one persistent fellow,' Harold Battiste remembered. 'He was used to getting kicked around because no one took him seriously. He had a big mouth and nothing to back it up – or at least that's how it seemed. But Sonny was a rock and roller, man. He was pursuing a dream a lot of people were chasing. There were dozens and dozens of cats in Los Angeles like Sonny, most of whom never made it big, most of whom ended up back at the grocery store baggin' food for old ladies. Not this guy. . . .'

Sonny once remembered seeing a photograph of himself taken in 1958 right before a concert date. His short dark hair was meticulously slicked back in the rock-and-roll tradition; his tailored white suit somehow seemed too big for him – it looked as if he were swimming in it. He stood in a dingy dressing room, and on a wall behind him hung framed photographs of Elvis Presley and Bo Diddley. Bono had stars in his eyes. 'Some band would play their set and I'd sit and wait my turn,' he recalled. 'Then I'd go out, stand in front of the microphone, and have my big chance, my big break. I looked at myself in that picture and I said, "Damn, Bono, did you really want to be a *singer*?"'

As a singer, Sonny had one major problem: he couldn't sing. It didn't matter what kind of gimmick he utilized or whom he tried to emulate. It was as if all that could even remotely be considered *musical* had somehow been sapped from his voice by the Lord above. Somehow, he knew that if he were going to be significant in the competitive entertainment world, it would be as a songwriter and producer. But the problem with that logic was that he wasn't a very talented or inspired songwriter or producer either.

Sonny Bono needed *something*, a hook, a magnet of some sort that would draw people to him, but that would also be so magnificent in itself it would draw attention away from him.

When Bono started his own Rush Records label after his other two record companies failed to make the grade, he issued only four singles (two he recorded himself as 'Don Christy' and two he produced for the team of Don and Dewey). His friends told him that his rock-and-roll music wasn't edgy enough; it was a bit too sophisticated; it didn't jump from the grooves . . . it just seeped into nothingness. But when Bono visited radio stations to try to convince programme directors to play his music and Specialty's music, he was in his element. As far as public relations went, Sonny Bono was a natural. He could talk a drowning man into a glass of water.

In 1963, Sonny took a job as promotion and artist relations representative for Philles Records, a burgeoning company owned and operated by Phil Spector. Spector was originally from New York, but he migrated to Los Angeles when the trends in popular music seemed to flow westward. He was an odd, ambiguous character his associates either revered or despised. 'There are only two kinds of people in this world,' Spector would say. 'Winners and losers.' Determined not to become the latter at any cost, Spector became notorious for his unethical business practices. He was a shrewd and, some have insisted, not a very trustworthy businessman.

That assessment, of course, comes from a lot of people who aspired to what Phil Spector had in the palm of his hand: success.

He was a thin man with a boyish-looking face that belied his sense of enterprise and ambition. His eyes never seemed to make contact with those of the person he spoke to. He was a suspicous man, but remarkably talented, trusting only his instincts.

He became a tremendously influential force in contemporary popular music. Before the onslaught of Motown's aggressive black sophistication and the British invasion's cockney-goes-pop, his music was one of the major forces in the entertainment world. Spector's story is a complicated one of musical groupings and record labels that flourished on both coasts, but by the time he and Sonny Bono crossed paths his operation was based in Hollywood, at Gold Star Studios on Santa Monica Boulevard.

His genius was best interpreted by The Ronettes, The Crystals, Bob B. Soxx and the Blue Jeans, and Darlene Love. The music was imaginative, vibrant, youthful, and, most notably, *loud*. He double- and triple-tracked instrumentation, and echoed the whole potpourri with reverberating voices. The result was called 'The Wall of Sound', and it was instantly identifiable as Spector's signature. All his major stars were black (he's white) and the music had the bite and grit of soul but the sweeping grandeur and 'class' of classical. It was all produced with assembly-line accuracy and with tremendous attention to detail and quality.

Harold Battiste worked at Philles Records as a session pianist and he encapsulated Spector's successful music this way: 'It was just a lot of echo when you boil it all down. It was using whatever was the available technology at the time to get the biggest sound. Gold Star couldn't do many things, but echo was one thing it could do very well. You could always get a *ton* of that.'

Jack Nitzsche, who arranged all of Spector's major chart successes, put it a bit more technically to writer Ken Barnes: 'Four guitars play eighth notes, four pianos hit it when Spector says roll; the drum is on two and four on tom-toms, no snare, two sticks – *heavy* sticks, and at least *five* percussionists. And all of that in the greatest echo chamber in the world.'

And that would be precisely the way Sonny Bono would arrange everything he'd do in the next couple of years. He was influenced by everything he saw and heard at Gold Star and around Phil Spector. Never had he seen a man wield so much power over so many. Spector became Sonny's idol, and he began to emulate his style of dress. Whereas before he had been a conservative person, he began to wear bright, mismatching colours and sunglasses – or *shades*, if you will. In years to come he would also copy Spector's concern, obsessive as it was, for sound quality in music, often recording a song as many as thirty times just to get the right sound (pity the poor singer who would have to bear the brunt of such excesses).

Unfortunately, Sonny Bono was also awed by Spector's private life. The man was as eccentric behind closed doors as he was in public. Tremendously jealous of any attention paid to anyone else by someone he valued, he was regarded by more than a few associates as a crazed monarch. 'That man was crazy as a dog run down,' said producer Snuff Garrett, an A&R (Artist and Repertoire) representative for Liberty Records, where Spector once worked.

Ronnie Spector was an ordinary-looking Brooklyn girl named Veronica Bennett before she met and fell in love with the president of Philles Records. Spector took this youngster and her limited vocal ability and transformed her into a pop star, as lead singer of a group called The Ronettes. The female trio, known for their 'other-side-of-the-tracks' posturings, became pop music's premiere vamps in the early Sixties. Bennett was a sight. All hair and eyeliner, she poured herself into a hip-clinging skirt and slipped into stiletto heels to walk out onto stages and melt into Spector masterpieces like 'Be My Baby', 'Walking in the Rain', and 'Do I Love You?'.

'Hey, they looked like three sluts, the Ronettes did,' Snuff Garrett noted. 'No nice way to say it. But, damn it, they made Spector a whole lot of money. . . .'

Sonny was enthralled with the way Phil Spector became obsessed with the waif Bennett. Bono was from the old Italian school, the one where you graduate with honours only if you know how to make a woman do what you want her to and make her believe it's what she wants as well. Stereotypical, yes, but that was Sonny Bono. So when Veronica Bennett became Ronnie Spector, Bono started to see the light. This woman's husband made her a star, and in becoming one she drew more attention to him than she did to herself. Her songs would bullet up the charts, but not so much because Ronnie was a resourceful singer as because she was Phil Spector's creation.

And as Spector's prize, she would allow him to choose her wardrobe, decide on the imagery she and her vocal cohorts projected, and mastermind her life and career.

At its peak (or nadir, depending on the way you look at it), Phil Spector's obsession with his wife became dangerous. He pulled her out of The Ronettes just when the trio was about to embark on its biggest and most prestigious concert tour as an opening attraction for the Beatles (they went without her) — not because he had decided that she should be a solo star, but because, as she has put it, 'He couldn't bear the idea of sharing me with the world.' He forced her into an early retirement.

Spector lavished his wife with money, jewels, servants, and a palatial mansion. But she was not permitted to socialize or leave their home without an escort. She could not listen to popular music in the house (only classical). In order to brainwash her completely of her show business identity, servants were instructed to refer to her as 'Veronica' instead of 'Ronnie'.

This Svengali approach to show business was nothing new, of course. While Spector was glossing up his wife, Berry Gordy had his eyes set on a skinny youngster from the Brewster Projects in Detroit. She was a member of the Supremes, but to Berry Gordy she was on her own planet. She would be nurtured, groomed and styled. She would have a romance with Gordy. And she would become Diana Ross.

It should be noted here that Gordy and Spector were very much alike in terms of the way they perceived the exploitation of popular music and their preoccupation with quality control. The difference between the two was that Gordy was a writer and producer who also had great business acumen and long-term vision, while Phil Spector was brilliant at writing and producing music for the period, but had no head for business – he burned many a bridge behind him – or commercial versatility.

Sonny Bono was influenced by Spector, and somewhat by Gordy. What he may not have realized, though, is that both of their women, Bennett and Ross, went on with their lives and careers feeling exploited and manipulated.

Ronnie Spector complained bitterly about the way her husband treated her, how he forced her into wasting the best years of her youth. Diana Ross, in years to come, would have the same kinds of charges to level at Gordy. Diana was thirty-seven years old by the time she freed herself from his control, and by that time, according to her, she couldn't even purchase an automobile without his signature – even though she had generated millions of dollars for Motown Records.

In time, however, Ronnie Spector and Diana Ross would have nothing on a woman named Cher.

... and cher

In November 1962, Sonny Bono was visiting the Programme Director of popular KFWB Radio on Hollywood Boulevard, the area's pre-eminent rock-and-roll outlet. Bono frequently socialized with the station's disc jockeys, who held his future in their hands. After all, they could transform whatever records Bono happened to be promoting into hits if he could convince them to play those records frequently enough. Whenever an important 'jock' went to work, that's when Sonny Bono punched in. If it was six o'clock in the morning, Sonny would be a 'Johnny-on-the-spot', coffee and doughnuts on hand, a stack of records in the trunk of his car and, for each one of them, a sales pitch on his lips.

One evening after work, Sonny was to meet some friends in a coffee shop next to KFWB headquarters. Bono had not been getting along with his wife lately and had been spending little time at home with her. One of his friends brought Cherilyn Sarkisian along to the coffee shop.

Cherilyn was sixteen years old and not much to look at. She was rail-thin with toothpick legs that were slightly bowed and better suited to trousers than skirts. A jutting nose was her most prominent feature. Her face was blemished, though she gallantly tried to cover the imperfections with a thick coat of meticulously applied make-up. She did have a winning smile, even though her teeth were arranged imperfectly, but her deeply brown and extraordinarily expressive eyes were her best physical assets. She dressed like a frumpish tomboy with no sense of style or finesse. She just *was*.

'There's Sonny!' someone said as he entered the coffee shop.

She glanced up over her menu and, for the next few seconds, she felt that her heart had stopped beating. Later, she would remember that 'everything around him went to star filter, like in the movies'.

Never before had she seen a man like this and even at her tender age she'd attracted more than her fair share of the male species. Way back when she was fourteen, her girlfriends used to brag about their sexual exploits, telling her that she, too, could have a satisfying sex life even though she was barely into her teens. The boy would respect her as long as she didn't surrender totally to her hormones, as long as she 'didn't go all the way'.

'But if you're going to go for it, then you should just *go for it*,' she told herself on the morning of her first sexual experience. She jumped into the sack with an older Italian boy who lived next door and who had been pestering her to give into an urge he felt much more strongly than she did. Though he'd have sex with her, he wouldn't be seen out in public with her; he thought she was too young for that.

'Okay, look, let's do this thing that you're always wanting to do,' she suddenly told him one day while unzipping her jeans.

Passion hit a new low; even she realized that, and she was only a fourteen-year-old beginner.

'Is that *it*? It's *over*?' she asked her panting partner.

'Yeah, I guess so . . .' he answered, gasping for air.

'Fine, then you can go home. And don't ever talk to me again. I don't want you *ever* coming over here again, and that's *it!*'

She may have had a tough façade, but inside she was like any other girl her age in search of her fairy-tale prince. Sonny Bono was dressed all in black: slacks, shirt, and high-heeled boots. Gold chains adorned his neck. He wasn't at all handsome and, in fact, could be considered rather on the other side of ugly. But she realized that she wasn't exactly Audrey Hepburn herself, so she could 'relate'.

'Too bad he's so short – those boots don't fool me,' she remembers thinking to herself. (Bono was five feet six inches.) Deep-set Italian eyes, smooth complexion, a gregarious personality . . . he did have some winning characteristics.

When he sat at the table, he gave her the once-over and then ignored her. She, of course, ignored him back. Later, he admitted that he thought she was conceited and he could see no physical reason for her self-absorption, 'so the hell with her'. But Cher was dazzled by him; she was trying to be coy and cute, and maybe a bit mysterious, but not stuck-up. From the way Sonny spoke, he seemed to her to be the most ambitious and intelligent man she'd ever met. He had a magnetic aura about him, she thought. She felt herself strangely drawn to him, as if they shared something rare. This even though she didn't know him. She decided then what was unfolding here in the coffee shop was a simple and obvious case of 'love at first sight'. And besides that, this guy knew show business people – chalk another one up for him!

She was taking acting lessons, and she thought that she was rather good. Playing characters seemed to bring her out of her shell of insecurity. Mostly Cherilyn managed to maintain an almost unnatural calm in the face of all of the domestic chaos in her life. But there were times when she wished she was anybody but a homely girl with a mixed-up mother who had more husbands than she could keep track of. Her appetite for gossip was hearty: she would purchase fan magazines and devour intimate details of the lives of every Hollywood star; when Eddie Fisher and Debbie Reynolds broke up she was convinced that she'd never be the same again.

In just a little over an hour, Sonny had boasted himself right into her heart. He spoke enthusiastically about record promotion, Veronica Bennett and Phil Spector – people that Cher had never heard of but who would soon become an important part of her life.

They went out dancing soon after that, and over the next few weeks Sonny would learn Cherilyn's story. It began with her mother's . . .

Jackie Jean Crouch was born in Kensett, Arkansas, in June 1927 to thirteen-year-old Lynda Inez Gully and her seventeen-year-old husband, Roy Crouch, a baker and sometimes-barber. Jackie's maternal grandfather, a railroad worker, had been killed in a dynamite accident when Lynda was five. From that point on, Lynda's relatives shifted her from one family to another, all the while spinning a web of the kind of dark, troubled history that would become the hallmark of two more generations of her family.

When Jackie was five years old, her mother walked out on her husband, an alcoholic who beat her mercilessly. By the age of seven, Jackie was singing on local radio stations, and soon she and her father began hitchhiking across the country to their destination: Hollywood, California. For the next five years, young father and daughter made their way from one hick town to the next, supporting themselves with the little money Jackie's voice earned in saloons and bars. Barefoot, she would stand before her drunken audience of farmers and salesmen and wail her country and western songs. After the show, her father would pass the hat. 'By the time I was nine, I'd sung in just about every gin mill and honky-tonk bar clear across the south Midwest,' she wrote in the book *Star Mothers*. 'That film, *Paper Moon*, was my life, only my daddy didn't sell bibles like Ryan O'Neal. He sold me.'

By the time she was seven, the youngster was a featured singer on a radio show in Oklahoma City with hillbilly group Bob Wills and his Texas Playboys. Roy was certain that his daughter's voice was the key to their financial stability, if he could just get her and himself to Hollywood. But success did not await them when they finally made it to the West Coast. Instead, once there, father and daughter slept in Salvation Army shelters and led a miserable, impoverished existence. Eventually, they would be joined by her brother Mickey, and the three of them settled into a one-bedroom apartment in the slums of Los Angeles. Welfare helped pay their bills. To help make ends meet during the holiday season, the two children hawked greeting cards and Christmas seals on street corners. 'Cher doesn't understand those times,' her mother now says. 'She doesn't understand what it's like to go hungry.'

At one point, Jackie Jean was offered an audition with Meglin's Kiddies (a school for young entertainment hopefuls where Shirley Temple got her first break). She never made it to the audition; Roy couldn't afford the required dancing shoes for his daughter and, out of frustration, he slipped deeper into a liquor-induced delirium.

When Jackie was eleven, her mother was given custody of the girl and her brother. Rather than let Lynda have them, Roy tried to kill them both by turning up the gas in the apartment in which they were living. Jackie smelled the fumes and managed to save herself and Mickey; she blocked the traumatic episode from her memory until it surfaced in psychiatric therapy many years later.

At thirteen years of age, Jackie became a maid for a wealthy family, working part time while attending junior high school. She has said that she was humiliated by this work, that she would cry herself to an uneasy sleep at night and wonder what her life would be like 'if only'. In the next few years, she attended seventeen schools, but she would never graduate.

When she was eighteen and working in a doughnut shop in Fresno, California, she met John Sarkisian. He seemed strongly masculine, handsome, with deep-set dark eyes and the kind of incendiary smile that could melt stone. He was Armenian, and all gloss and flamboyance. Gawdy rings adorned fingers on smooth hands that looked as if they had never been introduced to the concept of work. But he was a farmer and he had a farmer's psyche; he could handle anything, he was strong and forceful and enterprising. Or so he thought.

In eight months, they were married in Reno, Nevada, not because Jackie really loved him but rather because he was one of the most persuasive men she'd ever met.

The day after the wedding, she was certain that she had made a terrible mistake and decided to leave her husband. She didn't even know this man, and she didn't understand his sudden mood swings. Hoping to effect a reconciliation, he convinced her to stay with him for three months by telling her that if she was still unhappy she could leave after that trial period. During this time, the Sarkisians moved to El Centro, California, and Jackie became pregnant. Obviously, her pregnancy was not a joyous discovery for her. John, a heavy drinker and compulsive gambler, was always distant and unkind to his young wife and certainly not the perfect mate.

Her unhappiness was compounded by their extreme poverty. Sarkisian worked with his father as a farmer, but he barely made enough money for the essentials. Jackie was torn by her dilemma; her mother Lynda helped her make up her mind: she would have an abortion, and that would be the end of it. It was her only escape.

One awful afternoon, Jackie, frightened and alone, found herself in a dirty abortion clinic sitting in a cold chrome chair waiting to have this new life sucked out of her womb. At the last possible moment on the operating table she changed her mind. She couldn't go through with it. She wanted her child. 'Can you believe I came that close to not having Cher?' she would say years later.

On 20 May 1946, seven months before President Truman officially declared the end of World War II, Jackie Sarkisian gave birth to a daughter and named the child Cherilyn after Lana Turner's daughter, Cheryl. Truman optimistically predicted a prosperous year if workers 'will just stay on their jobs'. Jackie's husband couldn't stay sober long enough to find one, and he and his father weren't making enough money to support the new addition to the Sarkisian family. So they moved from one city to the next as John pursued harvesting work.

When Cherilyn was five months old, Jackie and her mother Lynda went to Reno to obtain divorces from their husbands.

Now Jackie was nineteen, destitute, and faced with raising a cranky infant alone. She took a job as a saloon singer for a dollar a night plus tips, and, while she worked, put Cher in a Catholic home that cost nine dollars a week. At the end of her shift, she would scoop her baby up and take her home. She almost lost little Cherilyn, though, when the Mother Superior discovered what she did for a living and tried to prevent her from taking the girl.

(Many years later, when Cher was in her thirties, she discovered that she had spent some time in an orphanage and also living with foster parents. She says that she spent 'from six months to three years' in those circumstances, which doesn't correlate with anything Jackie has ever revealed about those early days.)

No matter what her financial state, Jackie always managed to look groomed and stylish. She was proud of her blonde hair and green eyes and she felt that, if given half a chance, she could be competitive in Hollywood as an actress. Hours would be spent primping before a mirror and dreaming of the kind of opulent lifestyle she believed only a show business career would yield.

In 1947, she was offered a small role in an MGM motion picture and she gladly accepted the part, considering it the opportunity of her lifetime. She began securing bit parts and spending more time on the MGM lot, and then in 1948 she was offered a major role in a film. She claims that she didn't appear in the movie because she refused to have sex with the director, a married man. Soon after, she was offered a part in *The Asphalt Jungle* by director John Huston; the opportunity seemed too good to be true . . . and it was. A week later, when she called the studio to inquire about the status of her wardrobe, she was told that Huston had changed his mind about her and had given the job to another young hopeful – Marilyn Monroe.

In 1949, Jackie changed her name to Georgia because, to her, it sounded more distinguished and glamorous. Television was a booming new industry and in it she began securing steady work as an extra and a few bit parts on 'The Adventures of Ozzie and Harriet' and 'The Bob Cummings Show'. In the next couple of years, she would marry twice more and have another daughter, Georgeanne. (By 1989, she had been married eight times, three times to Sarkisian. 'In those days, it wasn't right to sleep with someone if you weren't married, so I ended up getting married a lot,' she explains.) Cher and her half-sister had a warm relationship with Georgeanne's father, John Southall, a young, charming and irresponsible playboy type who drank too much but had a good heart when he was sober, and a vicious streak when he wasn't. The marriage didn't last very long; Southall's drink-induced temper forced Georgia to leave him. One day he went after her and the kids with a butcher's knife, accusing Georgia of having a boyfriend. Georgia ran out of the house with Cher and Georgeanne and, in a desperate attempt to save both their lives, hurled them over a six-foot fence in the back yard.

It's been said that Georgia Holt became a humourless woman, embittered by the disappointments her marriages yielded and by the fact that fame and fortune always seemed to elude her. But, in fact, she's a pragmatic and very brave person who, though she may be considered rather superficial in many respects, learned the hard way to be realistic about a life so overpoweringly sad. When the girls were young, she leveled with them: she had rotten luck with men, life was a bitch, and they would have to learn to adjust to circumstances that might never improve. 'But in my eyes, their childhood was a day at the beach compared to my life with my father,' she said later of Cher and Georgeanne.

'I was poor when I grew up, and I couldn't bear that,' Cher says. 'Before getting a chance to tell people what I had to say, they would know I was poor by the way I looked. I was ashamed. I felt that somehow it was my fault. I didn't understand it but I figured it was something I was doing wrong.' A story often repeated has Cher recalling times when she attended school wearing rubber bands around her shoes to keep the soles from falling off. She explains that this may be the reason for her well-publicized spending sprees. 'She's the deadliest shopper I've ever seen,' says former boyfriend, rock star Gene Simmons, recalling a three-minute splurge at Fiorucci's in New York during which Cher 'spent the equivalent of the cost of a car'. In another charge-card frenzy she picked up seventy-five pairs of shoes.

Georgia craved show business so badly she could smell greasepaint in the air. She and her daughters would go into Hollywood, sit in their automobile on Hollywood Boulevard and watch the people walk by, hoping to catch glimpses of celebrities, or people who looked as if they could possibly be famous. Movie stars were 'happy', Georgia told Cher and Georgeanne, because they wore diamonds and led wonderful, privileged lives. They were never poor. On the way back home, Georgia would lead her daughters in song: 'We ain't got a barrel of money, maybe we're ragged and funny but we travel along, singing our song, side by side.'

Cherilyn never really seemed to fit the family mould, a fact which puzzled her. Georgia and Georgeanne were fair-complexioned and fairy-princess blonde with pure green eyes; Georgia's ancestry is mixed English, Irish, German and Cherokee Indian. But Cherilyn had deep brown eyes and dark fine hair. Her olive complexion resembled that of the father she didn't know. She had noticed that fair, blonde girls who looked like Sandra Dee always got the most attention in school, so she felt left out; Anna Magnani wasn't popular in her circle of ten-year-olds. Once, the three of them went to Mexico and the officials refused to allow Cherilyn access back into the country because they thought she was a Mexican being sneaked over the border by an American woman and her young American daughter. She would never forget that day.

'Honey, you won't be the most beautiful or the most talented but you have something else,' Georgia, always a very direct woman, told her eldest daughter. 'You have something special.'

When Cher was about eight years old, she overheard the news that her father had been arrested on a narcotics charge, the first of several such drugs and/or bad cheque charges. For the next three years, he would be an inmate at San Quentin. Later, he tried to explain that he was addicted to morphine as a result of treatment for a hiatus hernia. Cher was eleven when Sarkisian was released from prison and re-married Georgia. 'He was very showy,' Cher recalled in an interview with Barbara Walters. 'I mean, he was flashy. When I saw this dark man walking into the house for the first time, I thought, okay, now I understand everything. This is where I came from.'

Cher bore such a strong resemblance to her father – they had exactly the same smile – that she immediately bonded to him and began to adore him. Sarkisian, who had never known his daughter until now, noticed that she was the brooding type. 'She always kept everything in,' he once recalled. 'But she wouldn't keep it in without letting you know she was keeping it in. You never knew what she was thinking. She wouldn't show you that part of her. It came out only in witticisms. A lot of times it wouldn't come out at all. She was very self-conscious and never thought she was pretty. She would sit and draw sketches sulkily.'

The father-daughter relationship lasted only six months. 'And then he was such a let-down,' Cher has said, 'that it just crushed everything.'

First Sarkisian pawned all of Georgia's jewellery, and then he almost set their house on fire when he was high on either drugs or liquor. Georgia loved this man, though, and she would stay married to him. But Cher considered her mother's devotion to him 'some kind of special penance I just don't understand' and decided to keep her distance; he was self-destructive and she knew it, even at her young age. Eventually, Georgia divorced, remarried, and then divorced Sarkisian again.

Cher tried to disown her father – he wasn't around when she needed him, and when he did show up he was a disruptive influence in her life – but it was difficult because she still loved him and felt a special connection to him. Sarkisian took advantage of his daughter's vulnerability and when she and Sonny became popular he asked for a job with their organization. He was appointed as a so-called 'road manager'. It appears, though, that Sarkisian was actually being paid by Sonny and Cher's managers for his silence rather than for any services rendered. '[He] was just out of prison and started coming around looking for money,' recalls one of Cher's original managers, Charlie Greene. 'He was trying to blackmail her and we did pay off – about five hundred dollars a week. It was worth it to keep the stories [about Sarkisian] out of the papers.' Eventually – if only for a short time – Sarkisian was actually living with Sonny and Cher, this despite the fact that Sonny had promised Cher that he would never even allow Sarkisian in the house. When it came to powers of persuasion, however, it seems that Sonny had met his match in John Sarkisian. After Cher and Sarkisian had an argument over past differences, her father moved out and, at least for the time being, she was 'through with him'. Early press releases about Cher's career state that Gilbert LaPiere, another man in Georgia's marital parade, was her natural father.

Over the years, Cher would have an occasional bittersweet reunion with her father (such as the time she arranged to have him meet his granddaughter, Chastity). On 14 April 1975, Sarkisian filed a $4 million lawsuit in Los Angeles Superior Court against Cher, and *Time* and *People* magazines, over remarks attributed to his daughter during interviews in which she discussed his past. Cher was quoted as saying that whatever her father was doing at the time, it was 'probably nothing legal'. Describing her as a person of 'economic power and in the public spotlight', Sarkisian sought an injunction against Cher to prevent her from discussing 'certain unsavoury aspects' of his life. He admitted that he'd been imprisoned for narcotics and bad-cheques offences, but claimed that he'd abandoned his former life style and had lived 'an exemplary, virtuous, and honourable life for the past nine years'.

Cher's reaction: 'Bullshit.'

During a rare, light moment with her father and Chastity, Cher had a photograph taken of the three of them together. It was the only picture John had of daughter and granddaughter and Cher hoped he'd consider it a treasure. A while later, an Armenian rug dealer called her in New York to complain that her father had written him a bad cheque. The dealer said that Sarkisian assured him that Cher would cover the cheque and, to prove that he actually knew her, he sold the merchant the photograph. When she heard what John had done, she considered it a show of complete unconcern for her and her daughter. Choked with resentment, she vowed never to have anything more to do with her father from that moment on. 'That's it! To hell with him!' He died in 1985. 'And I don't feel anything about him at all.'

When Georgia married wealthy bank manager Gilbert LaPiere in 1960, the girls began attending private schools. From this point on, there would be periods of financial security for Georgia and her daughters. LaPiere loved the girls and adopted them when Cher was fifteen and Georgeanne ten.

Eventually, this marriage ended. 'I knew by this time that we didn't exactly live in a normal household,' said Cher. 'I grew up thinking of men as these things you loved against your will.'

'It was us on one side of the world,' recalled Georgia, 'and everyone else on the other side.'

'She [Georgia] was a demanding woman,' said a friend, 'and difficult to live with. She wanted stardom, and if she couldn't have that she wanted at least to have money. She put pressure on her men, first of all, and she made a lot of poor choices. But she loved the girls and tried to give them good lives.'

Cher and her mother have had an extremely stormy and adversarial relationship, marked by acrimonious quarrels and loving reconciliations. Most of their problems have stemmed from the fact that Cher has always resented her mother's intrusion in her life. 'When I was a child, she was everything to me,' Cher has recalled, 'but when I became a teenager she was this *woman* who told me what to do.'

The way Cher dressed, the boys she dated, her grades at school – topics that have been points of contention between mothers and daughters throughout the ages – were always volatile subjects that became heated arguments. Though Georgia's daughters fared rather well even without the stabilizing element of a father figure, the constant upheaval in their life styles, the dozens of schools they attended as they moved about, the many broken relationships they witnessed, all served to toughen their spirits and make them belligerent and difficult youngsters with tongues that could cut through leather.

'She was fearless, that's for sure,' said Della Farren, one of her childhood friends. 'When I backed down from doing something – like stealing my parents' car – she'd just go out and do it. She was tough and called all the shots with everyone – even her mother.'

Georgia didn't realize it at the time, but young Cherilyn had certainly inherited her interest in the opposite sex. Before she turned fifteen, Cher found herself having an affair with one of her mother's best friends, a blond, six-foot-four womanizer who was painting the house as a favour to Georgia. One summer day, he made a pass at Georgia's eldest and swept her off her feet. They had an affair that lasted about a year without Georgia being any the wiser. At fourteen and a half years old, a girl doesn't really know what good sex is, but now Cher admits, 'This guy was good sex. Now I know he was good sex.' If Georgia had discovered what was going on between her close friend and daughter, Cher has to admit, 'She would have killed him.'

About a year or so later, Cher ran across Warren Beatty in Hollywood and was flabbergasted to have the opportunity to sleep with him. Beatty was a young actor whose first three films were all released in the six-month period between October 1961 and April 1962; *Splendor in the Grass*, with Natalie Wood, is considered the best of the trio. Beatty had recently broken up with Joan Collins and Natalie Wood, and was on the prowl for 'sweet young things' on the Sunset Strip. Cher qualified. The fact that Georgia and her girlfriends all thought he was 'the most gorgeous creature on earth', and that he had 'known' the favours of gorgeous Hollywood goddesses like Collins and Wood, all gave Cher great incentive to have sex with Beatty and then brandish the experience about as a badge of honour and merit. It was only one night; Beatty must have been having a dry spell because even though she recalls him being 'technically good', young Cherilyn was far from satisfied: 'I didn't feel anything.'

Sleeping with Warren Beatty 'because he was there, and why the hell not' was certainly something Georgia would have done. Mother and daughter were a lot more alike than they probably realized. When Cher began practising her signature at the age of fifteen, fine-tuning it for a time when she hoped it would be in demand (it's the same signature she uses today), her mother realized that she and the girl did share a common interest in show business. She took her daughter to see Frankie Laine in Las Vegas; when he sang a number to Cher and the spotlight bathed the youngster in a warm show business glow, Georgia beamed with pride. It was a moment Cher has probably never forgotten. But this mutual interest in the entertainment world was not enough to sustain the mother-and-daughter relationship.

At the age of sixteen, in 1962, Cher dropped out of the eleventh grade and then moved out of the house.

catholic school

Though Cher knew that dropping out of school was the easy way out, she decided it was also the only way. She was a very poor student and every day she stayed in school was pure torture for her. This was another of the many disagreements straining the relationship between Cher and her mother.

Georgia believed Cher had talent, that perhaps she could even have the career as an actress that Georgia had fancied for herself. But she also realized that Cher wasn't focused; if she had any ambition at all, it was scattered in all directions. At the very least, Georgia tried to tell her daughter that she should finish school so that her chances for a secure future would be somewhat more hopeful.

'But I was never really *in* school,' Cher once recalled. 'I was always thinking about when I would be grown-up and famous and where I'd want to live or where I'd want to go, or what dresses I'd wear when I got there. All of these little scenarios – I'd be sitting in class thinking about how I would save people's lives. I was the great fairy angel who would find the cure for polio and save the entire world. I was real pissed off when Salk beat me to it. I really was.'

While Georgia was married to Gilbert LaPiere, Cher attended Julia Richmond High School in New York. On her first day, she sensed strong hostility from the other girls. She has said that they wanted to beat her up because she arrived in a taxicab. 'I didn't know any of the social graces of New York at that time; the chicks didn't like me because I was a lot different. Most of the time I just wanted to be alone. It wasn't a case where I couldn't be *in*. I just felt like, who the hell *wants* to be in?'

Cher once said that she had attended as many as fifteen schools as the family moved from one city to the next. Her least favourite was probably Mother Cabrini's High School in the San Fernando Valley of Los Angeles. The discipline of a Catholic school was something she could never understand or reconcile herself to. Cher believed that the strict nuns were after her. Chances are, they were. She certainly wasn't your run-of-the-mill obedient and subservient Catholic girl; she wasn't even Catholic and how her mother managed to enroll her in this school is still a mystery. If Cherilyn was 'pissed off' at a nun, the nun would know it – she'd be able to read it in the slant of Cher's expressive eyes. Cher wouldn't verbalize her hostility (she didn't dare?) which made it even more difficult for a suspicious nun to lash out at her – punishing someone for what she's thinking can be a tricky business, but that usually didn't stop the sisters at Mother Cabrini's.

'I went to schools where you couldn't wear patent leather shoes because there was some old lady who had a neurosis about it,' she told Andy Warhol. 'She was afraid your underpants would be reflected off the patent leather shoes and someone would peek. They were really sick. Once a nun beat me to a pulp. It wasn't nice what I said about her, but it was the truth.'

Young Cherilyn felt that this particular sister was a dead ringer for big-mouthed comedian Joe E. Brown. When she shared the joke with a friend, 'Sister Joe E. Brown' overheard it and 'beat me right into the ground'.

'The wildest girls I ever met were in Catholic schools,' Cher has said. 'I used to tell my mother she was going straight to hell when she died because she didn't do any of the things the nuns told us we were supposed to do.'

(While Cher was attending school at Mother Cabrini's, her father, John Sarkisian, was picked up on another narcotics charge and sent to a rehabilitation centre in North Corona, California.)

When Gilbert LaPiere enrolled Cher in Montclair, a private prep school in Van Nuys, California, she was surrounded by classmates who were particularly wealthy. The teachers constantly complained about Cher's long hair – which she would sometimes pile up on top of her head in an effort to look older – but she refused to cut it. Once, she was disciplined for coaxing her classmates to go to school barefoot. The dean of girls, Mrs Young, especially disliked Cher and suspended her for wearing clothes that she considered inappropriate school attire – slacks, T-shirts, boots.

Cher and her friends would holiday in exclusive Palm Springs, courtesy of Georgia's husband LaPiere. 'The story of the poor girl from the wrong side of the tracks is all publicity stuff,' Dr Vernon Simpson, former director and principal of Montclair, once observed. 'When Cher was here, her stepfather was a banker and she seemed to be from an affluent family. She was not a deprived child at all.'

At one point, Cher was employed by Robinson's department store in Beverly Hills as a receptionist. It was a dull job that she quit after a short time, as she did a part-time job at a See's candy store.

'I was a mess. I knew I wanted to be famous, but I didn't know what I could do,' she says. 'I would look in the mirror and see a not very distinguished-looking person. I wasn't good-looking. I wasn't even cute. I used to stand in my room and act out all the parts in *West Side Story*.'

School was difficult, and no matter how diligently Cher applied herself to her studies, she was never able to keep up. She believed that she was either dumb or just more interested in her 'fantasy world'. Cher didn't know it at the time, but she was suffering from dyslexia. Dyslexia, a brain disorder that causes letters and numbers to be transposed, makes simple reading and arithmetic very difficult for sufferers. Only in the past few years has it been widely recognized as a problem much different from retardation, low intelligence or 'laziness.

Cher's report card would indicate that she had great potential but simply would not apply herself. But Cher insists that she could not have tried any harder: 'I was busting my ass and getting nowhere.' Her problem was complicated by the fact that she was constantly changing schools; she was always the new kid on the block, yearning for acceptance.

She didn't realize the nature of her problem until years later when she was thirty years old, and her four-year-old daughter Chastity seemed to have the same kinds of learning difficulties. Cher had the youngster tested, and it was determined that she was dyslexic.

It was only then that she realized that she herself had been suffering from the same disorder for years.

Today, Cher is still a very poor reader. Simple tasks such as dialling a telephone number are arduous. Writing a cheque was extremely difficult for a long time (thank goodness for credit cards!). Scripts are especially hard work, and when she is confronted with one she absorbs it very slowly; but she's got a good memory and often memorizes parts during the first reading. Other actors, like Richard Chamberlain and Tom Cruise, also struggle with – and are successful despite – dyslexia.

When she was a student, her friends and even her family thought she was just lazy and unmotivated. The fact that she was a discipline problem was probably partly because she was so frustrated with her life. More than anything, Cher ached for approval and, though she would never admit it, acceptance. She wasn't receiving any at school so she dropped out at sixteen years old and would never go back.

Once, someone asked Cher why she had become a performer. Her observation was: 'I honestly think it has to do with something that was lacking when you are small. Because all it is when you perform and people clap for you – it's that these people out there love you for the moment. Certainly, you're expressing yourself. But what you're getting back is, well, it's just love.'

moving in with sonny

After their first date, Sonny Bono didn't feel as attracted to Cher as she did to him. He had to admit, though, that there seemed to be a sense of courage and determination about her, as if the skies were the limit . . . 'even though she doesn't really have any tits,' he told a friend. But as enthusiastic as she may have been about a career in show business – she told him that she was taking acting classes with Jeff Corey, a renowned drama teacher – she didn't seem motivated so much by a desire for artistic identity as by one to make as much money as she could and as quickly as possible.

It also didn't take him long to realize that this wasn't the most intelligent girl ever to walk down the pike. One evening soon after they met, she asked him to answer a question for her, one that had been nagging at her for years: 'Is it true that the sun is really the other side of the moon? Because when a solar eclipse comes along, I'm so banged up I don't know what the fuck is going on.'

Someone tried to convince her that Mount Rushmore was a natural rock formation. She believed him.

'Cher, either you are the stupidest person I have ever met,' Sonny told her, 'or you've got more faith than anyone in the world.'

Sonny had just separated from his wife and was interested in Melissa Melcher, a friend of Cher's who lived next door to her. To be near her, he also moved next door into an apartment building on Fountain Avenue in Hollywood, and then he acted surprised when he 'discovered' who his neighbours were.

Cher was infatuated with Bono. He was the first man she'd ever known to treat her like a lady, holding the door open for her, buying her meals. He covered her with a protective blanket of approval, encouraged her, and assured her that she was pretty. She was eleven years younger than he (in 1962 he was twenty-seven and she was sixteen), but she lied and told him that she was nineteen. It would be a year before Sonny would learn some of the truth – and even then he was lied to: she told him she was going to be eighteen in 1963 when actually she had turned seventeen.

One evening while out on a date with another fellow, she spent the entire evening fantasizing about Sonny. She cut the date short so that she could run back to Fountain Avenue and be close to him; she ran to his apartment and pounded on the door. When Sonny refused to answer, she realized that he was in bed with another girl. She was heartbroken and, as she would say years later, 'very pissed off'.

His interest in older women, the fact that he was married and had experiences she didn't have, all made Sonny Bono irresistible to this impressionable teenager. The first time Cher's mother met Sonny, he had a Prince Valiant-type haircut – this before long hair was in style – buckskin pants and 'Beatle boots'. As soon as Sonny left the room, Georgia went over to Cher and asked very urgently, 'What in the world was *that*?'

'That *happens* to be the man I am going to marry,' Cher shot back defensively.

'Everyone was aghast,' Cher's sister Georgeanne recalls.

The battle for power over Cher's life between Sonny and Georgia began on that day. 'I had been the power figure in Cher's life until then,' Georgia has recalled. 'But then Sonny came into the picture and . . .' Cher's mother made it very clear that she didn't want her daughter dating this older man, which, of course, made Sonny Bono all the more a prize to Cher.

When Cher's roommate moved out, leaving her with the responsibility of back rent and other bills, she realized that her prized independence from Georgia's grip was in great jeopardy. Cher didn't have steady employment – she didn't really want any – but worked at odd jobs, part time. Moving back home with Georgia was an option, but one that was obviously out of the question. She went next door to Sonny's and began to weep. 'I don't know what to do. You gotta help me.'

'Why don't you just move back in with your mother?' he suggested.

'My *mother*?' she screamed as she paced back and forth. 'My *mother?*' she repeated, melodramatically, pronouncing the word 'mother' with the same inflection most people reserve for words like 'malaria'. She looked up at Sonny with woeful puppy-dog eyes that spilled over in tears. Just the pitiful sight of her persuaded him to come up with a suggestion. He took the bait and made this proposition: 'Look, I really don't find you attractive at all,' he began (her spirits fell with a thud), 'but if you want, you can move in with me. Can you cook?' She shook her head no and held her breath. 'Well, can you clean?' Yes, of course, she could clean – sort of. ('She couldn't clean either,' Sonny remembered later.) 'Keep the house clean, and I'll pay the rent. You can stay here.'

Cher told her mother that she was moving in with a stewardess. It was the perfect story. When Georgia came to visit, she would kick Bono out of his apartment and then rush about collecting all his belongings and dumping them through the window to her friend Melissa Melcher's apartment across the way. Then she would simply explain to Georgia that the reason her roommate wasn't about was because she was en route to some foreign country. Once Georgia arrived unannounced and her daughter couldn't get all of Sonny's belongings out in time; she ended up desperately shoving his underwear and socks into the tea cupboard. When her mother announced her intention to go into the kitchen and 'fix myself a nice pot of tea', Cher panicked. 'No, mother! You stay out of my cupboards,' she demanded. 'When I come over to your house, do I go through all of your things? No, I do not! So stay out of mine!' Georgia says that it was then she realized her daughter was keeping a secret; it wouldn't be long before she would find out just what that was.

When Cher and Sonny began living together, he discovered what he called Cher's 'eccentric side'. She had no lingerie except for one bra. Before he knew it, she was wearing his Fruit of the Loom underwear. She had no sense of hygiene and she hated washing her hair. (She'd iron it to get it straight.) She had a favourite pair of worn jeans and a T-shirt that she especially liked, and she wore these clothes practically every day. She would spend most evenings dancing in clubs on the Sunset Strip. The next morning, she loved to sleep; Sonny considered it a miracle if she was out of bed by noon. She would lounge aound the apartment all day, watching television and eating junk food.

Sonny wasn't at all used to any of this; nothing irritated him more than laziness. There wasn't anything about Cher that he found particularly compelling or attractive – that is until he noticed her singing voice one afternoon. When she began singing around the apartment, he realized that she had talent. Her voice, a booming and unrefined sound, needed polishing but, to Sonny's way of thinking, it had great potential.

The two of them lived together for months, sleeping in separate beds in the same bedroom, but without having sex. 'It did take a long time for the relationship to get physical,' Cher has said. 'Sonny's into having a very mental relationship, and if he can't have it he doesn't mess with you. It wasn't a fiery, sexy thing with us, but rather paternal, like we were bound together, two people who needed each other almost for protection.' Sonny reserved his 'fiery, sexy things' for other women – most of whom would jump over Cher's twin bed while she was in it in order to get into Sonny's.

Interestingly, considering Sonny's lack of interest in Cher, Sonny and Cher's employees would, in years to come, talk among themselves about the couple's intimate moments. 'Cher used to complain about Sonny's sex demands,' Charlie Greene's wife Marci recalls. 'She said he'd chase her around the bedroom.'

'Sonny liked to see other women too,' Charlie Greene adds. 'When we stayed at hotels, Sonny would take an extra suite and when Cher was asleep, he'd go there and call out for hookers. Sonny would show them a big wad of bills, maybe $20,000, and he'd peel off $500 and give it to them. But he didn't go to bed with them. He would just talk to them – about himself.'

But in 1962, sex wasn't on Sonny and Cher's mind. If anything, Cher needed the so-called 'protection' Sonny offered her more than she says he did. But the trade-off was beneficial to both parties. She wanted to be in on show business and she could sing; he, who was in show business, couldn't sing a note. He was looking for a protégé and had apparently found one.

'I was twenty-seven and Cher was a resurgence for me,' said Bono. 'She was sixteen and needed a husband, a father and a brother. I loved giving that to her. I became a leader for the first time in my life.'

Cher remembers having a nightmare and asking Sonny if she could crawl into his bed with him. 'Oh, all right,' he said half-heartedly. 'But, look, just don't bother me.'

i met him on a sunday and my heart stood still . . .

When Sonny took Cher with him to recording sessions at Gold Star Studios, where he would sometimes play percussion on the musical tracks, she found herself surrounded by all of those wonderful flashy show business types she and her mother used to gawk at while sitting on Hollywood Boulevard. She noticed how the girl singers in the studio – Ronnie Spector, Darlene Love, and the others – seemed to treat her with respect and pay special attention to her just because she was with Sonny Bono. Bono wasn't top dog at Gold Star, but he was in the running as Spector's protégé. He was the guy to kiss up to if Phil Spector was someone you wanted to get to know.

Gold Star was always jumping with energy and activity. Singers clustered and rehearsed in every corner practising intricate harmonies, snapping their fingers, laughing and having a terrific time. Most of them have since recalled that they didn't care that Phil Spector was exploiting their talent, that he would make most of the money their art generated and then pay them just a pittance.

Sonny Bono wanted Cher to become serious about singing and to give up the acting classes she was taking with Jeff Corey. What could he do with her if she were an actress? If she were a singer, he could produce and arrange her music; she could be that magnet he was looking for, the one who would make him important but be magnificent enough to draw attention away from his inadequacies.

'If you wanted to impress someone with the music industry, Gold Star was a great place to take that person,' said Val Johns, a recording artist and songwriter who utilized the studio for many of his Sixties sessions. 'It was always bustling with activity. Musicians, singers, arrangers, producers . . . almost too much to take in, and Phil Spector ruling the rock-and-roll kingdom. But it was a strange little place, too. You could park in the back if you got there early enough – there were only four parking spots. When you walked in, there were two studios, A and B. B was a tiny little dump. A was a large room with state-of-the-art equipment, and that's where all the hits were recorded.'

On one particular day, Bono was playing percussion for a track that would go on to become 'Da Do Ron Ron' for The Crystals. As Cher legend has it, someone asked her if she could sing and she said no. Could she hold a tune? 'Yeah, she can hold a tune,' Sonny cut in. Before she knew it, she was part of a vocal ensemble singing background vocals to the song.

Phil Spector owned the names Crystals, Ronettes, Blue Jeans, and those of any other act that recorded for his label, and so he could substitute any vocalists he wished for the actual members of the group. Many of the fledgling singers who walked through Gold Star at one time or another in the early Sixties can be heard singing on Crystals and Ronettes songs.

Phil Spector thought Cher's voice was the oddest he had ever heard coming from a young girl. He favoured high-pitched vocalists and all his female artists had a light, piercing sound. Cher's was a booming rumble. At first, he didn't like the timbre at all. But after blending it in with the other singers and with all the elements that combined to build his 'Wall of Sound', he began to feel that her voice was a vocal anchor to the overall effect. In his mind, Cher's voice became a vital element to his concept, a bridge between the rock-heavy instrumentation and the flyaway lead vocals.

As usual, most of his associates thought he was talking through his hat. Cher's voice was as indistinguishable in the wash of noise he called background vocals as everyone else's was. But be that as it may, Cher recorded vocals for all of Spector's major records, including The Crystals' 'He's Sure the Boy I Love', 'Then He Kissed Me', and 'Da Do Ron Ron'; Darlene Love's 'Wait Til My Bobby Gets Home' and 'The Boy I'm Gonna Marry'; all of The Ronettes records, and innumerable album cuts and single B sides.

Cher fans insist that the sound of Spector's music changed when Sonny and Cher became popular and she stopped working for him. They claim that the timbre of Cher's voice made the songs on which she sang distinctive. In truth, the untrained ear would be hard-pressed to hear Cher on most of these songs (she's most audible on releases by The Ronettes).

For the record, the last release Cher sang background vocals on for Spector was his production of 'You've Lost That Lovin' Feeling' for The Righteous Brothers. (When it was finally released in late 1964, the record went to number one. Bono, incidentally, played percussion on the session.)

For the next few months, Cher's life was a fascinating series of recording dates and rehearsals. Sonny had opened a door to a world of possibilities for her, and she was grateful.

'Sonny Bono was Cher's idol,' said Darlene Love. 'Where he went, she followed. She was totally devoted and everyone knew it. She was also tough; no one messed with her. She'd shred you with her tongue. A tough, but lovable, chick. . . .'

There were others who didn't find her quite so 'lovable'. One Gold Star musician said, 'She was a pain in the ass. She really wasn't a singer and she had a tough time blending with the other girls she sang with. And she was *never* wrong in her mind. Sonny always backed her, and Phil wanted to use her, but there were a lot of people who didn't like it. It was tough enough meeting deadlines at Gold Star with Spector's off-the-wall mastering techniques, mixes that would take hours and hours, without having a fly in the ointment who couldn't sing.'

When Cher's mother discovered that she was actually living with Sonny Bono, Cher's life was thrown back into turmoil. Furious with her daughter for lying to her, Georgia gave her an ultimatum: either move home with her or move into a girls' residence. Cher opted for the latter, but when she got there, she hated it. She had no independence, and she had just begun to prize her freedom. 'There were ten truck drivers per room. Really heavy bull dykes,' Cher has recalled. 'I was introduced to a few of them my first night there.'

Many of the girl were from broken homes; others were there for minor criminal offences. There always seemed to be fear in the air. It was a stifling place to live, and she wouldn't be there very long. Most of the time she passed listening to the radio, hoping to hear one of the songs she had recorded background vocals for, and the rest of the time she waited for Sonny's call.

When she was gone, Bono realized how attached he'd become to Cher. She offered brightness and a sense of hope to his life as much as he did to hers. The two became determined to continue their romance.

'When I found out how old he was and that he had a wife and daughter, I didn't want him around,' Cher's mother stated bluntly. 'It's strange, but at the time Sonny was the spitting image of Cher's father. She had always longed for her father. It was apparent to everybody that he was a father image to this young girl, but I didn't think it would've helped if I had told her that.'

She wasn't convinced that Cher actually loved Sonny; she believed her daughter was simply trying to be defiant. The battle raged on – for years. Cher and Georgia would always be at odds over her fixation for Sonny. Bono would unwittingly drive a wedge between mother and daughter that would estrange them until he and Cher were finally divorced in 1975.

At one point, Georgia decided to put a little distance between her daughter and Bono, so she drove Georgeanne and Cher to Arkansas, where they stayed for a while. Cher hated Arkansas and missed Sonny terribly. While they were there, Georgia's husband, whichever one she was married to at this time, left her. 'And that was her just desserts,' Cher said.

When they returned, Sonny and Cher picked up where they'd left off. It wasn't a passionate relationship, but it was sincere. There was a brief break-up when the two disagreed about Cher's future. It was said that she still wanted to study with Corey, but Bono insisted that she pursue the music business. 'I knew she could be a great star with just a little work,' he said later. 'I knew she was a singer.' Cher finally agreed with Bono and dropped out of class.

This did nothing to encourage Georgia to warm up to this interloper; she wanted Cher to continue with Corey. 'In Cher, she saw herself,' said a friend. 'She knew she'd never make it as an actress, and she wanted Cher to make it for her. She felt that Sonny was being self-serving in convincing Cher to quit. The truth, though, is that Cher was so unmotivated that a slight push in any direction would be enough to change her course. Actress, singer, dancer, she really didn't care. This was not a girl who *planned* anything.'

Georgia has said that Cher was the youngest girl ever to qualify for Jeff Corey's Pasadena Playhouse workshop, but at the last minute Cher refused to join the group. 'I couldn't force her to go because by this time I didn't know *what* she wanted to do.'

In August 1963, Sonny's first wife filed for divorce. The name of her husband's eighteen-year-old lover was never mentioned in the divorce proceedings. Donna Bono complained bitterly that her husband was never at home and that when he did come home he smelled of perfume. When asked to explain the perfume, Sonny told her that it must have rubbed off from whomever he was sitting next to. She complained, 'He didn't pay attention to me or my little girl. We had no communication, no home life, no social life. It made me very nervous and unhappy.'

Bono did not contest the divorce and the decree was granted on 21 October 1963. Legally, as per California law at the time, he would have to wait one year before he could marry Cher. They had no intention of marrying, however. There were more important matters at hand.

In January 1964, Phil Spector established a subsidiary label to Philles called Annette Records (named after his first wife). Two young songwriters, Pete Anders and Vinnie Poncia, submitted a song to Spector called 'Ringo, I Love You'. It was a piece of nonsense that was meant to capitalize on the popularity of the Beatles at this time, and on Ringo Starr's growing following. Sonny hated the song, but he agreed to allow Cher to record it. Perhaps this would be her entrée.

Sonny wouldn't allow the record to be released under Cher's name, so they dreamed up the moniker Bonnie Jo Mason. The song was released in February 1964 and is considered Cher's first single. It failed miserably.

Former associates agree that Spector was playing a joke and that Sonny and Cher were the unwitting victims. Cher's voice was so deep, and she sounded so much like a man on the single, that it appeared as if 'Ringo, I Love You' were a tribute from a gay fan. 'I sounded too much like a boy,' Cher said later. 'Everyone thought it was a faggot song.'

It was said that Sonny put two and two together and realized what Spector had done. He also realized that Annette Records was a major tax write-off for Philles Records, organized to defray the enormous Internal Revenue bill that label had incurred the previous year. Bono was put off by the way he felt Cher was being ridiculed and exploited. To him, she was a major star. To everyone else, she was just a background singer. Spector never got the impression from her that she was serious about becoming a star; and to him all of this was just a bit of comic relief.

Eight months earlier, in May 1963, Sonny and Jack Nitzsche wrote a major hit for Jackie DeShannon ('Needles and Pins'). The song was recorded with terrific success by everyone from The Searchers and Bobby Vee to Gary Lewis and Del Shannon. Phil Spector had the idea of combining Bono's and Nitzsche's writing skills with his production work in a recording group they'd call The Philistines. But Sonny wanted nothing to do with that concept. His decision was made: he would now begin pulling away from Phil Spector in order to devote more time to Cher's career.

After Sonny Bono ended his relationship with Phil Spector in early 1964, he began working part time as a promoter for an independent promotion firm called California Merchandising, located in a heavily black area in Los Angeles on Washington Boulevard. Val Johns, who at the time was an aspiring pianist fresh in town from Oklahoma, recalled what he remembered as 'my Sonny Bono experience'.

'I was with Carlton Records,' said Johns, 'and had a new single, "The Theme to Ben Casey", which California Merchandising was working. The two men in the office who took artists out to meet disc jockeys and promote their records were Sonny Bono and Herb Alpert (Alpert went on to front the Tijuana Brass band and to become the co-founder of A&M Records).

'They assigned Sonny to me, probably because we're the same size,' said the slightly built Johns. 'It was extremely difficult to break this kind of instrumental record at that time, but Sonny was determined. We drove here and there, to one radio station and another, and he did his pitch. At the time he had an obnoxious-looking cream-and-green Nash convertible. He was personable, outgoing, and from the moment he picked me up until we parted company, he delighted in entertaining me.'

Bono was being paid by California Merchandising as a promoter, and he was also compensated by Johns' record label in the form of gratuities. 'After our business was finished that day,' Johns recalled, 'we immediately went to Sye DeVore's men's clothing store on Vine Street in Hollywood. There he was given a box of five shirts, each custom made and tailored expressly for him. He was much more excited about these terrific shirts than he was about his new artist with the doctor's theme.'

As Bono pulled up to the Carlton Records office complex on Argyle Avenue in Hollywood to drop Val Johns off, he invited him to 'come on by and see my show. Me and this girl I just met are working a club called The Parisian Room.' He gave Johns the address.

'As it turned out,' Johns recalled with a chuckle, 'Sonny and Cher were singing background vocals for Billy Daniels, the popular rhythm-and-blues star, at this club on Washington Boulevard in the heart of LA's black district. It amazed me. There were three white faces in the crowd. Mine, Sonny's, and Cher's.

'The two of them were just as rhythmic and black-sounding as they could possibly have been. Sonny hadn't grown his hair very long yet, and Cher had hers pulled straight back. And my God, she was so clumsy you felt as if she would fall off the stage at any moment. She did whatever Sonny whispered in her ear. She was the one with the obvious voice. Sonny just sort of sang around her, hitting notes now and then but mostly sounding off key. It was an odd, very early Sonny and Cher experience.'

Sonny Bono's strong connection to black music is interesting, first at Specialty Records with Little Richard and Sam Cooke, then at Philles with all of Phil Spector's black recording artists, and later in the background behind Billy Daniels.

Sam Cooke and Bono's friend Harold Battiste opened a recording studio in the centre of Los Angeles's black community and called it The Soul Station. Battiste explained the concept this way: 'Black talent was so buried in the black community that there was no way for many of them to understnd the mechanics of getting to Hollywood to present themselves to anyone who mattered, who could sign them to a deal. My own personal philosophy was that the ones who did make it to Hollywood were the more assertive ones, but not necessarily the most talented. Sam and I felt that there should be a place in the community that provided a more comfortable environment to nurture this great black ability.'

The Soul Station was official opened in early 1964. Eight months later, Sam Cooke was killed in a shooting incident in Los Angeles. Battiste continued with the worthy concept.

'Sonny was real convinced that he could something with Cher,' Battiste recalled. '"Look, man, this is what we can do," he said. "Cher's got this uncle and he's got some bread. Let's get a record made on her. She's *bad*!" There was a place on Hollywood Boulevard called The Cave, a nightclub, and her uncle had some interest in it. He was supposed to come up with forty thousand dollars to promote whatever we recorded on Cher. He never did.'

The 'uncle' Battiste referred to was Cher's stepfather LaPiere.

Sonny had an entire concept in mind for LaPiere to finance. 'But even though Cher's stepfather would do anything for Cher, I don't believe he trusted Sonny's business instincts,' said a friend. 'Cher's mother probably talked him out of giving up the money for what she thought was essentially a silly gimmick.'

Sonny's plan was to capitalize on the success of the film *Cleopatra*, starring Richard Burton and Elizabeth Taylor. He had his hair cut in a *Quo Vadis* style, and cast Cher as an Egyptian queen, with her long hair and exotic-looking eyes. The two of them rented Egyptian costumes, photographs were hastily taken, and 'Caesar and Cleo' were born.

In the spring of 1964, Sonny took the pictures, along with a recording of 'The Letter', which they had made at The Soul Station, to Jack Lewerke, president of Vault Records. 'The Letter' is an atrocious record; it doesn't quite sound like it's playing at the proper speed. Sonny and Cher's performance is primitive, harmonies clash, lead vocals are fuzzy. But Lewerke felt that the promotional hook was a good one, at least for a one-record deal, and for the duration of the film's popularity. The song was issued but did nothing significant on the record charts.

So it was back to The Soul Station in April 1964, where Sonny and Cher cut a remake of the 1956 Mickey and Sylvia record 'Love Is Strange'. This time out, Bono produced a stronger effort. The song was tailor-made for vocal interplay between a male and a female singer, and Cher's performance is stronger than before. But still, the final outcome was a very weak single release, badly in need of re-editing. Bono used another of his record business connections and convinced Mo Austin, president of Reprise, to sign Caesar and Cleo to that label.

'That was very typical of Sonny,' said a former associate. 'He would play both sides to the middle. Lewerke hadn't even released the one record, and here was Sonny signing a deal with Austin. He didn't always know what he was doing, though, and more than anything he needed strong management at this point.'

This is where Charles Greene and Brian Stone came into the picture. The two would become a couple of the most controversial figures in Sixties rock management as a result of their outrageous dealings with Sonny and Cher, Buffalo Springfield, and Iron Butterfly. They were less than conventional career strategists, and Sonny was awed by their drive and ambition. 'They were some heavy fast talkers,' Battiste said of Greene and Stone. 'They could talk you into opening an ice-cream parlour in Alaska.'

Sonny and Cher first met these two before they had officially started their management careers, at a recording sessing at Gold Star on 4 May 1964. Jack Nitzsche was producing an all-star recording of Gus Kahn's standard 'Yes Sir, That's My Baby', which, in its new Spector-style trappings, was barely recognizable. Instantly identifiable, though, in the wash of heavy background vocals is Cher's robust, throaty sound.

Nitzsche recalled: 'On the song, that's Brian Wilson [of the Beach Boys] singing falsetto, with Sonny and Cher, Darlene Love, The Blossoms, Jackie DeShannon, and Albert Stone. It was an all-star session. The guy singing bass is someone who was in the lobby at the time. Honest to God, a black guy was in the lobby and I asked him if he could sing bass. He said he could and I told him to come on in and sing on the record. That's Edna Wright singing lead. [Wright, sister of Darlene Love, would go on to become lead singer for The Honeycone, a Seventies female singing trio best remembered for its record 'Want Ads'.] We did the session at RCA's recording studio, and the Rolling Stones sat and watched the whole thing.'

'The room was as big as a basketball court, but Cher's voice cut through everyone's,' recalled Charlie Greene. 'We had to put her way in the back of the studio.'

No one was paid for the session. (It was said that Nitzsche organized the date as a charitable effort to help pay outstanding bills Greene and Stone had accumulated in premanagement ventures.) The record was issued on Reprise under the group name Hale and the Hushabyes in August 1964.

That night at the session, Greene and Stone became friendly with Sonny Bono. Bono told them about his plans for Cher, how she could be a major star 'in two weeks, that's all we need, two weeks.' Greene and Stone encouraged Sonny's enthusiasm by suggesting that he and Cher could fill a void in the popular recording industry because there were no successful male/female duet acts at the time (Peaches and Herb probably didn't count, in their eyes). Sonny was convinced; Greene and Stone would be their managers. But Cher was sceptical.

It was said that Greene–Stone Management was started when the two of them climbed over the fence at the Universal lot and took over a bungalow. One of them called the next morning to ask where the furniture was. And they were at this Universal Studios lot for a year, rent free, without anybody asking how they got there or what they were doing there. They did all of their business from that locale, and became Greene–Stone Management. They muscled their way into show business on pure guts. That was their style.

Back in the Sixties, no one made it as a rock-and-roll representative unless he had the kind of determination Greene and Stone prided themselves on. They knew that progress wasn't made in the Sixties record industry by moving into an office in a tall high-rise where your quarters weren't visible to your peers. The proper way to ensure recognition was to secure a building of your own, hang a sign out front that said you were there, and then go into business.

A week after he signed Sonny and Cher to a management contract, Brian Stone got a phone call from Bono, bubbling with excitement over a song he'd just written called 'Baby Don't Go'. He sang the three-chord repetitive riff to Stone over the phone, and his new manager booked Studio C at the RCA recording facility. He felt he should impress his new client, so Stone picked up the tab for the recording date. He had no money, though, so he pawned his typewriter and two adding machines to finance the $2,000 session.

Harold Battiste, who arranged the song, recalled, 'I believe the original intention was that this would be a Cher single. Sonny didn't want to be on the record; he wanted to launch her as a solo. We laid down some of the tracks at The Soul Station before they finished it at RCA. Cher got into the studio and froze up. She was so nervous about being in there alone, having all of that attention focused on her, and she was so insecure about her voice that she couldn't sing a note. So Sonny went in and started harmonizing with her. It sounded so pure and full, we decided to keep him on the record. Neither of them had the best voices, but somehow they sounded so full together.'

The safest way Bono knew to determine whether or not a record was a hit was to play it for his mentor Spector. 'If Phil Spector wanted to buy it from you, you knew you had a hit,' he said to friends. Spector thought 'Baby Don't Go' was a winner and paid Bono $500 for half of the publishing rights. Charlie Greene convinced Mo Austin at Reprise to issue the record, the first with the label copy 'Sonny and Cher'. The song was released on 16 September 1964; the same day, oddly enough, saw the release of 'Love Is Strange' by Caesar and Cleo.

Even odder is the fact that Cher's performance on 'Baby Don't Go', an early single release that most people don't even know about (though it did go top ten when it was re-released in 1965), is really one of her better efforts. She is full-bodied and vital-sounding here, not yet influenced by Bono's off-key style. The song has an interesting lyric, too, expressly written for Cher by Bono, about an eighteen-year-old wanderer searching for her niche, looking for affection and support. Cher sings the song in a brooding, very convincing manner.

The music to 'Baby Don't Go' seems heavily influenced by

the burgeoning British invasion, and sounds like a copy of what McCartney and Lennon were just beginning to popularize. At first, it was only a regional success in Los Angeles and Dallas. But the record caught on enough to give Greene and Stone access to some nightclub work for Sonny and Cher.

Sonny and Cher's first engagement was an opening act for Ike and Tina Turner at the Purple Onion nightclub in Los Angeles in November 1964.

At this point, Sonny and Cher were living with Cher's mother and Gilbert LaPiere on Beaumont Drive in upper-class Truesdale Estates, outside of Los Angeles. The couple could no longer pay rent now that so much time was invested in Sonny's own business ventures instead of in Phil Spector's. Bono wasn't making much money, and it has been said that he wasn't enchanted by the idea of living with Cher's mother and stepfather, especially given Georgia's low opinion of him. 'She didn't think I was bright, just because I had long hair,' he recalled. 'She couldn't relate to me in any way, especially when it came to my relationship with Cher.'

She and Sonny were a couple, and her family would just have to accept that, Cher decided. 'Even if they didn't approve of Sonny, Georgia was probably glad to have Cher in the house where she could keep an eye on her,' said a friend. 'Sonny just came along as part of the deal. They had the most incredible bathroom you've ever seen. People would come from miles around just to go to the bathroom in their home.'

Sonny and Cher didn't have much going for them at this time in terms of musical arrangements or stage presentation. They had no musicians they could call their own, so for the Purple Onion and all the other early gigs they had to hire independent players and teach them the weak arrangements to the songs Sonny decided they should perform. Harold Battiste had the unenviable job of teaching these haphazard charts to the musicians.

Sound check for the Purple Onion opening night was a disaster. It turned into a full-blown rehearsal, and when Ike and Tina Turner showed up, Sonny and Cher were still rehearsing 'Baby Don't Go'. In true Bono fashion, they practised the song until their throats were raw. 'It's just not right, damn it!' Sonny shouted at Battiste. 'These musicians sound like *shit*!'

Cher, in her jeans and T-shirt, sat on the stage, her legs crossed in front of her. 'I'm bored,' she complained to Sonny. He ignored her, saying to Battiste instead, 'Harold, what can we do? This is going to be humiliating.'

There wasn't much time to do anything. Ike and Tina were quickly ushered backstage so that they wouldn't be able to hear just how poor their opening act really was.

Sonny was right; the show was humiliating. The audience sat stone-faced as the couple performed a few numbers. As they left, there was a smattering of applause. When Ike and Tina Turner came on to the stage, the Purple Onion rocked with loud music and a fully fledged show, Ikettes and all.

'The Purple Onion gig was an odd experience,' recalled Bob Johnston, a former stagehand who freelanced as a security guard for nightclubs on the Sunset Strip. 'Sonny had to push, and I do mean *push*, Cher out onto the stage. Someone told me she even pretended to faint before the show, and that Sonny bent over her and whispered in her ear to get the hell up and get out and onto the stage. She wore a shell-beaded blouse, off-white crepe pants, and high heels. It wasn't your Sonny and Cher look that was popularized years later. Sonny was in a suit that matched Cher's inexpensive ensemble. Dick and Dee Dee were a brother–sister act Sonny and Cher were trying to copy at the time. Charlie Greene sold all his suits to buy stage wear for the two of them. After the Purple Onion, they were booked with Tom Jones in Long Beach, California. I think it was a skating rink or something. They were probably paid about a hundred bucks a night back then.

'I recall Cher as being this very disagreeable character, street tough and with a vocabulary like a truck driver's. Belligerence took on new meaning. . . .'

Sonny Bono, Charles Greene and Brian Stone continued to pool their money so that Cher could record some material on her own at Gold Star Studios. On 7 February 1965, she recorded the first of many Bob Dylan compositions she would rework over the next couple of years. Cher had the perfect voice for Dylan. Hers was a sad, dejected sound. She sounded as if she were always on the edge of tears. 'All I Really Want to Do', a simple plea for friendship, was to become a top-twenty record for Cher when it was finally released in July.

Sonny produced three more sessions for Cher in the next couple of months ('Needles and Pins', still another version of his biggest-selling composition at this point, 'I Go to Sleep' and 'The Bells of Rhymney'), and then in April he secured a major deal for Cher at Imperial Records, a subsidiary of Liberty. At last Cher had her own record deal with a major company. It's said, though, that Bono didn't have much confidence in the message-oriented material that Cher told him she wanted to record at Imperial. So for her first release he wrote and produced a piece of fluff called 'Dream Baby'. It's no doubt the biggest Phil Spector rip-off of all time. The production had all the typical Spector elements: heavy on the indelible hook lines, fully realized background arrangements, and double- (or was that triple-?) tracked lead vocals from Cher. In fact, Bono speeded up Cher's voice in the final mix so that she would sound more 'commercial'.

Her performance on this record is tenderhearted and memorable. It's a true teen lament, even if it does not provide the most imaginative setting for Cher's voice. The sound on the single issue is so muddy that one reviewer said, 'You keep taking the needle off the record to clean off the dust, only there's no dust on your needle.'

When the Imperial Records staff got hold of 'Dream Baby', they thought they had the greatest hit record of all time. They didn't realize that the Phil Spector sound was all but dead and buried by 1965. Motown was monopolizing the spots on the charts that the Beatles hadn't already cornered.

The song was issued with the label copy reading 'Cherilyn' because Sonny felt that at one point he might want to secure a new deal for Sonny and Cher and he wasn't sure he'd be able to do this if Cher's name was tied up at Imperial. As it turned out, her future Imperial releases were issued as 'Cher', and Sonny and Cher continued recording for a competitive label. 'It's all in the contracts,' said Sonny with a grin.

first road tour

Sonny and Cher's first concert tours are textbook examples of the kinds of hardships young rock-and-roll upstarts endured in the Sixties. They were paid roughly $350 a week to appear at thirty concerts over a forty-five-day period. They carried very primitive amplification gear and used the house's lighting and sound systems. Old-timer stagehands who knew nothing about rock and roll would never allow them to play their music loud enough.

Harold Battiste recalled, 'This is when things started to get sticky. I would have to hire different musicians in every city, and that was crazy. We'd get local cats in every town, and they had to be young because the older guys would never be able to understand Sonny's musical arrangements. The guys we used in the studio didn't want to go out on the road. Sometimes we used musicians from other bands who were on the bill. The only thing that was consistent was that it was always a mess.'

Sonny and Cher would appear at rock-and-roll concert events with groups like The Dave Clark Five and The Animals. The acts always caused a panic wherever they appeared, and even though Sonny and Cher were not popular yet, they were still 'stars' and fair game for over-zealous souvenir seekers. All the groups were told that if the audience started to converge onto the stage the show would have to stop. The youngsters would have to control themselves before the performance could continue, and an announcement to that effect would be made if necessary. Promoters were responsible for the safety of the youngsters who paid to see these shows.

'You mean, they're going to come up on to the stage with *us*?' Cher asked, horrified at the thought. She was terrified of performing in the first place, and she only did it because Sonny made her. But the idea of being mobbed by a team of wild youngsters was more than she could bear.

'In her own mind, I'm sure Cher was more afraid than anyone else could ever be in this world,' Harold Battiste said. 'But Sonny was very confident and reassuring. She could afford to be frightened because he was there to support and encourage her. She was his creation, after all – his baby.'

'In the old days when I first started, I was terrified of the crowd,' Cher told a reporter years later. 'When we were doing the rock-and-roll shows and stuff like that, you never got to finish a song. You took the money and ran like hell. . . .'

Musician Ted Wright described the atmosphere of these first road tours: 'The tour promoter would send someone out with all the young kids to act like a commanding officer. He'd bully them about being on time and threaten to leave them behind if they were late getting to the bus. I'm sure that scared the shit out of Cher. Sonny and Cher did a lot of bus work, which meant they'd travel from one city to the next with thirty other young singers and musicians all crammed into a smelly, dirty bus. Your seat was yours and yours alone for the whole tour. In the back of the bus is where all the wilder kids got high on drugs or had sex. Sonny was very conservative, always; no drugs and no sex. He and Cher sat in the front of the bus.

'Everyone on the bus had transistor radios, and all of the radios were set to different stations because the groups wanted to hear their hits as they passed from one town to the next. The noise was unbelievable. The bus would never be clean; every time it turned a corner, soda and beer bottles would go rolling across the middle aisle. Some of the so-called "stars" were pigs; they'd urinate in the back of the bus if they couldn't wait for a rest stop.'

Most rock stars had an unkempt look about them, and they also maintained a bad reputation for stealing from the hotels in which they stayed. So, as soon as the bus would depart for the next stop, maids and managers would take quick inventory and report all thefts to the authorities. In no time, the state police would overtake the bus, sirens wailing and lights flashing. Pillows, towels, small televisions sets would all be discovered by the police and taken back to the hotel. Sometimes charges were pressed against the thieves; sometimes the hotel didn't bother.

All of this was exciting to Cher, but it was hard work, and after a few weeks of it she grew to hate it as much as that job she'd held at See's Candy Store. 'But she was pretty quiet, not assertive at all then,' Battiste confirmed. 'She was passive, usually receptive to whatever needed to be done. She was a novice, and Sonny was the cat she knew had the experience to make her a star. She was obedient as hell. . . .'

The arena house lights would dim and the young crowd would begin to wail and scream as the excitement built. Cher would stand in the wings frozen in her miniskirt as the announcer introduced them. 'Son, I can't,' she pleaded. And then before she knew what was happening, she'd feel his hand on her back and she would be very literally launched onto the stage.

Afterward, many of the artists would congregate backstage in the dressing rooms, eating snacks and smoking dope. Sonny wouldn't allow Cher to socialize with the musicians; he was strictly opposed to drug abuse, saying that he'd had his share of it when he was a youngster and he didn't want Cher exposed to it at all.

Cher was dead set against drugs, anyway. 'Once I asked someone to tell me about cocaine and he said, "Well, it makes you high and it makes your heart beat fast,"' Cher recalled. 'I said, "It makes your heart beat fast?" and he said yeah. I said, "Okay, pass. . . ."' When I used to get nervous my heart would beat really fast and anything that would make it beat faster I wanted nothing to do with. I can't even take aspirin.'

(When Cher was fourteen years old, she and some of her girlfriends had attended a party, and in all the excitement she was coaxed into taking two benzedrines. She stayed wide awake for two days, chewing the same piece of gum for the whole weekend. When she finally recovered from the effects of the drug, she said she felt as if someone had broken her jaw. 'Mother!' she screamed. 'Look what I've done. Am I gonna *die?*' 'My mother said, "I hope you've learned your lesson from this." And I said, "I swear to God, I have." That was the first and last time for me.')

By June 1965, Sonny Bono had produced at least a dozen demonstration tapes of songs he had written for himself and Cher. With Cher secure at Imperial, her first release scheduled for July, he suggested to Charlie Greene that they contact Ahmet Ertegun, president of Atlantic Records, to see if he would have any interest in signing Sonny and Cher as a duo. Ertegun and Bono were acquainted with each other because of promotional work Bono had done for some of the Atlantic roster.

Ertegun had founded Atlantic Records in 1947, and had been a friend of jazz bands, rhythm-and-blues singers, rock and rollers and cabaret performers for years. Atlantic's R&B stars are legendary: The Drifters, The Coasters, Ben E. King, Booker T and the MG's, Esther Phillips, Roberta Flack, Otis Redding, and Aretha Franklin, to name just a few. Its rock line-up has included Led Zeppelin; Crosby, Stills and Nash; Buffalo Springfield; and the Rolling Stones.

Ertegun is the eldest son of Turkey's ambassador to France, England, and later the United States. While studying at St John's University in New York as a graduate student in philosophy – with a special interest in Aristotle – Ertegun decided to go into the music business. He and Herb Abramson started Atlantic; the first two signed artists were Tiny Grimes, a jazz guitarist, and Joe Morris, a trumpet player from Lionel Hampton's band.

With no experience, Ertegun became a record producer. Later, he would be joined by *Billboard* columnist Jerry Wexler; together they produced some of the most astonishing and imaginative rhythm-and-blues music of the decade. In 1968, Atlantic became the largest seller of soul music, surpassing its chief rival at the time, Motown.

'It's not surprising that Sonny Bono singled out Atlantic as the label he'd like Sonny and Cher to record for,' said Barry Ginsmore, a pop music archivist. 'The label was chiefly known for its black music at the time, and Sonny's roots were strongly black-influenced. It's odd, when you consider the total picture, to think of Sonny Bono as a soul music enthusiast, but that certainly was the case.'

Ertegun played Bono's music and was duly impressed. Though he didn't know it at the time, Ertegun was also a friend of Cher's mother, Georgia. 'Ahmet is one of the most unique men I have ever met,' Cher once said. 'He could sit down with James Brown and then go out with Henry Kissinger, and it wouldn't faze him.'

Ertegun gave Sonny and Cher their first big break. He offered them a small-money recording deal: two thousand dollars as an advance against 7.5 per cent royalties on all product, with the proviso that Bono produce all the team's material for the next five years (that was Sonny's idea; he would not work with any outside producers). Eventually, Ertegun sweetened this deal, but not until Bono proved himself a commercial success.

On 7 July 1965, Sonny Bono walked into the Gold Star complex with the song that would change the course of his and Cher's entire life. Sonny wrote 'I Got You Babe' as an expression of his feelings for Cher and hers for him. They aren't the most exalted lyrics, but they addressed the hearts of a restless generation of young people.

Val Johns, who at this time was recording his final album for Carlton, *Mashin' the Classicks* (sic), recalled the session. 'My time slot at Gold Star followed theirs for "I Got You Babe". Sonny had every balalaika, mandolin, and guitar player in town squeezed into the studio. Literally, there must have been fifty people at that session. All of the musicians were laughing about it because it was so obviously wasteful to have so many people playing virtually the same simple chords. "I Got You Babe" isn't the most revelatory arrangement ever written.'

Harold Battiste, the song's arranger, concurred. 'We stretched the capacity limit for musicians in a studio, that's for certain. But it was that way on every single Sonny and Cher session. Sonny got that from Phil Spector. If the fire marshal had come and seen how many musicians were squeezed into the studio, we'd all have been arrested. I used to say that the real technical achievement wasn't in recording Sonny and Cher, it was in getting everyone into that studio and then still finding room for instruments and mikes.'

Bono recorded 'I Got You Babe' (a 'fun session, we had a real ball,' said Battiste), and over the next couple of days (7–9 July), five more songs for Cher that, combined with the four he'd already produced, would be consolidated into Cher's first solo album for Imperial, *All I Really Want to Do*. The album would include her interpretations of Dylan's 'Blowin' in the Wind' and 'Don't Think Twice'.

'Sonny would always take Cher further than I thought he needed to take her,' Battiste recalled. 'He'd push her to the limits of exhaustion in the recording studio. Often I felt he was pushing the girl too hard. Sometimes she would sing a song twenty times, and then look at me for emotional rescue. She would be inside the booth, Sonny and I on the outside, and when he'd turn his head she'd give me an exasperated expression as if to say, "Harold, is all *this* necessary. What *is* he trying to do?"'

Bono, again, was utilizing what he'd picked up from Phil Spector, and the manner in which Spector had recorded Ronnie Bennett. The first dozen or so takes were never good enough. Spector believed that an artist never reached the pinnacle of his ability until he was exhausted. Recording was always a trying experience for Cher, who much preferred spontaneity over Bono's technique.

'Sonny had very grandiose ideas about musical composition as well,' Battiste continued. 'He was much more extrovert artistically speaking than I was, but then I'd have to arrange the music. I kept hearing myself say, "Oh, man, you can't do *that* in a song, it'll sound crazy." But he thought he could do anything, and he was right. There are no limits to art.

'The joke, though, was that he really couldn't play the piano. We used to laugh about whether he could play two chords or three. So I would have to take this massive arrangement he had in his head and translate it onto paper for the musicians. He always wanted to surround Cher with big, enveloping productions.

'After she was finished recording, we stayed on that record mixing and mastering forever and a day. He was never concerned about what Imperial or Atco, the record labels, would say about the money he spent on studio time. My personal background had shown me that we didn't need all that studio time for these simple Sonny and Cher records, but Sonny was sometimes obsessed.'

i got you babe . . . but not legally

It was 1965. The year of the Motown regime. The year John Sebastian and the Lovin' Spoonful offered 'Do You Believe in Magic?' and the Rolling Stones countered with 'Hey You, Get Off of My Cloud' and 'I Can't Get No Satisfaction'. It was the year The Righteous Brothers lost 'That Lovin' Feeling' and Pete Seeger adapted a passage from Ecclesiastes for 'Turn, Turn, Turn', later recorded by the Byrds. The Beatles continued to record the purest of pop music experiences. It was the year of Dylan's 'Like a Rolling Stone' and 'Mr Tambourine Man', and a year in which the United States resumed air attacks on North Vietnam.

Sonny and Cher's first single release for Atco was 'Just You', an absolute clone of Phil Spector's production of 'Baby I Love You' by The Ronettes. In his excellent analysis of Cher's recorded work in *Goldmine* magazine (October 1980), Rick Wilson said of 'Just You': 'It was a sumptuous and magnificent piece of folk-rock history. Heavily indebted to Spector and a tribute to Gold Star Studios, it can only be called three and a half minutes of heaven. The lyrics were strictly teen lament, but it was nevertheless a technical masterpiece in aural dimension. The majority of the backing was far, far in the background, but deafeningly so.'

It really was a strong single, and went as high as number twenty on the charts, an impressive Atco debut. The flip side of the release, 'Sing C'est la Vie', a silly little ditty that lent an Italian-style production to Doris Day's 'Que Sera Sera' theme, was a strong seller in Europe.

But nothing the two of them had recorded until this point was as riveting as 'I Got You Babe'. Bono decided that this should be the next release, and he produced a truly maudlin B side for it called 'It's Gonna Rain'.

He sent the master to Ahmet Ertegun in New York for his approval.

The next day, the phone rang, Ertegun calling Bono. 'This new single, "It's Gonna Rain", is a solid hit. It'll be top ten in four weeks,' Ertegun predicted.

Sonny was stunned. 'Get *serious*, Ahmet. "I Got You Babe" is the A side. You got the songs mixed up. "I Got You Babe" is the *hit* side.'

Ertegun wasn't convinced; he thought "I Got You Babe" was trite silliness and he ordered it released as the flip side to 'It's Gonna Rain'.

'Sonny was pissed off. He was a promotion man, he felt he knew music, and he was determined about his choice,' said a friend. 'So he did what only Bono would do. He defied Ertegun, a cardinal sin, and used his own connections at the popular KHJ radio station in Los Angeles to get "I Got You Babe" played once an hour as an "exclusive".'

In no time, the radio station's phone lines were lighting up with requests for Sonny's preference. Ertegun had no choice. 'It's Gonna Rain' became the B side. 'Please, Sonny, don't try anything like that again,' he begged as Atlantic was flooded with shipping orders for 'I Got You Babe'.

On 14 August 1965, 'I Got You Babe' topped the *Billboard* pop chart and became the number-one song in the country. 'I Got You Babe' is by far Sonny and Cher's best recording. Here it becomes apparent that Cher is singing in Sonny's register. He really had no range to go to, so she had to go to his. In a short while, Cher would begin sounding a bit flat and off key in her recordings, mostly due to the fact that she was so strongly influenced by Bono. (On 'All I Really Want To Do', Cher sings a call-and-response delivery, and her responses sound almost exactly as they would had Sonny recorded them – their voices slowly became almost identical.)

Cher's tonal quality was interesting because she had one of those voices that went 360 degrees around a note but never really centred on it. Sonny never even came close to the note. Oddly, when the two voices were paired the result was never a true tone, was not perfectly pitched, but somehow sounded *warm*. With Sonny and

Cher, the warm harmony made them sound as though they could really sing.

'Sonny and Cher began to fill the social aspirations of a lot of kids,' said Harold Battiste, who also arranged 'I Got You Babe' (and was responsible for the striking use of the 2/2 timed flute and oboe on the track). 'They were saying in their music that adults don't really understand us and so they try to keep us away from love. But we *can* love and we don't need the Establishment. The lyrics to "I Got You Babe" pretty much say it all as far as Sonny and Cher's entire career is concerned.'

Sonny and Cher quickly became the perfect commercial realization of the Sixties hippie. They were one of the first acts in popular music to combine music and fashion. The appeal was not simply aural; it was visual as well. Two young female designers who, Cher has recalled, 'were really weird and freaked out', designed the outrageous stage wear for which Sonny and Cher would become known.

Cher's trademark elephant bell-bottoms and fur vests would become as integral to her persona as her straight raven black hair and heavy eyeliner. 'Everyone thought the look was odd, but it caught on,' she said of the bell-bottoms. (According to most fashion journalists, Cher was really responsible for the popularization of the bell-bottomed look.) 'That taught me to dress how I feel. One of my pride-and-joy outfits was red, white and blue striped bell-bottoms, an industrial pants zipper with a huge pull ring, and bell-sleeved blouse.'

Life magazine said in November 1965: 'Cher does not own a dress, and Sonny doesn't own a tie. Her trademark is slacks which are snug around the hips, then flare out below the knees. She has hundreds of them, every color, and thousands of her fans regard her as a style setter and have taken to wearing them, too.' Bono's costumery was equally outrageous: Phil Spector-inspired bobcat fur vests, fur slippers, paisley prints, beads – sometimes he even wore short pants with black socks.

With 'I Got You Babe' and the hit records that followed it, Sonny and Cher, along with the Byrds and the Mamas and the Papas, became West Coast purveyors of the folk-rock sound Bob Dylan had defined and popularized on the East Coast. In terms of rock and roll, they were the bridge between the dying Phil Spector girl group sound and the new American music as it recouped its losses after the British invasion. Historically, though, Sonny and Cher have never been recognized as part of the revitalization of American pop, or as being at all integral to contemporary Sixties music.

'It's a rewrite of history,' says one industry observer, 'mostly due to the fact that they never appeared *serious* the way the Byrds, the Mamas and the Papas, and even the Beach Boys did. Sonny Bono was an important figure in rock history; you can't really credit Cher with anything more than just being with him. He produced a healthier and more imaginative collection of music than any of Phil Spector's other protégés. But it wasn't respected because so many people believe Sonny was a thief when it came to his art.'

Sonny and Cher were happy in their relationship, and their contentment was obvious in their performances together. They made love and marriage very fashionable in a period when free love was the catch phrase. The irony, of course, is that the two of them were not married. Had it been revealed in 1965 that they were simply living together, their innocent image would surely have been shattered.

Exactly when the two of them were married has always been somewhat of a mystery. When they became role models for young people, they claimed in press interviews that they were legally married on 27 October 1964, in Tijuana, Mexico. The date seemed legitimate, as it was a little more than a year after the first anniversary of Sonny's divorce.

Another version of the story had it that the two discovered after the Tijuana nuptials that Sonny had forgotten to have his divorce papers finalized; he hadn't signed the interlocutory decree. When he finally did, he and Cher were remarried on 13 December 1965.

Still another story, and this one from Sonny Bono years later, has it that he and Cher weren't married 'until sometime in 1966 or 1967. We were living together,' he admitted, 'but you couldn't just live together in those days. So my lawyer arranged for a wedding in our house in Bel Air. There were no guests or reception. It was very quiet.'

Bono's story seems to jibe with those by others who worked with him and Cher at that time. Charlie Greene had insisted that he tried to convince the two of them to marry before some clever newspaper reporter discovered their secret. But Bono realized that it would be impossible for them to walk into the office of a justice of the peace and have a marriage ceremony without also having a great deal of publicity. So, according to Greene, he and his partner Brian Stone engineered it so that Sonny and Cher could go to Tijuana and pay $7,500 to a marriage registry official to marry them and backdate the documentation. But Bono thought that was a waste of money, and the idea was scrapped.

The truth is that the wedding Sonny and Cher said they had in Tijuana in 1964 really took place – but Cher performed the ceremony herself in a bathroom of the hotel they had checked into. The two of them exchanged twelve-dollar silver rings with their names engraved on them. They were married in their hearts, and that's all that really mattered as far as they were concerned.

Sonny and Cher were legally married in 1969, right before Chastity was born.

bittersweet success

With the success of 'I Got You Babe', Sonny and Cher became regulars on all the teen-oriented dance and rock-and-roll television programmes of the period. Exposure on these shows gave the two a strong boost of publicity and promotion. They were favourites on NBC's 'Hullabaloo' and its ABC counterpart, 'Shindig' – both rare attempts by television programmers to give Sixties rock a big-budget showcase in prime time. Each week, top recording artists lip-synced (performed to a pre-recorded track) their current release, backed by elaborate productions and frantic miniskirted dancers.

Sonny and Cher's first appearance on 'Hullabaloo' was in September 1965, with The Everly Brothers, Neil Sedaka, and Nancy Sinatra – three acts you couldn't exactly call outrageous dressers. During rehearsal, everyone on the show would have lunch, socialize, and talk shop. But Sonny and Cher weren't really accepted because of the way they looked. That was part of the hypocrisy of Sixties pop stars. They were all fighting for acceptance and recognition, but within the ranks they snubbed each other. Nancy Sinatra said that they looked like two clowns, and someone went up to Charlie Greene and told him, 'You got yourself a great little circus act here.' Greene shot back, 'Yeah, I know, and I'm gonna make big stars out of these clowns, and a lot of money off them too.'

Peter Matz was the musical director of 'Hullabaloo', and when Sonny and Cher walked in, she with the flower-patterned bell-bottoms and fringe vest, he in some kind of animal fur with woolly boots, Matz shook his head and said, 'Christ, pop music is going right down the toilet.'

Greene and Stone arranged a tour budget with Ertegun so that Sonny and Cher could test their appeal internationally. 'Sing C'est la Vie' sold fairly well in Britain, and with the success of 'I Got You

Babe' in the States, bookings were not difficult to secure in England. 'It was easy because they were promotable,' Ertegun has said. 'They were in the vanguard of the times, not only in music but also in fashion.'

At first, the British press paid no attention to Sonny and Cher. They looked ridiculous; so what else was new? 'But in one day our lives totally changed,' Cher recalled in an interview. 'We got thrown out of the London Hilton Hotel at about nine o'clock in the morning and by seven that night we were famous. All of a sudden everyone wanted to know who we were.'

What Cher didn't know then was that Charles Greene, always the unabashed promotional wizard, arrived at the Hilton five minutes before his clients, and then paid £100 to the hotel manager to have the two of them thrown out when they tried to check in. Greene had notified the press corps ahead of time that a major story would be breaking at the Hilton. Reporters were positioned when Sonny and Cher showed up at the ritzy hotel dressed in their 'work clothes', and camera flashes popped when the manager dramatized the eviction scene. It was masterful, and the con would go on for months.

Back in the United States, the word was out: Sonny and Cher, who were riding the charts with 'I Got You Babe' (and Cher with 'All I Really Want to Do'), were getting thrown out of the best hotels in Europe and at one point had to stay at Ahmet Ertegun's flat in London at 6 Thurloe Place because no one would have them. 'And to think,' one reporter noted, 'all they really want to do is be friends with you,' he wrote, quoting Cher's hit song.

Teenagers everywhere began to identify with these young rebels who were simply trying to pass on a message of peace and love to an unsympathetic Establishment. From this point on, Sonny and Cher were expected to be completely revolutionary. In reality, they were very traditional (apart from the fact that they weren't married) and when it came right down to it, they would stick to their conservative values and not represent youngsters in a revolutionary manner.

But Sonny and Cher were not complete frauds. The way they felt about each other was real affection, if not passion. They spent as much time with each other as possible, sharing and growing. Bono nurtured Cher, protected her, and loved her. To her, he was everything that mattered. She would continue to sing in concert and on records to satisfy Sonny's ambition more than her own.

Still, walking out on that stage was a terrifying experience for Cher every time she had to do it. She would sit in the dressing room, numb and sick to her stomach, wishing that somehow the concert would be cancelled. Greene and Stone would try to convince her that she would be fine, that the crowds would be controlled, and that the show would be a success. Then Sonny would help her apply her make-up. With Greene on one side of her, Stone on the other, and Bono walking ahead clearing the way through crowds of reporters and fans, Cher would make her way to the stage. She would perform, but she wouldn't remember any of it afterwards because she was paralyzed with fear.

Sonny had his own problems to deal with. He was suffering with gallstones and was in almost constant pain. A shot of bourbon, though, and he could pull himself through a performance.

When Sonny and Cher played the Hollywood Bowl in Los Angeles, the show was sold out in twenty-four hours; the two of them had to be smuggled in and out of the stadium in an armoured car. They had reached the pinnacle of their first cycle of success by January 1966.

In the audience sat Cher's mother, Georgia, and as she watched her daughter's performance she saw mirrored in the girl all of her own aspirations for a career in show business. Georgia's own dream would never materialize. It was a proud, but also a painful, moment. 'My father lived to see Cher become a star,' she said. 'We sat together when they appeared at the Hollywood Bowl, and he kept telling me, "That's *you* up there, Jackie, that's *you*."'

When they continued the concert tour to San Francisco, the crowd of youngsters who came to see the performance became hysterical with excitement. Cher's coterie of protection was somehow scrambled in the ruckus and a security guard, mistaking her for a fan, pushed her aside. She hit a wall with a thud. 'Have that ass fired,' Sonny fumed to the nightclub manager when he realized what had happened.

'That's it, no more of this for me,' Cher decided aloud when they finally made it to the dressing room. 'I'm finished.'

'She almost quit right then and there,' said Battiste. 'But Sonny convinced her that they should hang in there for just one more year, and then that would be the end of it. He knew this gimmick couldn't last forever.'

Cher began to wonder how much concern Sonny had for her safety and welfare, and how this compared with the way he felt about the creation he'd molded called 'Sonny and Cher'. If he really cared, she thought, he wouldn't force her to be so miserable.

Cher was petrified of flying. Buses were an uncomfortable method of transportation – but at least they didn't leave the ground. 'She was afraid to step on a plane,' said Charlie Greene. 'And the only way we could get her to fly was to start her drinking vodka hours before the flight. Charlie and I would walk on either side of her, holding her, while Sonny would walk ahead, pretending he wasn't with us. Eventually, some of the airlines would help us with getting Cher on the plane. They would supply us with a wheelchair.'

Greene's comments were to Brian Haugh of the *Star*. Harold Battiste refuted them. Said Battiste, 'Cher hated to fly, yeah, but vodka? How's she gonna perform on stage with a vodka hangover? Maybe she had a couple of drinks, but she wouldn't get loaded, not so drunk that they had to wheel her onto the airplane.'

But another source added, 'It depended on how far they had to fly, how long she had to be in the plane. Cher hated to drink, as much as she hated drugs. But I think she hated flying more than anything, and she'd throw a couple down if it meant she'd be knocked out for the flight. She was only nineteen years old. My God, what a life she must've been leading. When was she ever happy?'

'It was on a European trip that I first realized how limited Cher's life had become,' said Battiste. 'Much of what a tourist could do in a foreign country, she couldn't even think about doing because she was so recognizable. Sonny would set up special activities for her; he was like a teacher and she was a student on a field trip. He'd hire a movie house after hours, just so she could see a film and not be bothered by fans.'

The next few months were exciting ones. Sonny and Cher hosted cocktail parties for pop phenomenons like Twiggy, and when the Rolling Stones came to the United States on their first tour, they took refuge at Sonny and Cher's and slept on the living room floor. The couple appeared on an episode of the popular 'The Man From UNCLE' spy series starring Robert Vaughn and David McCallum, with Sonny playing a dress manufacturer and Cher a high-priced model. (They became embroiled in an inane espionage plot line that involved a multicoloured dress and pattern that contained a secret code. Their acting was horrendous and they didn't sing, though strains of 'I Got You Babe' played in the background as the plot thickened.)

In September 1965, socialites Mr and Mrs Charles Engelhard gave a black-tie party in a suite of New York City's Waldorf-Astoria Towers for former first lady Jacqueline Kennedy. In planning the chic event, Jane Engelhard asked Mrs Kennedy who she would like to have perform. Amazingly enough, she requested Sonny and Cher. Charles Greene and Brian Stone were contacted, the Sonny and Cher camp was astonished, and the evening was planned.

First order of business: what should they wear? Greene suggested that Cher wear a dress. 'I hate dresses,' she complained. 'And I have terrible legs. I'm bow-legged. I won't wear a dress, even for Jackie Kennedy.'

Cher would wear her bell-bottoms, Sonny his bobcat vest. 'This is what Mrs Kennedy wants to see if she likes Sonny and Cher,' reasoned Bono. 'Why disappoint the woman?'

Charles Engelhard offered to compensate Sonny and Cher for their performance at this intimate gathering (only eighteen people attended), but Brian Stone felt the evening would hold better publicity value if it was a gratis show. This would be Sonny and Cher's 'coming-out party', their introduction to high society, he decided.

Dinner would include champagne, saddle of lamb, and *profiteroles au chocolat*. But Sonny and Cher would not eat with the socialites, and would later explain that they simply wouldn't have known how to act, eating with the former first lady. The truth is that Jane Engelhard didn't invite them to eat dinner – they were the entertainment and, in her mind, on a par with the people who *served* the food, not the ones who were to eat it. 'If we're good enough to perform, and we're doing it for free, the least they could do is feed us,' Cher lamented.

After the meal, Sonny and Cher were introduced. Mrs Kennedy watched intently; the whole room was fixed on their performance. Cher was tall, glamorous, and insouciant, regardless of the fact that she wore brown bell-bottoms and matching boots (Mrs Kennedy was wearing a pink satin evening gown). Jackie Kennedy lapped up Sonny and Cher's performance like cake frosting, and afterward she cornered Cher to tell her how much she had enjoyed the show. Lowering her voice an awed octave, Cher told Sonny, 'She said she thought our clothes were very *Shakespearean*! She's so down to earth.'

Later, she told friends, 'I have to admit that Jackie Kennedy looked a lot older than I thought she would. I thought she was better preserved. And her hands! They are so *big*! That woman has the biggest hands I think I've ever seen.'

Sonny, brimming with self-confidence, mingled with the black-tied socialites who pretended not to notice his fur vest. Cher tried to fit in with the other women there, acting as if she belonged when deep down she wished she were somewhere else. She moved about in a slow, studied manner, trying to appear chic in her bells, when she and Diana Vreeland made eye contact. Vreeland, grande dame of the fashion world, stared intently at this five-foot-seven-inch, 102-pound waif trying to melt into the wallpaper. She sidled over to Cher and gushed. 'Oh, my *dear*, you have a *pointed* head! You're beautiful! Look at you! You're so skinny, why aren't you in magazines?'

'All I could say was, "Uh, I dunno. . . ."' Cher once recalled. 'I was like that then.'

Vreeland, the then-editor of *Vogue* magazine, introduced Cher to photographer Richard Avedon, and a photo session was arranged. The original concept was to run two pictures of Cher, featuring her as a fashion innovator and doing a complete makeover of her dark aquiline face. She and Avedon ended up spending ten days on the project and Vreeland was so enthusiastic about the results she ran twenty photos in *Vogue*.

Cher wondered aloud if she would ever make the cover of *Vogue*. Avedon discouraged her. 'You just don't have that *Vogue* look,' he said. (Years later, Cher would appear on *Vogue*'s cover, three times.) 'The first layout was Cher's big break,' recalled a columnist and former friend of Cher's. 'She was amazed at how they made her look. She never dreamed she could look like that. She was tall, dark, and provocative and she'd never envisioned herself like that. The reason the sessions were so time-consuming was because they experimented with make-ups and hairstyles. Cher was never the same after this. There would always be a sense of elegance and glamour to her, even though she would continue to downplay it for years.'

Sonny and Cher may have been trendy and interesting-looking to avant-garde socialites, but the news media didn't share in the enthusiasm. 'The only way to distinguish man from wife,' said a *Newsweek* reporter of their performance at the Engelhards' gathering, 'was that Sonny's hair ended at his shoulders and Cher's fell to her waist.'

Hedda Hopper, infamous gossipmonger who held the Hollywood studios in a tight publicity grip for years, devoted space to Sonny and Cher in her 30 September 1965 column in the *Los Angeles Times*: 'Five producers, including Joe Pasternak, Steve Broidy, Peter Lawford, the Mirisch brothers, and Allied Artists, are after Sonny and Cher to star in a movie. If you're like me, you just said "Sonny and *who*?" Tuesday they flew east to entertain at a private party for Jackie Kennedy. A friend of mine thought they were a couple of girls; his hair is almost as long as hers. A couple of weeks ago I predicted that good music would be back shortly. My crystal ball has got to go. . . .'

A month later, Hopper reported that the couple had purchased a $75,000 home in Encino, 'and the real-estate man who made the sale is still numb. Sonny peeled off 150 one-hundred-dollar bills as a down payment. *Vogue* shot them last week,' she wrote. 'I'd like to shoot them too, but not with a camera. . . .' (Hopper wrote in another column that she received a letter from someone who admitted, 'I never liked Jackie Kennedy until she invited Cher to her party.')

Sonny did purchase a home on Academia Street in Encino for the amount Hopper quoted. Friends of the couple had to admit that this was the tackiest house they'd ever seen. 'The home was decorated in early American plastic,' said one friend. 'They moved into it as a model home, and they kept the furniture the house came with. Every room looked like something out of a Ramada Inn furnishings catalogue.

A few weeks after the Jackie Kennedy gala, Princess Margaret requested that Sonny and Cher perform at the World Adoption International Fund (WAIF) charity ball. The black-tie event would take place at the Hollywood Palladium on Sunset Boulevard. The Engelhard affair had been a success both in terms of acceptance and recognition and Sonny and Cher hoped the WAIF function would be more of the same. It didn't turn out that way.

Sonny wore a yellow turtleneck sweater, a white double-breasted and wide-lapel jacket, white slacks, and black boots. Cher was a matching book-end in a yellow-and-white-striped suede top and white bell-bottoms. Their look was toned down tremendously; it was apparent that they were hoping to be accepted by the more conservative show business elitists in the audience this evening.

Frank Sinatra was scheduled to perform, but he bowed out because of an illness. The audience was disappointed by Sinatra's no-show, and the function seemed endlessly boring. Bob Hope, in a white tuxedo, was to introduce Sonny and Cher after Jane Russell concluded a long-winded summation of 'why we are here tonight'. As he waited for Russell to finish proselytizing, Hope noticed Cher standing in the stage wings, frozen in anticipation. 'Why, how *are* you?' he asked, sizing her up. 'Terrific,' she thought to herself, 'I'm scared to death and now I have to make small talk with Mr Show Business.' 'I'm fine,' she responded glumly.

'It's terrible,' Hope continued, turning to Bono. 'Princess Margaret, she's got the flu or something, and this whole thing is taking forever.' Cher squeezed Sonny's hand so tightly she threatened to cut off his circulation. But Sonny, looking out past the footlights at the faces of Doris Day, Rock Hudson, Andy Williams, Danny Kaye, Zsa Zsa Gabor and Mary Pickford, had his own nervousness to deal with.

Hope walked out onto the stage and then, said a reporter for *Variety*, 'he made the worst mistake of the evening. He introduced Sonny and Cher.'

Cher picked up her hand mike as her legs carried her out from stage right and she sang 'Baby Don't Go'. Sonny made his entrance from stage left. They met in the middle, locking gazes, trying to ignore the audience in front of them.

Peter Bogdanovich, who would go on to direct Cher in her fifth motion picture some fifteen years after this night, was a young writer at this time for the *Saturday Evening Post*. He wrote of Sonny and Cher's performance: 'It sounded almost like a howl, and, with their heads thrown back, necks arched, facing each other, they called to mind a pair of lovesick coyotes on a solitary mountain. Cher held her microphone as though it were a goatskin wine bag and she were going to drink it dry.'

Princess Margaret sat ringside in her conservative blue chiffon ensemble with a smile frozen on her face. The people in her party conversed among themselves as if Sonny and Cher didn't exist. Cher began her solo, 'All I Really Want to Do', and her low vamp voice rumbled thoughout the theatre. Princess Margaret leaned over and whispered into the ear of an aide at her table. The small round man bolted from his chair and cut a beeline through the audience to the backstage area.

'You gotta turn her down,' he demanded of a stagehand. 'She's too loud for the princess's ears.'

The word was passed quickly to the sound technician; as he tried to adjust Cher's audio output, the power went dead and her solo was lost among the first couple of tables. Finishing the number quickly, she pretended not to notice the problem. She took her bows and retreated to the safety of the musicians' area, far from the spotlight's eye.

Sonny made his way to the front of the platform to address the crowd. Somehow, tonight he felt like a bumbling idiot. He wore his outfit as if it were the greatest afterthought of all time; he looked uncomfortable in it as he peered out among the tuxedos and gowns in the theatre. His awkwardness made everyone else even more aware of the fact that standing before them was a very insecure entertainer. 'We do, in a way, represent the *young* people. But it's nice to perform for you . . .' he began.

Well, it *seemed* funny when he thought of it.

The joke fell flat. Several people began to jeer as Bono searched for an apology. 'What I *meant* to say was, it's nice to perform for such *mature* people. Okay?'

'No, it's *not* okay, lunkhead,' someone shouted from the back.

'No? Well . . .' He was at a loss for words. The band struck up the dramatic flourishes to Sonny's solo, 'Ebb Tide'.

He began to sing, but he couldn't hear his own voice because the band was playing so loudly and the sound adjustment on Cher's performance made it impossible to hear the monitors. He strayed off key. A fat drunk in the middle of the theatre stood up on his chair and shouted at Bono, 'That's gotta be the *worst* thing I have ever heard!' The theatre erupted into laughter.

Cher, still standing among the musicians, suddenly looked stricken. She turned her back to the audience and began to cry. And then she counted the minutes, wishing the evening would end. Sonny finished his number like a seasoned trouper and after 'I Got You Babe', the two of them got off that stage so fast there were probably skid marks on the wood.

'They couldn't *hear* ya,' Joe deCarlo, who was hired by Greene and Stone as road manager for Sonny and Cher, tried to explain as the two entertainers walked dejectedly out onto the parking lot. 'They couldn't *hear* you, that's all it was. The mikes, they went dead, Sonny. They just couldn't hear what you were doing.'

'Sonofabitches didn't *want* to hear us,' Sonny snorted. 'Let's get the hell out of here. Cher, get your coat.'

She grabbed a ratty looking rabbit-skin coat and raced after Bono. Outside they walked in silence, Cher with their coterie of roadies, Sonny ahead of the party lost in anger and humiliation. All of the old fears and insecurities began to surface. 'Sonofabitches,' he kept repeating to himself.

To be faced with blatant hostility and cynicism from a show

business audience was demoralizing to Sonny Bono, and he suddenly realized that he wanted more for himself and Cher than the terrific pop gimmick they had become. Cher's wants and needs may have been undefined at this point, but Sonny's were not. He wanted respect.

In 1965, Bono had his first and only solo hit record: 'Laugh at Me' made it to the top ten on *Billboard*'s charts. Most people have forgotten that Cher had nothing to do with the song.

'Laugh at Me' was written by Sonny after a couple of unfriendly encounters in Los Angeles restaurants. At Martoni's Italian eatery, an expensive restaurant he and Cher frequented, Bono almost ended up in a brawl with a customer who came over to his table and called him a faggot. The maître d' offered to move the Bonos to another table on the other side of the room, but Sonny insisted that the offending party be moved. 'I've spent thousands of bucks eating at this joint,' he complained as Cher self-consciously shifted from one side of her seat to the other. 'All we're trying to do is eat a decent meal in peace.'

Later, a man stopped Charlie Greene, tweaked his beard, and gushed, 'Hey, you're cute!' Sonny's bodyguard rushed to Greene's aid and demanded, 'Whatdya want, mister?'

'What do *you* want?' the inebriated flirt responded.

'We don't want no trouble here,' the bodyguard, a menacing-looking character, said firmly. 'We're just trying to eat. Stop pulling our manager's beard.'

The owner of the establishment eventually asked the man and his friends to leave the restaurant. Shortly after, he came over to the Bonos' table and asked why there always seemed to be trouble whenever they came to his place of business for a meal. 'It's not our damn fault if tourists are always coming over to us and acting like asses,' Sonny defended.

'But it is,' the manager insisted, 'because you *dress* so funny.'

'I know that. But if you want our business, then the way we dress shouldn't matter.'

'Look,' the manager suggested matter-of-factly. 'Why don't you do us all a favour and dress your wife up and wear a suit and tie yourself next time you come here?'

Cher was mortified and she could feel the tears welling up in her eyes ('I cried a lot back then,' she remembers).

'No way,' Sonny countered, getting very angry. 'This is what Cher and I wear. Would you rather we didn't eat here?'

'Yes, now that you mention it,' the manager said.

The Bono party rose from their table and walked out as the other customers gawked at them suspicously.

'This image thing has gotten out of hand,' Cher moaned to Sonny as they walked to the car. 'It was okay at first, but now I'm really sick of it.'

It was almost midnight by the time they got back to Encino, and when they arrived home Sonny went straight to the garage in which he kept his piano. As Cher slept, he wrote 'Laugh at Me', a song whose lyrics asked why people couldn't accept one another at face value, the way they *really* were. The paradox here is that the way they appeared was not the way Sonny and Cher *really* were. The whole thing was an act – their marriage, getting kicked out of hotels, wearing the outrageous costumes. But Bono wrote the song anyway and the lyric is a heartfelt, thought-provoking one. 'I'm writing this for myself, and for Cher,' he said in the song's opening monologue.

The next day, before noon, he assembled a group of musicians together at Gold Star and cut 'Laugh at Me'. It was a rare experience for everyone involved because Bono didn't belabour the effort. His raw voice on the song is so unabashedly off pitch the record is almost comical. But the young buying public felt that Bono was speaking for them (as well as 'for Cher') all along, and this song seemed like a natural as soon as he finished it – in three hours.

By four o'clock that afternoon, Sonny had taken the tape over to the KHJ program director who had broken 'I Got You Babe' to the Los Angeles market. In two hours, the radio station was airing the tape and the disc jockeys were getting requests to play 'the new *SonnyandCher* record', a record that hadn't even been transferred onto vinyl disc yet. When it was issued, it sold more than 700,000 copies, and Bono made eight cents from each one. He also had a copy sent over to the manager of Martoni's.

By the end of 1965, Bono had placed five songs in the top twenty on *Billboard*'s charts: 'I Got You Babe', 'Laugh at Me', 'Baby Don't Go', 'Just You', and 'But You're Mine'. The first three were top ten.

In early 1966, it seemed as if Sonny and Cher had the recording industry by the horns. Bono would purchase new cars every month. A friend owned a foreign car dealership and when he had an automobile he thought Sonny would like, he'd place an ad in the *Los Angeles Sunday Times*: *'Sonny, come on in, I've got a great car for you.'* And Sonny would go down to the dealership and charge it.

'We had six cars and he collected cameras,' Cher said. 'I used to think, what's he going to *do* with fifty camera bodies? I noticed rich kids like Jane Fonda couldn't care less about clothes, houses, whereas poor people who suddenly get rich like we did, they want to buy *everything*. Somehow I never *felt* rich. Even when we made thousands a week. . . . It's not *organic* with me, richness. To be poor, now *that's* organic.'

Sonny and Cher had been advanced $100,000 to do a twelve-city tour of Australia. In January, they appeared on NBC's Danny Thomas special, 'My Home Town', with Mitzi Gaynor and Jim Nabors. The show was taped on the sets of MGM Studios and the couple sang 'I Got You Babe' and 'Sing C'est la Vie'. Thomas treated them with the greatest respect. An old vaudevillian himself, he understood visual theatre and showmanship, and buffed their egos by praising their success.

Cher designed a line of clothes for teenagers, an 'exclusive' collection of pants and tops ('sizes 5 to 15, $19.95 and up') for Gordon and Marx clothing manufacturers of California. She also designed two fake fur vests for Lou Nierenberg of New York.

In promoting her new venture, Cher was interviewed by Lydia

Lane for the *Los Angeles Times* (January 1966). For someone who was supposed to be representing the youth generation, Cher's comments were a bit surprising. 'I don't understand these dirty people or what they are trying to prove,' she bristled. 'If you wear your hair long, it has to be clean and attractive. Sonny washes his hair every day and I give myself a shampoo every other day. When a girl is cheap looking,' she said (and this showed just how far she had come in a couple of years) 'or if she has bad manners, she probably has had no one help her form her tastes. There are classes at school to teach you grammar, but there should be classes to teach you how to act and dress as well.'

On 12 January 1966, Cher recorded what Ahmet Ertegun called 'one of the greatest songs written since World War II: 'Bang Bang (My Baby Shot Me Down)'. Bono's composition is a mini opera, a pop tragedy about two youngsters who play cowboys and Indians as children, become engaged as adults, and have a bitter parting of the ways when he jilts her at the altar.

The song was a risk for the market at the time because Bono's production violates one cardinal rule of pop music: the song stops in the middle, and then starts again. The melody is written in a minor mode, is heavily eastern European, and sounds as if Bono stole the idea from a half-dozen gypsy laments.

Released in March 1966, 'Bang Bang (My Baby Shot Me Down)' became Cher's first major solo record (peaking at number two on the pop charts). An album, *The Sonny Side of Cher*, was recorded in January and February of 1966 and, sparked by the success of 'Bang Bang', became a great success.

Sonny was faring well on the charts, but if it was respect he was after he was going about it the wrong way. He may have been inventive, but he was forever stealing ideas from everyone else. He's most remembered, unfortunately, as someone who became successful by appropriating melodies and hooks from other sources into his own work. It's not difficult to hear 'Zorba the Greek' in 'Bang Bang (My Baby Shot Me Down)'.

'Sonny is very good at picking out certain commercial aspects of hit songs,' said Charlie Greene in an interview with *Rolling Stone*'s Chris Hodenfield. 'Just listen to "I Got You Babe" and Donovan's

"Catch the Wind" side by side. It's an influence. Sonny's clever. He's not a good songwriter, but he's a clever thief. No, thief is the wrong word. Influence . . . he uses *influence* well.' ('I Got You Babe' matches the melody of 'Catch the Wind' almost note for note.)

Charlie Greene also tells the story of Sonny's 'But You're Mine' (another top-twenty hit for Sonny and Cher in 1965): 'Sonny and Cher were on an airplane returning to the States from the 1965 British tour and Bono noticed Cher singing The Fortunes' "You Got Your Troubles I Got Mine" over and over again to herself. When the plane landed in New York, Bono called Jerry Wexler at Atlantic and played him an impromptu tape he'd made of his new song, "But You're Mine".'

'I got a *hit*! I got a *hit*!' he told Wexler. The Atlantic producer heard the tape and said. 'Okay, what's the joke? C'mon let me hear the hit.'

'I always tend to think we move in a continuum of whatever we are,' says Harold Battiste with a grin. 'We're the sum of whatever we've been. No doubt there was some influence. Sonny formulated a basis for producing around material he was familiar with. He found new ways to work within that framework. I would attribute his genius to the fact that he could steal without really stealing.'

Sonny and Cher's 'Baby Don't Go' is, to a large extent, a rewrite of Gale Garnett's 'We'll Sing in the Sunshine', while Sonny and Cher's 'Little Man' (number twenty-one on the charts in 1966) has strains of 'Hava Nagilla' in it. 'You and Me' imitates the Turtles' 'Happy Together', and Cher's 'Where Do You Go?' (October 1965) is yet another rewrite of 'Catch the Wind'.

Bono almost found himself in court over his composition 'Just You', because the melody is dangerously close to the one Phil Spector, Jeff Barry and Ellie Greenwich gave to The Ronettes' 'Baby I Love You'. The principals passed on the legal battle in the end, probably because Sonny and Cher's first album, *Look at Us*, included a couple of legitimate Spector/Barry/Greenwich compositions on it. The record sold more than 2 million copies. The not-so-great fortunes that were made from the single issue of 'Just You' were certainly recouped, if indeed any theft was involved, from the sales of that first album.

Sonny would continue to be 'influenced' for years to come. Sonny and Cher's 'The Beat Goes On' sounds exactly like Bob Dylan's 'The Trip'. And Sonny wasn't above being inspired by his own work. Soon Cher would have a hit single release called 'You'd Better Sit Down Kids' that was really a slower version of the hook to 'Sing C'est la Vie'.

Cher has said she liked the simplicity of Bob Dylan's work. To her, it somehow seemed less artificial than the material Sonny was writing. So she concentrated on expressing herself through music by Dylan, Bob Lind (she covered 'Elusive Butterfly'), Phil Ochs ('There But for Fortune'), Tim Hardin ('Reason to Believe'), John Sebastian ('Do You Believe in Magic?'), and other folk composers. She was also experimental in what she enjoyed, with material popping up on the Imperial solo albums like 'I Will Wait for You' (the love theme from 'The Umbrellas of Cherbourg'), Burt Bacharach's 'A House Is Not a Home', Joe Darion's 'The Impossible Dream', Miriam Makeba's 'The Click Song', and Rodgers and Hart's 'Sing for Your Supper'.

On her five solo Imperial albums between 1966 and 1968, Cher showed great insight in selecting material. These solo ventures were the first indication that she had any kind of taste in music – that, indeed, there *was* a mind at work, albeit quietly.

'Sonny wasn't crazy about the material on the solo Cher albums,' said Stephen Bradford a former Imperial Records executive. 'He felt that he could write his own classics. He kind of fancied himself a little Dylan, but his mind didn't work that way. He could fashion a hit, but he wasn't a *poet* like Dylan. Still, there *is* something to be said for being able to compose a hit no matter how you go about it. You can't take that away from the guy. Personally, I have never believed that Cher had anything to do with the selection of all those great folk songs for her albums. She never struck me as being intelligent enough to know good music that would last. But I did hear that she had to argue those songs onto her albums. . . .'

Said Harold Battiste, arranger of all the material, 'Sonny was Spector-influenced, but Cher wasn't. She was a folk singer at heart and the solo albums were a reflection of her personality while the duet albums were a reflection of his.'

Battiste offered a diplomatic appraisal of Cher's voice: 'She sang fairly in time, fairly in tune. But there was a sincerity in her sound, which in my opinion was the most important thing. She surrendered to her emotions and, I felt, really gave the material her all.'

The problem with Cher's solo work is that it was generally poorly produced; the Sonny and Cher albums got Bono's undivided attention. So, on her own, Cher's voice usually sounded harsh and painfully self-conscious. Most of the material screamed out for better delivery and the kind of quality treatment Bono gave all the duets for Atco. The solo albums, though, are rare expressions of Cher's early personality and are considered valued treasures by her fans.

In Feburary 1966, Joe deCarlo heard that Paramount was looking for an artist to sing the title track to a new Michael Caine film set for release in July called *Alfie*. Hal David and Burt Bacharach wrote a mellifluous theme song, and they wanted Dionne Warwick to record it for the original motion picture soundtrack album. Both had enjoyed great chart success with material personalized by Warwick, songs like 'Anyone Who Had a Heart' and 'Walk On By'.

Paramount executives felt that Dionne Warwick's career had peaked, that she wasn't contemporary enough, or gritty enough, to interpret a song for a movie as controversial as *Alfie* (the film was about the sexual exploits of a young gigolo).

Associate producer John Gilbert was contacted by deCarlo, who suggested that Cher would be perfect for the song. Her voice had depth, he said, a lot more than Warwick's, and it also had a sense of heartbreak about it that the song somehow demanded. Sonny agreed to produce the Bacharach/David composition.

But, again, Paramount thought this was a terrible idea.

'Who is this woman, *Cher?*' one out-of-touch executive demanded. 'She's a nobody. She's a step down from Diane [sic] Warwick.'

'Cher is the future,' Gilbert allowed, unrelenting. 'She's got a voice you can't beat. She's got *pathos*.'

The Paramount brass yielded to Gilbert, and Cher went on to become the first American artist to record 'Alfie'. (A British recording star, Cilla Black, was actually the first to record the song, but her version went by unnoticed.)

Cher's version was produced by Bono and arranged by Battiste. It made the *Billboard* charts in August 1966, but only got as far as thirty-two. It sold about 200,000 copies.

Bacharach and David were certain the song could do better than that. They felt that Bono's production was all wrong; it was all gusto and no subtlety. So a year later they produced the song for Dionne Warwick at Sceptor Records. This version, of course, went on to become a tremendous success for Warwick, considered today to be one of her signature songs.

The next major Sonny and Cher record wouldn't hit the top ten until January 1967. 'The Beat Goes On' was actually recorded back on 13 December 1965, at Gold Star. The song has become, along with 'I Got You Babe', as closely identified with Sixties culture as with Sonny and Cher's career. In fact, 'The Beat Goes On' is a pop music catchphrase still used in radio station promotions today. 'No matter how our careers went,' Bono said, 'I could always say that "The Beat Goes On" is mine, and that phrase will be around forever.'

The composition seems fresh even though there are elements of other popular arrangements of the period in it. It is classic commerciality, with a 'let's comment on trendy things' lyric line from Bono and a guttural bass and guitar arrangement from Battiste. Cher's performance here is influenced by Cass Elliott's wistful, soaring style, and Sonny tried to out-Dylan Dylan in nasal tones.

good times

By the mid-Sixties, the idea of pop stars making motion pictures was certainly not innovative. In the Fifties, *Rock Around the Clock* made a powerful statement that rock and roll was a visual as well as a musical experience. Elvis Presley's movies were the precursors of Prince's 1984 opus, *Purple Rain*. And after Presley's first couple of movies, the success of the Beatles' *A Hard Day's Night*, widely considered a pop masterpiece from director Richard Lester, inspired Sonny Bono. He and Cher were as *visual* as pop stars come. If their relationship could be captured on celluloid, if they could find a script that would allow them to play themselves, perhaps they could break into the film world.

He ached for 'credibility in this damn town', but the people around Sonny felt that this quest for approval from people who really didn't care about Sonny and Cher was unrealistic. Why exchange the security of their recording career for the uncertainty of a film venture? A movie would sap everyone's creative energy; there'd be nothing left to give to the music.

'Because I want *respect*, damn it, not more teen fans,' Bono countered. 'Doris Day and Rock Hudson did it. They made silly movies that earned money. We'll do it too.'

Colonel Tom Parker, who managed Elvis Presley, called Charlie Greene one day to tell him how much he enjoyed the Sonny and Cher creation. Just out of curiosity, he wondered what the next step in their career strategy would be. Greene mentioned Bono's film idea, and much to his surprise Parker agreed that this was the next logical move. Furthermore, he suggested they call the movie *I Got You Babe*. 'Do it real cheap,' he warned, 'and nothing artsy-fartsy. Just a movie. . . .'

Sonny was thrilled with the validation. He signed with Steve

Broidy Productions to develop a film starring Sonny and Cher for Columbia Pictures, called *I Got You Babe*, as Parker suggested. (Eventually the film's title would be changed to *Bang Bang* and *New Times, Happy Times* before Bono finally settled on *Good Times*.)

Cher hated the whole idea. To her, the only important thing right now was her relationship with Sonny. It was strained; he seemed more interested in business than in her. She knew that this movie would mean that she'd be separated from Bono while he was involved in production. Furthermore, she knew that she'd have no input into its creation.

'I don't want to do this movie,' she said to Sonny. 'Doesn't that count for *anything?*'

It didn't.

The film was sold to television for about $800,000, which is about how much it would cost to produce, before it was even shot. After that, most of the money generated would be profit; Sonny and Cher would own 33⅓ per cent of the movie.

In an interview for *Variety*, Sonny noted, 'MGM and Warner Brothers were very interested in the idea, but they wanted album rights too and we record for Atlantic. Joe Pasternak was willing to make the film without album rights, but MGM wouldn't go along. So Columbia gave us the best deal.' He then admitted that he was 'not the world's greatest singer. I was just gonna produce Cher's records at first; she is the singer. But how ya gonna fight City Hall?'

Cher cringed when she saw the *Variety* story; they were really going to make this movie. In the next couple of years, she would play Trilby to Sonny's Svengali through two rocky film experiences.

Sonny knew that he and Cher had box-office potential, but he was certain they would need a strong director to ensure that they'd be presented in the proper light. William Friedkin was hired for the job. Friedkin, a native of Chicago, started out as a director of live television at the age of eighteen. His shoestring-budget documentary, 'The People vs. Paul Crump', which explored the psychology of a man who had spent eleven years on death row, won an award at the San Francisco Film Festival and led to a position with David Wolper Productions.

With Wolper, he produced three documentaries for ABC. After

Good Times, of course, Friedkin would go on to direct The Exorcist
(for which he won an Academy Award, the youngest director until
that point ever to do so), and The French Connection (The French
Connection and The Exorcist won a total of seven Oscars). Most
recently, Friedkin directed the flim To Live and Die in LA (1985)
and Barbra Streisand's 'Somewhere' video from her The Broadway
Album collection.

Good Times was his first major work; he was twenty-nine years
old.

'Sonny was looking for a guy he could communicate with,'
Friedkin recalled. 'He had seen a couple of my documentaries and
was impressed by them. We met and liked each other immediately.
I thought he was a terrific songwriter, that he was saying things that
were very close to young people. I felt we could express visually
some of the things he and Cher expressed in their music.'

As sketched out in a screenplay by Tony Barrett from a story by
Nicholas Hymans, Good Times is a movie about a movie that was
never made. In an early scene, Sonny and Cher are walking lazily
down a quiet street, smiling and holding hands. 'Hey, wanna make
a movie?' Sonny asks nonchalantly.

'Naah,' Cher answers indifferently.

'Why?'

'Because I like what I'm doin' now, that's why.'

As the story goes, Bono signs a contract with a powerful film
tycoon played by George Sanders. He commits himself and Cher
to a hoary rags-to-riches potboiler of a script. But after considering
the matter, the two decide that they don't want to do the movie
because 'it's a cop-out and it doesn't reflect our lives or even our,
you know, personalities.'

They have just ten days to come up with a better idea; if they
don't they'll have to do Sanders' film.

In Walter Mitty daydreams, Sonny fantasizes about being 'Sheriff
Irving Ringo', a lawman whose bullets keep dribbling though his
gun belt. And then he's 'Jungle Morry', a Tarzan type in the bush
who yells ape calls in distress and alienates all the animals. Then
he's detective 'Johnny Pitzcatto', who shoots up everyone but the
gangsters pursuing him. It's all very silly. There are plenty of colours

and pop art designs with monochromes of reds and blues flashing about through Bono's fantasies.

After a few more movie parodies and visual gags, Sonny and Cher are threatened by the movie tycoon either to do his movie, 'or you'll never work in this town again.'

The slice-of-life Bono dialogue went like this:

CHER (hopelessly): 'You mean we gotta make that rags-to-riches junk? You said we didn't *have* to, Son.'

SONNY (sadly): 'Well, we do.'

CHER: 'And that's all you have to say? You just gonna let them tell us what to do?'

SONNY (getting angry): 'That's not it. We got a contract, don't you *understand*? It's either that or we're in a lot of trouble. You know nothing, *nothing* about business.'

CHER (sobbing): 'I don't care anything about business. I just care about what you said and you *said* we wouldn't have to do it. Now I *told* you not to get involved with those people.'

SONNY (furiously): 'Now I get "I told you so", right? I don't want to hear about it anymore. Just leave me alone . . . *get out*! Get outta here. . . .'

(And then he speeds off on his motorcycle, leaving Cher dejected and miserable.)

In the end, though, the film producer surrenders to Sonny and Cher's personal integrity (even though to most people watching this movie his concept seemed a lot more interesting than anything Bono dreamed up). Sonny and Cher remain free, a part of the love generation, as they go about their happy lives running through fields of flowers and among neon city lights, all of which are shot from every imaginable angle. The film begins and ends with 'I Got You Babe'.

Filming began on 24 January 1966 at their Encino home, the plastic wonderland.

Said William Friedkin to *Variety*: 'This is anything but a Watusi picture. There won't be one frug in the entire film. It's actually very moral [and] has something to say. It will not be like *A Hard Day's*

Night. That was more like a camera exercise. You never got to know the Beatles themselves. You'll get to know Sonny and Cher as a result of this film.'

In his *Saturday Evening Post* article, 'Sonny and Cher – They're What's Happening' (23 April 1966), Peter Bogdanovich painted a rather interesting picture of Sonny's paternal relationship with his lover.

He observed as Bono and writer Nick Hymans conducted a script meeting at the Encino home. According to Bogdanovich, it went like this:

'Now, for this one dream sequence,' Hymans was saying, 'we have Cher dressed up like Marie Antoinette. . . .'

'Why don't you do some work on your own?' Cher asked, turning to Hymans. '*You're* the writer – why don't you leave Sonny alone?'

'C'mon, Cher,' Sonny poked at her.

Sonny picked up the script outline and read from it. 'I say: "There's something sinister in the air." Cher says, "It's known as fog." Sonny: "What is?" Cher: "The something sinister to which you refer. . . ."'

'I *never* say "refer",' Cher broke in. 'I'm just gonna look at your words and say what I feel.'

Sonny read on. 'I say, "Isn't this what we always wanted?" Cher: "Sure, we worked our fingers to the bone. . . ."'

'I *never* worked my fingers to the bone. I *hate* this movie. *Roll 'em!*'

Sonny turned back to the script and read a page of dialogue. Cher interrupted him. 'We have a lot to say in this movie,' she said. Picking up on of a pair of dueling pistols on the side table, she cocked it. 'Why can't we have a Beatles movie?'

'Cause I don't *want* a Beatles movie?' Sonny was emphatic.

Cher aimed the pistol at one of the flickering candles and pulled the trigger; the hammer clicked. 'I shot the candle out.'

Sonny grasped the pistol. '*Leave that alone.*'

'Can I ask a question, Sonny?'

'You're starting to drive me crazy, Cher.'

'Has this pistol ever killed anybody?'

'*I* don't know.'

'What good's an authentic dueling pistol if you don't know its history?'

'If you don't cool it, Cher, I'm gonna make you go sit in the kitchen.'

'No, I'll be good, Sonny.'

'What're you gonna call this movie?' Cher asked after several minutes. 'Why don't you call it *A Stitch in Time is Worth Two in the Bush*? I think that's a great title. Or *Mary Poppins is a Junkie*.'

'We'll do it later, Nick. I can't work like *this*.'

Sonny slumped unhappily on the couch. Cher cocked the pistol and pointed it across the room at Theresa [Rinaldi, Bono's secretary], who smiled at her sympathetically: she pulled the trigger and the hammer clicked.

It was said at the time that Bono was furious about the Bogdanovich profile, the first that portrayed him as an aggressive career strategist ('Under this easygoing guilelessness is a seed of corruptibility') rather than a hippie pop star who often invited youngsters to the Encino digs to 'rap about their problems'.

Cher wasn't happy about the article either, mostly because Bogdanovich referred to her as 'a sexy broad'.

It was the first and last time a reporter would be allowed such intimate association with Sonny and Cher in the Sixties.

'I hated the idea of doing a movie,' Cher said later. 'It took too much of Sonny's time and I figured we were doing all right without it. For four months I was a movie widow. I got told to go to my bedroom while he and Billy Friedkin sat until two in the morning figuring out what they would do the next day.'

Perhaps if Cher had been allowed some input she would have been more interested in it. But Sonny was certain she had no mind of her own, and no real imagination. Even if he did feel that she was, as he put it once, 'a pain in the ass', had he looked deeper he might have found that she was quite creative. Cher became frustrated; she felt that *Good Times* was an ego trip for Sonny.

'On the other hand,' said a former associate, 'it's possible that

Sonny knew Cher better than she knew herself, and that she really had nothing going for her except for him and his motivation. That's the way it appeared to most people, anyway.'

'The problems started cropping up early on, even before shooting started,' Brian Stone has recalled, 'when Sonny started calling us at three in the morning asking for writers' conferences. He didn't like the script. He thought he was a big hotshot producer or director. His ego was taking over.'

Shooting *Good Times* took about two months, but it monopolized their time for over a year, time Sonny and Cher should have been recording, time that would've been better spent solidifying their positions and reputations in the record business.

After the movie's postproduction, and while they were waiting for Columbia to decide when it would be released, Sonny and Cher went to Europe for a concert tour. They left on 22 August 1966. Cher was relieved that the movie was finally behind her. Though she hated the idea of *Good Times*, she couldn't argue with the fact that Bono had got them this far and that life was sweet.

'He had a dream; it was Sonny and Cher,' she said years later in an interview with Lynn Tornabene for *Ladies Home Journal*. 'He built us. But it was all built on truth, on reality. We were with each other twenty-four hours a day – and I don't care what anyone says, there's no need fo me to lie – we fought less than any other couple I have ever known. And he never lifted a hand to me. Never. And I never lifted a hand to him. The idea of lifting a hand to Sonny Bono! I would sooner lift a hand to the pope.'

She wasn't quite as articulate back in 1966, though. In an interview with Digby Diehl for the *Los Angeles Times*, (in which Diehl noted that Cher looked too young 'to be served a watered-down Fresca'), she said rather vaguely, 'Our marriage is different. We're best friends. When we go out onstage, sometimes I hold his hand or something. . . .'

When a reporter for the *New York Sunday News* interviewed the couple, he noted that Sonny did all the talking; Cher spoke one sentence. He asked her why, though she was wearing rings on all her fingers, she wasn't wearing any on her thumbs. 'I don't want to be too gaudy,' she responded.

Their month-long European tour was a resounding success. Greene and Stone were long gone, though. The relationshp deteriorated when the managers became as newsworthy as their clients. They were both young and aggressive, a 'new breed of entertainment representatives', as one reporter put it. They were masterminding Sonny and Cher's career as well as that of Buffalo Springfield. When *Life* magazine did a profile of Sixties rock and roll and gave Greene and Stone more editorial space (including a large photograph of the two men in a black stretch limousine) than they allowed Sonny and Cher, Bono was reportedly furious. 'You're supposed to be *behind* the scenes,' he charged. '*We're* the stars!'

Sonny was also anxious about the fact that his managers were spending so much time developing interests that had nothing to do with Sonny and Cher's career. So on 30 December 1965, he had his lawyer send them a letter terminating their contract. A fair settlement was reached. Greene and Stone maintained publishing royalites from Bono's music, and management and recording contracts were dissolved. It is supposed to have cost Sonny Bono about $250,000 to break his ties with Charlie Greene and Brian Stone. The two continued managing Buffalo Springfield for a time, and then Iron Butterfly.

So in Europe it was up to Joe deCarlo to see to it that Sonny and Cher were kicked out of hotels for publicity purposes. They were barred from hotels in Hamburg and Copenhagen (though in Copenhagen it was probably for real; the management didn't want them to stay at the hotel because of previous bad experiences with rock-and-roll stars).

'I told them, "If you have laws in this country, I'll *sue* you,"' Sonny said dramatically to a battery of press people at a news conference held when they returned home on 19 September 1966. 'I insisted on an apology, and I got one.'

In London, they played the Royal Albert Hall to a capacity crowd. In Rome, there was an audience with Pope Paul VI.

'What do you wear to visit the pope,' Cher wondered, 'a miniskirt, or bell-bottoms?'

'Please, Cher,' deCarlo begged. 'Just this once, wear a dress.'

Cher agreed. This was, after all, *the pope*. She wore a black crepe dress.

'It wasn't a private audience,' Sonny explained to the reporters. 'But it was stirring just the same. We both got shook.'

When asked to confirm a rumour that she was pregnant, Cher did a double take and responded, 'I've been pregnant twenty months now.'

The truth was that she *was* pregnant. She was amazed at how quickly the news got back to the press.

On Tuesday, 11 April 1967, *Good Times* had its world premiere at the Paramount Theatre in Austin, Texas. Columbia engineered a most bizarre promotional plan for the occasion: Governor John B. Connally of Texas issued a proclamation declaring that on the day of the first screening, the name of Austin, Texas, would be changed to *Good Times* for a period of twenty-four hours.

Following the premiere, Sonny and Cher embarked on a seven-city tour: El Paso, Dallas, Fort Worth, Denton, Tyler, Witchita Falls and Waco with concerts and interviews at each stop.

The Dirty Dozen was the year's top-grossing film. Other popular films of the period included *In the Heat of the Night*, with Sidney Poitier and Rod Steiger, and *Bonnie and Clyde*, with Warren Beatty and Faye Dunaway. A piece of fluff like *Good Times* seemed doomed. The movie's only hope was a youth audience, but the kids who weren't flocking to Sean Connery's James Bond epic, *You Only Live Twice*, were drifting over to a feature documentary on Bob Dylan's career, with guest stars Joan Baez and Donovan. The Dylan film kicked the wind out of *Good Times*.

Richard F. Shepard reviewed the movie in the *New York Times* (3 August 1967). He called it 'a nice unexpected summer bonus in the shape of a colourful, sprightly, bit of good-humoured silliness'. Of Sonny and Cher, he observed, 'They are an ingratiating couple, he long-haired and comic in a way that recalls a touch of Harpo Marx and The Three Stooges. She is long-haired and attractive, robustly voiced. Lively bits of fun are evidence that Sonny doesn't have to rely on music for a living. . . .'

Sonny was thrilled with the review from the prestigious *Times*, and particularly with the special accolade. It's true that Sonny hammed it up throughout the movie to exhilarating effect. He was irresistible and, as a comic, Bono could have been quite a threat. Cher sleepwalked her way through the film in a variety of wigs and costumes. It wasn't much of a vehicle for her, and her unwillingness to participate was fairly obvious on the final print.

'Sonny not only possesses a fine sense of comic delivery, but he manages to communicate an edge of pathos that many attempt and few accomplish,' said a review in the *Hollywood Reporter*. 'He carries a demanding amount of the footage and emerges as an individual of complexity and depth. Cher's performance seems almost effortless. . . .'

The *Reporter* also enthused that Friedkin had made 'the most impressive directorial debut since Francis Ford Coppola's *You're a Big Boy Now*'.

Bono was amazed at the attention the film received from the media. 'What gives *Good Times* its charm is the naturalness of Sonny and Cher's relationship,' wrote Charles Champlin for the *Los Angeles Times* (26 May 1967). 'There isn't a heavy clinch from first footage to last, just a peck on the nose and lots of handholding. Friedkin documents them as I think they see themselves.'

Cher's assessment of her performance in the film: 'I didn't want to do the movie. I was terrible in it.'

The original soundtrack album to *Good Times* was an odd collection of songs with polka, vaudeville and big-band influences combined with the ever-present Phil Spector trappings.

The album's arranger, Harold Battiste, recalled, 'We were really jammin' the musicians into the studio for that one. It was my first movie score. I went and picked up a book about scoring, looked it over, and said, "Oh, is that all there is to it?" But it was really due to Sonny's strenuous encouragement that I was able to do this. "Oh man, you can arrange a *movie*. You're better than all them other cats," he'd say.

'We were all just taking a shot at it. It was Sonny's boldness that made him feel he had a *right* to do this movie, and he convinced people to let him in. It was Friedkin's first big break. Mine. Cher's too, but she wasn't that interested at the time. And all because of the little Italian.'

The album received terrible reviews. 'This collection of songs really exposes how bad Sonny and Cher are,' said one critic. 'Cher's performance is lifeless, but you can only rise so far above the given material.'

William Friedkin attempted to explain the failure of *Good Times* at the box office: 'As soon as the film was released, acid rock came in and wiped out the whole message of Sonny and Cher. They were singing about emotions that were now passé. The film opened to an audience that was rapidly losing interest in Sonny and Cher. But it was made with two people who had absolutely no acting experience and a director who'd never made a feature and whose future was highly questionable. I'm not at all disappointed in it. I can still watch it today and not be embarrassed.'

'We did this picture to show people what we're like and what we have besides music,' Sonny told a reporter. 'A singer is only as good as his last record, but a picture can prolong his career because it provides a new form of communication. We gave up $500,000 worth of dates for this movie.'

William Friedkin went on to direct *The Night They Raided Minsky's* and Sonny and Cher announced that they would star in their second film, *Ignatz*. ('It's a man's name,' Cher feebly tried to explain. 'I think it kinda means *stupid* or something in German slang.')

'From now on, we intend to make two pictures a year,' Sonny boasted, inflated by the favourable reviews *Good Times* received, even though the box-office receipts were low. The second film was to be shot in Rodenburg, Germany (near Hamburg), and was scripted by Jack Guss. Friedkin was supposed to direct, but the whole project was scuttled when Steve Broidy Productions realized how much money everyone, including Bono, had lost on Sonny and Cher's film debut. *Ignatz* was shelved. When the project was cancelled, Sonny was crushed. For the first time in years, they had nothing in the offing.

'I thought it would be easy,' he confided to friends about his first movie experience. 'But it wasn't. I've come close to costing us our career. It's eaten up almost every dollar we have.'

'Sonny and Cher have had it. *They're kaput!*' said Hedda Hopper with wicked zeal.

The press continued its assault. The reviews for *Good Times* were generous, but now it was time for the backlash, since the movie was not a success. 'How can a hippie in good standing let her hair get oily and unkempt when there's a hairdresser on the set of *Good Times* to see that it's freshly shampooed every morning?' asked Dorothy Manners, a gossip columnist who took over for the ailing Louella Parsons. She was implying that Cher was a fraud. 'And what's a hippie doing wearing a twelve-carat diamond solitaire on one hand and three beautiful rings of precious stones and diamonds on the other? Exponents of the so-called mod generation are not supposed to be rich and successful.'

Sonny and Cher's record sales were slipping. Bono no longer cared that much about the music, and it showed. Single releases were going nowhere. After 'The Beat Goes On', Imperial issued two consecutive flops by Cher, and Atco released three stiffs by Sonny and Cher.

The writing was on the wall. Sonny and Cher were about to see their careers explode, and neither one of them was prepared for the fall.

cher-wanna-be's

Sonny Bono attempted to become a bit more radical in his musical approach. 'We just did a thing called "Plastic Man",' he offered in a *New York Times* interview (6 July 1967), 'in which each verse moves from contemporary rock and roll to Salvation Army band music – which shows you that it's missionary work. It's a rebuttal to Timothy Leary and other extremists. It's a warning not to be drawn into a plastic world, to draw your own conclusions. I didn't limit my plastic man to so-called leaders of the hippies, though. A lot of people are recruiting the adults, too. And conning them tremendously.'

'Plastic Man' peaked at seventy-four on the top one hundred. Most of Sonny and Cher's fans had no idea what Bono was talking about. If Sonny and Cher hadn't spent so much time on the film, they could have hung on to their music. Now it looked as if they were going to lose it all.

The *Good Times* soundtrack album was even less popular than the movie; the single release, 'Little Things', didn't even crack the top forty.

Back in November 1966, Sonny wrote a song about a father explaining to his children that he and their mother were divorcing. Bono has said he penned 'You'd Better Sit Down Kids' with his own parents' divorce as inspiration.

Cher performs the song from the male point of view, and the record is considered one of the first experiments in what pop culture historians have coined 'gender bender' (where males perform female roles in films, or points of view in songs, and vice versa).

'You'd Better Sit Down Kids' is one of the best records Cher ever recorded, and certainly one of the finest productions Sonny Bono ever released. The arrangement was unique, breaking pop music's house rules by changing rhythms in mid-song, stopping and starting the orchestration when least expected. Finally, it was a record by Sonny Bono that did not resemble anything else; it was his first truly *original* composition.

The end of the song doesn't sound arranged: the musicians jam in an impromptu session that has nothing in common with the rhythm of what preceded it. It's an imaginative tag, a touch of jazz fusion in a pure pop experience. Battiste said that Cher rarely performed the song in concert because they could never find musicians in the cities they worked who could play the arrangement properly.

The song soared into the top ten in November 1967; it would be Cher's last hit record for four years. Her performance is remarkably expressive and vital. The song appeared on Cher's *With Love* album, released by Imperial in 1967; produced, as always, by Bono; and arranged by Battiste. (Bono took the cover photograph of Cher himself.)

In July 1967, Sonny and Cher were packing to leave for a concert performance in Minneapolis, when Cher became ill and doubled over in pain. Something was wrong with the pregnancy, and she was afraid she was about to have a miscarriage. (Cher suffered an earlier miscarriage sometime in 1966, she revealed years later.)

After some discussion, it was decided that she would not perform in Minneapolis, that they would not take the chance. As it turned out, she did miscarry and Sonny went alone.

Harold Battiste recalled, 'We left for Minnesota either the day she miscarried or the day after, I can't recall. There was the thought that Cher might be able to make it, but we wound up in Minneapolis with no Cher. Someone got the brilliant idea of advertising this dilemma on the radio. I thought to myself, "Man, these cats always got some brilliant scheme – if it's a lemon, make lemonade out of it." To promote this gig, they announced that Cher had suffered a miscarriage.

'It was played as a heart-wrenching thing, that here was this ideal couple all the kids were crazy about, and look what she's going through and yet he's out here doing the gig anyway. On top of that, he's going to let some other girl have an opportunity to replace Cher. People were coming in and auditioning for her spot.'

The whole scenario sounds exploitive and callous in retrospect. Six girls, all 'Cher-wanna-be's' with long dark hair and heavy lashes, became runners-up in 'the contest'. Rather than choose a single winner, Bono performed with all six shaggy-haired blue-jeaned hippies, and the show was probably more comical than it was an actual performance.

'I don't know how Cher felt about this,' offered a source. 'My guess is that she was hurt, but it's hard to tell. Even if she had suggested that Sonny go on ahead without her, she probably didn't think he'd actually do it. Capitalizing on something like this seems a bit strange, to say the least.'

At the end of 1967, Sonny purchased a thirty-one-room Tudor-style mansion from Tony Curtis for a reported $900,000 (with a $100,000 annual maintenance cost) on Carolwood Road in Holmby Hills, a high-class area of Los Angeles.

'People ask why you need anything larger than twenty-two rooms,' Cher said to a reporter. 'You don't *need* any more than a living room, kitchen, bedroom and bath. But what you *want* is something else again.'

Cher has said that she drove Sonny 'crazy' to purchase that house for her, that she'd longed for the mansion ever since the two of them were invited to attend a birthday party for Curtis at the house. 'When we came up to the gate, we looked at each other and said, "What are *we* doing *here*? We don't *belong* here." After we left, I turned to Sonny and said, "Son, someday we're going to live right here in this house." Five years later, we were.'

As Harold Battiste said to writer George Carpozi Jr, 'The house was a castle, that's what it was. I asked Sonny what prompted him to buy digs so wild and rampant. He said, "Look, all broads want money, man. If you can't give it to them, you're in trouble. Some other cat will come along and give it to her."'

He also bought Cher an Excalibur automobile, and himself an Aston Martin – and four motorcycles.

'Why shouldn't entertainers live high if they want to?' Cher asked defensively. 'If people work hard for money, they should be allowed to do anything with it because they earned it.'

Sonny and Cher over extended themselves when they decorated their new home with seventeenth-century antiques, early English portraits, Scottish lace curtains, and white silk damask embroidery.

'It was as funny as anything you've ever seen to see these two goat-skinned hippies with fur leggings coming out of this mansion, being whisked off in a limousine to "work",' said Val Johns.

'Beneath that pop imagery, Cher really wanted to be as suburban as Donna Reed and her television family. You couldn't talk six sentences with her before she'd let you know what she wanted out of this business – security.

'She and Sonny were typical of a Sixties youth generation in Los Angeles who would live in squalour in groups of fifty, knowing all the time that as soon as they made some money they'd want a pink refrigerator in their conservative kitchen. It was the man's responsibility to take care of his lover and make sure she got that refrigerator – two, if possible. If you were to ask Cher what she wanted next after they moved into that home, she would have probably said she wanted a bigger kitchen.'

'They were going out of their minds spending money,' said Harold Battiste. 'Camera, clothes, antiques, everything.'

Sonny cared for his first wife by allowing her to live in the Encino home he and Cher had just vacated. He purchased a car for her birthday present. When he wanted to send his eldest daughter to Europe, he and Cher paid for airline tickets for the child and her mother.

When Cher would purchase kitchen supplies, she would buy two of everything and put one away, just in case one day they couldn't afford to buy it. She had a stockpile of electric frying pans and blenders.

By 1967, Sonny Bono was thirty-two years old. His ideals were becoming more conservative; he was a part of the so-called Establishment. Kids on one side, adults on the other. For a while, he was perpetually twenty-seven, and now he's not sure why he continued trying to relate to the youth generation on its level. 'There's little they wouldn't have accepted,' he said. 'I was always trying to make sure I didn't say anything that would contradict something I had said before.'

Everything was out of control. Part of their appeal was that they were supposed to be married, though they weren't. They were supposed to be revolutionary, but they were conservative. Bono was supposed to be in his twenties and he wasn't.

'College campuses are booking speakers like Jane Fonda, who gives me a pain right in my ass,' he said publicly. 'Then you have Adam Clayton Powell, and they're getting two thousand a shot to sing the woes and shove more negativity down the throats of kids. Nobody has the courage to tell them that this country is enterprising enough to cope with overpopulation and pollution and that people can make it working within the system.'

The widespread drug culture was a movement Sonny felt his and Cher's fans wanted them to support. Chances are, Bono probably could have slipped by unnoticed without commenting on the perils of drug abuse, especially since any conservative statement could jeopardize their already flagging image. But Sonny and Cher spoke out against drugs and even made a film for the federal government to distribute to high schools on the evils of narcotics. It was a sincere effort, but how could their fans know this? To them, Sonny and Cher were hippies, and hippies used drugs. The film seemed to be the height of hypocrisy.

Sonny spoke out against legalized abortion, and even 'love-in' demonstrations. ('What do they achieve by that sort of thing?') If Cher could have related to the youth of the Sixties, and she probably could have, she wasn't talking.

When Sonny and Cher expressed sympathy for youngsters who were protesting against curfew laws and police brutality on Sunset Strip in Hollywood, representatives from the New Year's Day Tournament of Roses Parade in Pasadena, California, banned the couple from the parade. They were to have been part of a 'pop-music float'.

Joe Flaherty, parade chairman, said that Sonny and Cher were scratched from the roster of events because of 'adverse publicity by participating in the teenage rebellion on Sunset Strip'. But instead of supporting the teenagers' actions, Bono countered, 'We took no part in the activity. We were merely observing what was going on.

We're victims of guilt by association.' They were replaced by Buck Henry.

'If they were going to be involved, they should have just *been* involved,' said an observer. 'The kids would have respected that. As it was, it looked like a total cop-out.'

'Hippies thought we were square. Squares thought we were hippies,' Cher offered, years later. 'And Sonny and Cher were down the toilet. The kids who came to see us thought we were stupid.'

All of this adverse publicity was reflected in their record sales in the next couple of years. They were washed up on the best-selling charts by 1968. Four single releases that year didn't even make the top hundred. Four more consecutive singles the following year didn't crack the charts. And in 1970 there would be three more consecutive duds.

Cher was only twenty-two years old in 1968, but it seemed as if her career was over.

Bono didn't know what to do about the poor record sales, so he attempted to generate publicity by becoming more vocal on social issues.

He wrote a musical entitled *The Beat Goes On* about the pop world and 'the terrible influence of pot and LSD'. He said at the time, 'My agency wouldn't even take it to the networks because it's too rough. But I think that these things need to be said because there are getting to be too many of these hard-core hippies. All the public sees on "The Huntley–Brinkley Report" are hippie gatherings that end with either Huntley or Brinkley chuckling.'

Sonny campaigned for Robert Kennedy in 1968 and financed lobbying for a plank in the 1968 platform that said, 'We will institute a youth commission.' 'That was my contribution,' Bono said, 'my political involvement.'

Cher tried to follow Sonny's lead and appear socially conscious, but it never worked. 'I correspond with a whole platoon of guys in Vietnam,' she offered in an interview. 'I ask them what's happening there, and they say they don't know. That's very sad. It's so *weird* because they don't know why they're being killed. If you're asked to give your life, you know, you kinda should know why, ya know?'

She wasn't convincing or articulate because she really didn't care one way or the other about the passionate ideals and burning issues of the Sixties. Most of her thoughts were Sonny's. She was just an echo, rummaging through his philosophies, picking and choosing the ones she could understand and liked best.

She never watched the news on television. She knew nothing about politics. Privately, she said that the first president she knew anything about was Eisenhower, and all she knew about him was that he enjoyed playing golf . . . and that his wife Mamie had beautiful bangs. She hated to vote 'because I always go for the charisma of the human being and that usually doesn't mean shit.'

Cher really had no reason to appear to be socially knowledgeable, except for the fact that she was at Sonny's side and he felt that he needed to make a statement. 'I didn't care about *thinking* much back then,' she admitted. 'I was thinking I was going to be rich and famous and that was very exciting to me.'

As Cher was about to discover, though, fame and fortune can be very short-lived.

'why can't I get a break?'

Christmas 1968 was a desperate time for Sonny Bono. He and Cher had spent much more money in the last year than they had made. The pressure on Bono was doubled because not only was he responsible for pulling himself and Cher out of this financial quicksand, but he also had to do it without her knowing what was happening. He told friends and associates that Cher was not to know how serious their money problems had become. It had been his decision to forsake their recording career and risk it all on *Good Times*. Cher was against the idea. He was determined to keep his pride intact. Hiding their financial woes from Cher was not difficult, though, because she wasn't interested in their business and depended on Sonny to handle everything.

'I do not want to be involved in any of the money deals,' she insisted. 'All I want to know is that if I want to buy something, the money is there.' Cher didn't even know the name of the bank in which they kept accounts. Sonny had two instructions for her: *Stop* spending' or 'Everything is cool, *spend.*' (And then she'd 'charge it'.)

Keeping up the pretence of security, Sonny bought Cher a boulder-sized emerald, never asking the price (about $30,000) or the size (between thirty-six and forty carats). He borrowed the money to pay for the ring, hoping that he would at least be able to carry the interest on his loan until he sold a screenplay he'd just written called *Chastity*.

'Since we'd been big names, people let us have a lot of credit,' Sonny recalled. 'That's why so many stars announce that they're bankrupt to the tune of $1 million. I was scared when the reality hit me,' he told Henry Erlich in a *Good Housekeeping* magazine interview. 'Where are you going to go? What are you going to do?'

Sonny completed the screenplay for *Chastity* in four months and then went about the business of trying to line up a distribution deal, front money, so that he could film the movie and star Cher in it. Hollywood wasn't interested. It appeared that Sonny and Cher were finished as a viable property, and no studio was about to finance a project that would be produced by one of them and star the other. But Sonny felt that even if *Good Times* didn't generate the revenue everyone hoped it would, it did, at least, garner favourable reviews. Didn't that count for anything? Apparently not. 'What does this town expect from me?' he complained to friends. 'Why can't I get a break? *Why can't I get a break?*'

To Sonny Bono, *Chastity* was a last hope. He mortgaged their home and borrowed more money to pull together $300,000 to finance the film himself. 'Who knows how he did it?' commented a former associate. 'But he got the money and now he was deeper in debt than ever before. The only thing that could save him was a film that would be an unqualified success. But when he told Cher he was going to have her star in a movie, she said "Forget it."'

'You are going to do this damn movie, and that's that,' he insisted.

'One thing: you do not disagree with Sonny,' Cher said later. 'You never disagree. So I would always find a way to make it easier on me, and easier to be with him. Anyway, most of the time he was right. I mean, if I went on my own judgment, I *had* no judgment, so there was no way of knowing if I was right or wrong.'

So Cher would do the movie.

'If it's controversy these people want, if that's the only way to make a buck, if good clean fun doesn't count for anything, then we'll give 'em controversy,' Sonny promised. 'We'll do a movie people will never forget, and you, Cher, will become a major star.'

'I saw the two of them in action backstage at a "Kraft Music Hall" TV show they were doing with Bob Hope and Phyllis Diller,' said one source. 'Sonny would always be promising stardom to Cher. She'd heave a heavy sigh and shrug her shoulders. "There he goes again," she'd say to herself.'

chastity

The year 1969 was a year of oddities in the film industry. It was the year a new sense of permissiveness invaded the American pop consciousness, and this was reflected in cinemas across the country. Movies such as Vilgot Sjoman's Swedish imports, *I Am Curious: Yellow*, revolutionized the pornographic film genre, making soft-core porn acceptable to the masses and changing the status of the so-called 'blue movie' to the kind of entertainment that could be seen in suburbia. The motion pictures' censors would come up with a rating system and the letter 'R' would now have a new meaning: 'Restricted, under seventeen not allowed without a parent or guardian.'

A series of European imports became critical and commercial successes in 1969: *I, a Woman, Part II*, a sexual coming-of-age story, from Denmark; *Baby Love*, the story of a carnally demented youngster, from Britain; and *99 Women*, a women-in-chains prison farce, also from Britain. In the States, Andy Warhol made good on his promise to produce and direct an American porno/political docudrama called, appropriately enough, *Blue Movie*.

This was also the year music and television personalities tried their luck at controversial character portrayals. Dionne Warwick was an abused and neglected indentured servant in *Slaves*, while Patty Duke lost her virginity in *Me, Natalie*, and Lena Horne played a gun moll in *Death of a Gunfighter*.

For years, Cher had been seen as a confused, bad girl from the wrong side of the tracks. She was the overly made-up, combative, tormented and misunderstood waif, and this persona was the result of story-line songs for Imperial Records like 'Where Do You Go?' (in which not only her parents rejected her, but so did the Lord), 'Bang Bang (My Baby Shot Me Down)' (in which she was jilted at the altar), 'Magic in the Air' (a pregnant, unmarried teen), 'Mama (When My Dollies Have Babies)' (a pregnant, unmarried teen who gives birth to a child who becomes, yes, a pregnant, unmarried teen).

These songs, combined with Cher's hard-bitten selection of songs for her solo albums, from Milton Bennett's bitter 'Go Now' to Bob Dylan's 'Masters of War', gave Cher an image of sad bonhomie and desperation. It was a persona that was very unlike the happy-go-lucky hippie-in-love image she was known for when paired with Sonny at Atco Records and in concert.

Sonny took Cher's solo image and wrote a script to exploit it. In *Chastity*, Cher would star as a rebel runaway who searches for her distant soul after a childhood of incestuous attacks. The dialogue would be salty to suit the times. There would be sexual overtones and Bono hoped it would be controversial. There would be a lesbian love scene in which Cher would be seduced by a bordello madam. In another scene, she would do a striptease.

When she first read the script, Cher thought it was one of the best ideas for a film she'd ever heard of. At last, here was something she could really sink her teeth into. She identified with the confusion and heartbreak, with this character Chastity's complexities, and with the way she masked a softness in her personality with a tough façade.

Cher had no idea, though, that Sonny would finance this movie by mortgaging her security blanket, the Holmby Hills mansion. 'Sonny has to be crazy,' said television producer Geroge Schlatter years later. 'He shouldn't be allowed out without a leash. Every cent he could round up went into that picture. No one with any brains *ever* puts his own money into anything but the bureau drawer.'

'I was defensive and mad,' Sonny explained in retrospect. 'I wanted to be a part of show business and they wouldn't have me. So I invested everything I had – emotionally and financially – into that movie. I was trying to say, "Look, we are solid entertainers. You have got to accept us."'

The movie began filming outside Phoenix, Arizona, on 4 May 1968.

At first Sonny had hoped William Friedkin could direct *Chastity*, but he was involved with *The Night They Raided Minsky's* at this point in his career. Allessio dePaola, a former stills photographer and successful director of television commercials, was his next choice. 'From the moment I read the script, I understood this girl,' said dePaola of *Chastity*. 'I could see her and Cher *is* Chastity. She does incredible things. She performs beautifully and her face is fantastic on the screen.'

Sonny objected to the word 'perform' and corrected dePaola in the interview. 'What Cher does is *react*. When I see her get her heart torn out on that screen, I am awestruck.'

When *Daily Variety* asked Bono which major studio would distribute *Chastity*, he responded, 'That depends on who will understand it. The Hollywood film industry is very narrow-minded in its understanding of today's problems. The faster the industry changes, the better off we will be.'

Just as they started shooting the movie, Cher discovered that she was pregnant again. They were both overjoyed, but apprehensive as well because of Cher's history of miscarriages, and also because this would be a physical movie. Production schedules on the film were pushed forward and Cher was put under the care of a specialist. *Time* magazine carried the story that Sonny and Cher were expecting a child and that they were giving 'very deep thought as to what the baby's name will be'.

In its original form, the script to *Chastity* was strong for the times. But as he watched dePaola direct Cher in the suggestive scenes, Bono began to bastardize his original concept by watering down the content. Cher was hesitant about the rewrites. She believed that the strength of this film was in its brash honesty, and if that were sacrificed the movie would be nothing but amiable trash. So the two of them battled over Cher's dialogue and the film's point of view.

'It was probably the first time Cher actually spoke her mind about *anything* to Sonny,' said a former associate. 'And Sonny didn't take the suggestions very well. What the hell did she know about anything, anyway? was his position. So he shot her down at every turn. Cher probably thought that if they'd listened to her, *Good Times* might not have been such a bust. She was eager to attack the controversy in *Chastity* head on . . . but Sonny copped out on his own script.'

'Cher had definitely changed by this time,' observed Harold Battiste. 'I saw her as becoming more confident as an artist, performer, and person. It was a natural personality growth. But all of us had a perception of her as Sonny's lover and little child. I think we underestimated how mature and savvy she was becoming.

'In career decisions and in social presentation, Sonny was more attuned and sensitive to the way the masses perceive public figures,' he continued. 'Cher was much more liberal-minded. "No, you can *not* do this and you can *not* do that," Sonny would say, as a father would to a daughter. "I'm not going to *let* you." He was conscious of the image of this piece of art he'd created; it was all fuelled by feelings and emotion.'

By the time *Chastity* was revised to appease Sonny's conservativism, the writing was all high-minded clichés. As the story went, Chastity (who chose her name from the dictionary because 'it denotes purity and abstinence') hitchhikes her way through the Midwest and is picked up by a truck driver (played by Elmer Valentine). He takes her to a motel, where he makes a play for her. She thwarts his advances and ends up sleeping on the floor. Later she is picked up by a college student (Stephen Whitaker) and, after a confrontation, a similar sexless scenario takes place. ('Do me a favour, will ya,' Chastity says in typical Cher deadpan. 'Don't try to make me. I'll tell ya if I feel like it.')

Chastity gets involved with a taxi driver and, though she refuses to have sex with him, confides a secret ambition to become – of all things – a prostitute. He directs her to a popular bordello, where she becomes a sex slave who refuses to have relations with her johns; instead, she steals their money. She is, indeed, chaste.

Eventually, she has a one-night encounter with madam Diana Midnight (Barbara London), but the lesbian activity is no breakthrough in terms of on-the-screen sexual moxie. In another benign scene, Chastity re-enacts the madam's life story, doing a striptease and peeling down to 'almost nothing'. Direct dePaola's lack of sophistication and Cher's inexperience killed the scene, making it laughable instead of tantalizing. Through the rest of the film, Chastity, tough and unsmiling, lapses into protracted monologues, babbling on about the meaning of life and love, criticizing conservative morals, and, as one observer put it, 'passing off her own nonmorality as a new morality'.

It's a frustrating film that Sonny described to a reporter for the *Washington Post* (29 March 1968) this way: 'A girl doesn't know whether to be a virgin or whether to go ahead and be modern. This conflict creates pressures on the girl, whatever she decides. It has caused a large increase in frigidity and lesbianism among modern women. Today, women are as independent as men, but they don't really want to be. Every woman wants a man to take care of her and protect her. A woman will always test a man to see how far she can go, but she wants *him* to set the limits.'

Cher was said to be horrified by Sonny's blatant and public sexism and by his comments. 'Is *that* what this movie is about?' she asked friends.

'My husband Sonny Bono is such a male chauvinist,' she said later. 'I swear to God! He's a stereotype . . . like a woman could be a great doctor, but when she goes home she cannot bring being a doctor into her house. She must be just a woman, and the moment she becomes that woman she must do what the man says. Walk three steps behind. That's Sonny. . . .'

Meanwhile, because Cher was pregnant, Sonny was having her chauffeur-driven in a limousine even though he couldn't afford the luxury. He was borrowing money from the chauffeur.

He was absolutely stubborn about all of his concepts during the filming and postproduction of *Chastity*. It was understandable, of course, considering what he had at stake: his career, his reputation, his home, Cher's respect and confidence. He had been very outspoken against the Hollywood system ('This industry thinks singers are nobodies who pick up a million bucks by being lucky – Cher can act and we'll muscle our way in') and now he had to wonder whether or not 'this damn town' would actually let him and Cher 'in'. If this film didn't prove that he was seriously talented and not just a lot of hot air, he knew that he and Cher would be washed up once and for all.

'I've got all of Hollywood back there, watching and waiting for me to fail,' he said bitterly. 'Well, I won't. I hope that after seeing *Chastity* people who've been labelling us *SonnyandCher*, like we're Siamese twins, are finally going to realize that we're two separate people.'

This was the first time Sonny's associates had ever heard him complain about being part of a team. He had to admit that even though he wrote *Chastity* as a vehicle for Cher, he was also hoping to make a name for himself in the film industry so that he could branch off and involve himself in productions that had nothing to do with Cher. 'I want my last name back,' he told friends.

'Sonny wasn't really himself,' said a source. 'He became totally obsessed with *Chastity* and with Cher's performance. He and dePaola told Cher not to discuss any of her problems on the set with Sonny unless he was present. This, of course, put even more pressure on her. Eleven weeks were spent editing in the cutting room, and then Sonny went back to do more editing. It was a miserable experience for everyone.'

March 1969 was a more optimistic time. The future looked as if it could be bright, with just a bit of luck. American International Pictures (AIP) had acquired *Chastity* for distribution and the movie would premiere in April on the East Coast (but there were problems distributing the film and it would take seven months before it was finally shown in Hollywood).

On 4 March, Cher went into labour at seven in the morning. She gave birth to a seven-pound, ten-and-a-half-ounce baby girl at Cedars of Lebanon Hospital in Los Angeles. Georgia was at the hospital. 'When I saw the baby, I just knew what I was going to name her,' said Cher. They named the baby Chastity. (Later she and Sonny explained that they thought Cher's pregnancy during production of the film might be a good omen for the fate of the movie, and that's why they named their child after it.)

The movie's notices, however, were poor. The *Los Angeles Herald Examiner* commented: 'Cher gives a performance that, in its simple way, is as ghastly as the movie. Most of her part – when she's not philosophizing – consists of pushing her glum face into the camera. At her best, she looks like a grade-B Dietrich and acts perpetually stoned.'

'Completely banal,' wrote Vincent Canby of the *New York Times*. 'There may be a movie out there but it escapes Sonny and Cher and Alessio dePaola, who seems to have directed *Chastity* simply by keeping Cher in focus.'

(It should be mentioned here that *Chastity* was, indeed, extraordinarily photographed, and it was wonderful to see Cher so magnificently captured at the peak of her sloe-eyed Sixties perfection.)

The *Hollywood Reporter* gave the film a particularly scathing assessment: 'Cher's sense of economy shines through as she runs through the whole eighty-five teasing minutes in the same sleeveless violet jersey and corduroy jeans, unencumbered by such excess baggage as bra or range of emotion. What this movie lacks is conviction, coherence, or the slightest capacity to compel sympathy for Chastity, a ruthless bitch-hiker, a callous, contempt-spewing, self-pitying man-hater who stalks the land flaunting her mammaries, always talking about sex and never doing anything about it. Peroxide-blonde madam Diana Midnight proves that you don't have to look to another picture to find a more inept performer than our leering leading lady.'

'Maybe she didn't want to do the movie, but once she committed herself to it, she put her whole heart and soul into *Chastity*,' said Harold Battiste. 'And when the reviews came out I'm sure she was crushed. Didn't anyone care about her feelings, she wondered. How could they be so cruel when she had tried so hard?'

And she also had mixed feelings about Sonny because this was, after all, his concept, 'and now they're making fun of me'.

Bono, too, was stunned by the mean-minded reviews. But he quickly forgot them when he read *Time* magazine's opinion (18 July 1969). The critic agreed that the movie was 'arch and inconclusive' but pointed out that Cher was 'more than creditable in her acting debut. True, the messed-up youth scene can hardly be new to her, but Cher is on-screen for virtually the whole film and still handles herself with an easy flair. She clearly enjoys playing a side-of-the-mouth post-teeny-bopper bitch and even brings off the role's dark comedy. *Chastity*'s primary virtue is that it serves as a showcase for an engaging performer.'

Sonny was jubilant about the review. Finally, someone saw matters his way, and it was *Time*, no less.

But Cher, always the pragmatist, was said to have been unimpressed. She felt that her performance in *Chastity* was amateurish, that she was in over her head and shouldn't have taken on the challenge without dramatic coaching. The film was trite, and Sonny was deluding himself. She has recalled going to a screening of the film and watching everyone laugh at the parts she felt were most dramatic. She left crying, vowing never to make another movie.

'*Please*, Sonny,' she begged, 'let's forget about this. Let's act like it never happened.'

She wanted nothing more to do with this nightmare, and masked her hurt pride and bruised ego by telling friends, 'It's a toilet movie.'

Years later, she'd explain that 'I really didn't know what I was *doing* in those first two movies. Also, I was not *thinking* of myself as an actress. Sonny didn't want me to.' But Sonny had too much riding on the success or failure of this movie to 'act like it never happened'. If the movie wasn't a box-office success, he'd lose everything. So he went about the business of promoting it with a vengeance, and he insisted that Cher do the same.

In a prepared statement from AIP, Cher was quoted to have said, 'This girl, Chastity, is actually me. I don't mean to say all the risqué situations figured into my life, but I was the same wide-eyed searching girl trying to explore every nook and cranny of today's society. I was also the same girl standing on the corner with my thumb extended trying to hitch a ride.'

'This picture is about as serious as you can *get*,' Sonny hyped to a reporter. 'It's not kindergarten time. It's so adult, it's frightening. It's not a hippy-dippy teenage film. It's today and it's going to offend some people,' he said, hoping to tantalize the public.

Sonny went on to say that *Good Times* was 'an Establishment product. We had nothing to say, and we were just puppets.'

He continued to reject their past credentials, and in doing that he lost even more credibility in Hollywood. 'This isn't a cop-out, but *Good Times* was an error in my judgment. *Chastity* is a different story. The industry knocked me around a lot. I made *Chastity* for $300,000 and raised it all myself. I sold it after I made the movie on a percentage deal with an up-front advance. [The advance was said to be a very small one.] I made every bit of it on location,' he boasted, 'and with a fifteen-member crew.'

The movie's code board decided that *Chastity* would have to be rated 'R'.

American International Pictures had no idea how to promote this movie. Sonny and Cher's audience was a youthful one, many of whom would not be permitted to see the film without being accompanied by an adult. As usual, everything was out of balance.

At a loss for ideas, AIP's promotional division sent a list of 'directives' to all the cinemas running *Chastity*. The checklist included eighteen suggestions on how to generate public awareness and interest in Cher's movie, such as:

'#11: Make blow-ups of Cher in the hitchhiking pose and station them on busy intersections so she is hitchhiking rides in the direction of the theatre.' And:

'#13: Where usherettes are used, dress them in Cher's *Chastity* costume for advance sell. Later, use them on the streets with signs that read: "I'm hitchhiking to the (*fill in the name of theatre*) to see Cher in *Chastity*."'

The rest of the advertising campaign for *Chastity* was just as humorous. Two ad proofs were utilized. The first shows Cher in jeans and halter top, her head cocked playfully, a deadpan look on her face, straight hair hanging over her chest. In her left hand, an overnight bag; her right hand is outstretched, thumb out, hitchhiking. The ad copy read, 'Meet Chastity . . . she picked out her name herself, but not for any reason you'd think. She's a *bummer*, a *loser*, using men like a drunk uses drink. Pick her up if you want, but *be warned*. She's not just a girl, she's an *experience!*'

Another concept was a campaign with similar photo and copy but with the additional teaser that after Chastity 'uses' her men, 'there's *nothing* left but a hangover at the end of each spree.'

Meanwhile, Sonny wrote another screenplay called *Editha* from a story by nineteenth-century writer William Dean Howells, and he also penned what he described as 'a soul opera showing that if youth isn't in revolt, it's already dead.' He was probably hoping to warm up to the youth generation again, but the time for that was long gone. Also, for television, he planned an animated 'Odyssey of Sonny and Cher', and for Broadway he was preparing a musical starring Cher called (what else?) *The Beat Goes On*.

'The guy was ambitious and would not take "no" for an answer from show business,' said Harold Battiste. 'You gotta hand it to him.'

But all of Sonny's ideas and plans went up in smoke when *Chastity* failed miserably at the box office. Hollywood would no longer take him and Cher seriously. Their recording career was also a shambles. All the doors were being slammed in his face. By this time, Sonny Bono couldn't get a doghouse financed and he was up to his moustache in debt; 1969 would end the way it had begun – desperately.

'There's a possibility Cher may go off on another project as an independent artist,' Sonny Bono told a reporter for the *Los Angles Herald Examiner*. 'So I'll have to do a picture that won't require Cher.'

The truth was that Cher wasn't doing any more motion pictures. Period. If her husband had aspirations for the film world, he would have to attain his goals without her, because she was going to Muscle Shoals, Alabama, to work on an album – the first that would not be produced by Bono.

'I don't know whose idea it was, hers or Sonny's, but Cher wanted to get deeper into music that was closer to rhythm and blues, black music. I thought the idea was a great one,' said Harold Battiste. 'I would've liked to have been able to produce her in that vein. I was a little shaken when Jerry Wexler was called in. I wanted the opportunity and couldn't understand why I wasn't asked to do it. It messed with me for a while.'

'We're in a cocoon stage again,' Cher said at the time. 'But with a difference. When we were in that stage before, no one knew it. We weren't anybody – then.'

The Jerry Wexler-produced album, *3614 Jackson Highway*, was Cher's only solo album for Atco (she was no longer with Imperial) and it's a strong, surprising effort. Wexler, whose background

Left; Sonny and Cher, 1964. *(London Features International)*

Below; Cher was so nervous about performing that Sonny literally had to push her out onto the stage. Here they are in 1965. *(Topham Picture Library)*

Above; A rehearsal for an early club date. *(David Redfern)*

Right; Though they told the world they were married, they really wern't. 'But living together in 1965 wasn't a cool thing to do,' explained Sonny. 'So we kept it a secret.' *(Topham Picture Library)*

Left; When Cher left Sonny, she married rock musician Gregg Allman. She says that Gregg's drug addiction ruined the relationship. *(London Features International)*

Below right; Cher, 1976, with Nilsson. *(Topham Picture Library)*

Above; Cher, 1969. She didn't even know where her bank account was, or how much money she had. 'I just lived my life knowing Sonny was taking care of me,' she said. 'Then I found out he really wasn't.' *(Topham Picture Library)*

Left; In 1972, a soft look…
(Topham Picture Library)

Below left; …ten years later, and tough as leather. *(London Features International)*

Below right; 'People actually treated me different, better, when I was a blonde,' she said in 1985. *(Topham Picture Library)*

Right; Cher: One of the most famous, most admired and most trashed women in the world. Leicester Square, 1988. *(Topham Picture Library)*

Below; Son Elijah Blue, boyfriend Josh Donen, and daughter Chastity. *(London Features International)*

Right; The spiked hairstyle, another of Cher's many looks. *(Topham Picture Library)*

Below; In 1977 with heart-throb boyfriend Rob Camilletti. *(London Features International)*

Above; In March 1984, during a
break from filming *Suspect.*
(Topham Picture Library)

Right; With her Oscar for Best
Actress in 1988, 'I don't think
this means I am somebody, but I
guess I'm on my way.' *(Topham
Picture Library)*

includes producing some of Aretha Franklin's post-Columbia soul
music for Atlantic, provided a terrific showcase for Cher: colourful
horns and clever backing with strong supporting female voices in
robust Memphis-sounding material. The material included Bob
Dylan's 'Lay Lady Lay' (retitled 'Lay Baby Lay'), Don Penn's 'Do
Right Woman', and Don Mize and Ira Allen's '(Just Enough to Keep
Me) Hanging On'.

Cher was on the cover in a beaded Indian ensemble surrounded
by Wexler, arrangers, and musicians (Sonny was in the picture as
well, and the album is dedicated to him).

The album should have established something solid for Cher
in terms of a new recording identity, but it was a flop. The
part of young America interested in this kind of earthy music
was getting plenty from Aretha Franklin and Janis Joplin. Single
releases culled from *3614 Jackson Highway* didn't even make the
Top 100.

Jerry Wexler, attempting to describe Cher's voice said: 'I don't
think Cher has a conscious, sophisticated head appreciation of
music. She's not formal or academic. Just flows, you know? No
sense of propulsion. It's a sublimation of personality and suppression
of the personal musical signature in favour of complete surrender to
the music.'

At the end of 1970, Sonny broke the news to Cher. They owed
the Internal Revenue Service $190,000 and they had no money.
They might have to move back into the Encino home; the Holmby
Hills mansion would be just a memory. Cher's worst fears were
coming true. Her pet nightmare for years was that one day she
would be broke, and now it was actually happening.

'I am not leaving this house,' she said firmly. 'You'll have to do
something because I'm *not moving*.'

'That's the way it is with Cher,' Sonny said later. 'She's very
demanding of the men in her life. She expected me to lead the way
to success. . . .'

In November 1970 the 'California Living' section of the *Los
Angeles Times* featured a picture layout of Sonny and Cher at home
'cooking steak and never drinking anything stronger than wine'. A
portrait of a carefree couple was painted. 'Sonny says that meat

tastes best when grilled over the fire,' wrote the reporter. 'And Cher agrees. She usually does.'

And then Cher gave her recipe for 'Groovy Steak'.

The last few years had been difficult ones. It seemed as if Hollywood was forcing Sonny and Cher into obscurity. But Sonny Bono was still attracted by the possibility of once again achieving the kind of success he and Cher enjoyed in the mid-Sixties. Cher was a mother now, and that responsibility kept her busy, which was probably best. She had satisfied her lust for celebrity a long time ago, and if Sonny and Cher had now reached a career impasse, so be it. As long as there was money and they didn't have to move out of Holmby Hills, she would do whatever her husband told her to do. 'We'll be back on top in three years,' Sonny promised. 'Just give me three years. . . .'

Bono felt that if the young people weren't interested in Sonny and Cher, then, as he put it to a friend, 'who the hell needs 'em?' When Cher recorded Leon Russell's 'Superstar' and it didn't even crack the Top 100 but went on to become a Grammy Award winner for Karen Carpenter, Sonny and Cher knew that the record-buying audience had abandoned them. (Carpenter recorded the song because she had enjoyed Bette Midler's version. She once said she didn't even know Cher had recorded it first.)

'Let's do some heavier things,' Cher suggested. 'Let's get into some of the acid-rock material. Let's redesign our image and get funkier. We're still young; let's act it.'

Sonny thought that was a terrible idea. At thirty-four, he no longer felt that young, and furthermore, there are no guarantees in the record business. He believed that they'd been in show business long enough to expect a modicum of security. Redesigning their public persona was the way to go, he agreed, but it would be a revamping not geared to young America but to its parents.

'Cher, go out and buy a dress,' he said one day. 'A long dress. Don't spend a lot of money.'

'Go out and get a *what?*'

'It's time for you to start looking like a *woman*, and it's time for us to start appealing to adults – that's where the money is.'

'I've got to admit that I fought him all the way,' Cher conceded to *Life* magazine two years later, in February 1972. 'I remember the very first time I went and bought a long dress. Sonny kept saying, "You've got to do it. You've got to change." So I went to a store on Sunset Strip, and it was a terrible store. I don't know why I went there, except that it was the only place I could remember that had long dresses in the window.'

The Bono mind began to click off ideas. Sonny borrowed more money from some very loyal friends and, with Joe deCarlo's financial assistance and input, fashioned a new stage act. There would be an emphasis on stage patter, they decided. But Cher was uncomfortable when she was performing and they knew that she would resist having to relate to an audience. So Sonny would address the crowd, and she would talk to him, criticizing his Italian ancestry, his mother, his height, and his off-key singing. Sonny would counter with barbs about her Indian heritage, her prominent nose, and her pencil-thin figure.

Everyone agreed that Cher was great with a deadpan rebuke. 'We'll just be ourselves,' Bono said. 'And we'll see how *honesty* works for a change.'

'A form developed that must have been natural,' Cher recalled later. 'Because that's the way it felt.'

Bono and deCarlo spent a week in Las Vegas watching other entertainers strut their stuff, scribbling notes, and incorporating all the best elements into the new Sonny and Cher stage act. 'I feel that Cher was never really recognized as a *woman*,' Bono told deCarlo. 'She was even almost in between male and female in the public mind. But,' he predicted, prophetically, 'if she listens to me I think she'll become *the* woman of the decade, very glamorous and even setting new trends.'

Booked by the William Morris talent agency, the new act made its debut in Vancouver, Canada, at the Cave nightclub; from there the act went to the Elmwood Casino in Windsor, Ontario, and on to the Twin Coaches in Monroeville, Pennsylvania. The revised show, all polish and gloss, went over fairly well. Sonny and Cher sang other recording artists' current fare and pretty much ignored their own material. A major emotional adjustment had to be made, though, along with the change in direction. 'We're only pulling in two hundred people for the second show,' Cher complained. 'Remember how we used to pull twenty thousand kids for a concert? They really cared; these people are falling asleep in their drinks.'

On March 30 1970, Sonny and Cher were booked into Los Angeles, at the Century Plaza Hotel's small West Side Room, a plush supper club. The date was a coup for the William Morris Agency, and its office would promote it as if it were the second coming of rock's premiere song and music stars.

'A nightclub performer wants the audience to tell him that he's good,' Sonny observed to Digby Diehl. 'If you don't please the audience, you want to slash your wrists. We're a little nuts to try this. Something is wrong with us when we say, "Now look at me for an hour and like me". When you're on a nightclub floor, you can feel the dead air. Either you talk or you sing forty songs. We can't sing forty songs, so we'll talk.'

The day of the opening night was filled with confusion and apprehension. When performing at the West Side Room, as at most hotel dinner clubs, the artist has to come down through a service elevator from a dressing room and walk through the kitchen and out onto the stage. Sonny and Cher had never heard of such a thing. They were used to being introduced with great fanfare, having a curtain rise in front of them, and then facing an audience with authority. Working a floor show, on the same level as paying customers, was foreign to them.

'It's idiotic from a standpoint that when you come out onstage you're supposed to feel important. That's part of the game,' Sonny complained to the hotel manager. 'But [here] you gotta stand in the kitchen listening to waiters yelling "Hey, Charlie, bring me some more soup". It's just demoralizing to wait for your cue and be pushed around while the roast beef is flying all over the place. . . . We're gonna get all dressed in new gowns and suits and walk on *this* dirty floor?' he moaned, motioning to the greasy wooden deck. 'A door separates you from total glamour and this mess. That door opens and Cher and I are supposed to suddenly sparkle? That's *nuts*.'

That's entertainment.

'It was tough and scary,' he recalled years later. 'Sonny and Cher were synonymous with Tiny Tim. We were a freak show and now we were going for acceptance from a different audience. We were scared to death.'

So there they stood, Sonny in a blue paisley tuxedo and Cher in a matching sequinned gown her husband said was 'a St Laurent, or a Givenchy or something like that.' Waiters pushed them from side to side as they took one collective breath and walked through the kitchen door, hands joined. 'Ladies and gentlemen,' announced Bill Cosby, acting as master of ceremonies as a favour to Bono, 'Sonny and Cher!'

The complete line-up of conservative Hollywood's who's who was in the audience: Joey Bishop, Al Martino, Steve Allen, Jackie Gayle, and others.

'Sonny never believed it, but Hollywood wanted to give him a chance,' said Snuff Garrett, record producer. 'He had a chip on his shoulder because he'd been bounced around so much. But if there's one thing this city enjoys, it's to see someone pull himself up from a disastrous career. Then, of course, when you do, they try to knock you back down.'

> Sonny: 'Cher, look, you were in such a hurry you left this big mess in the dressing room.'
> Cher (a long, sombre gaze): 'And how *is* your mother?'
> (Two beats.)
> Cher: 'We should take her home tonight, throw a sheet over her, and show home movies.'

'They didn't get the feel of the audience and vice versa until halfway into the show,' wrote John Scott in his review of the show for the *Los Angeles Times*. 'Much of Sonny's performance consisted of straight comedy lines, with Cher deadpanning the toppers, à la Steve Lawrence and Eydie Gormé. Now, if only Sonny could sing like Steve. . . .'

'the sonny and cher comedy hour'

There were no album releases for Sonny and/or Cher in 1970 because they didn't have a record deal. Most of their young fans thought they'd finally been divorced (ironically, they'd just recently been married), gone their separate ways, and retired from show business as wealthy people. For the next year, they would play the nightclub circuit, working to pay off their tax problems and to keep possession of the Holmby Hills mansion. Chastity would travel with them from time to time; they were loving and good parents, very attentive to her every need. If anything, she inspired them to straighten out their lives and careers.

If Irving Berlin had written 'There's No Business Like Show Business' in 1971, it would have been with Sonny and Cher in mind. Just when it seemed as if they were destined to become friendly with every kitchen waiter and cook in nightclubs across the country, they were 'discovered' by Freddie Silverman at the Americana Hotel in New York City.

Silverman watched their performance one evening and was impressed with their imagination and creativity. 'They were like a modern-day Louis Prima and Keely Smith, or George Burns and Gracie Allen, Mickey Rooney and Judy Garland,' he has recalled. 'As singers they were just okay. But as comics, they were really quite funny.'

Silverman arranged with the William Morris Agency to have Sonny and Cher substitute as hosts for 'The Merv Griffin Show' on 20 April 1971, the night of that year's Academy Awards. If it hadn't been for Freddie Silverman taking a chance on Sonny and Cher, their future would have been bleak. But he enjoyed the basic premise Sonny and Cher had decided to exploit: she glamorous and aloof, he a bumbling fool; she witty and sarcastic, he lovable and apologetic.

With their guest stint on the Griffin show a success, Silverman offered Sonny and Cher the opportunity to tape a summer pilot. CBS had planned a mini-series on the six wives of Henry VIII (each wife would get her own night of prime-time drama) and the network was shopping for six one-hour frothy variety programmes to lead into the heavier historical programming. Seventy-five thousand dollars was allocated for each of the new Sonny and Cher shows; it was a small budget that would double in time.

'Sonny's feet never touched the ground for a week after the decision was made,' said a friend. '"See? What'd I tell ya, huh? What'd I tell ya?" he kept saying. He was like a kid in a candy store now that Hollywood had let him in. Cher was as excited as Cher ever is. . . .'

Silverman approached George Schlatter with the concept of 'The Sonny and Cher Comedy Hour', hoping he would produce it, but Schlatter, a veteran of 'Rowan and Martin's Laugh-In', passed. He suggested Allan Blye and Chris Bearde, both of whom had been writers on 'Laugh-In' and had just completed work as producers of 'The Andy Williams Show'.

'"The Sonny and Cher Comedy Hour"? Why not just go and do a television series starring Peaches and Herb?' someone joked. 'Or how about "The Jerry Butler/Betty Everett Show"?'

To most people the idea of Sonny and Cher starring in a prime-time vehicle seemed a little odd. But Silverman's vision would pay off.

The first time Chris Bearde had paid any attention to Cher was in 1968, when she appeared as a guest on a Don Adams NBC special, 'Where the Girls Are'. She struck him as being a limited performer with no self-confidence. Later he saw Sonny and Cher's stage show at the Waldorf-Astoria Hotel, and he wasn't particularly impressed. But he and Blye took on the challenge of presenting the Bonos in a weekly format. The two of them would be best, it was decided, if they were surrounded by other elements. The producers began a search for a group of young comics who would support Sonny and Cher.

Freeman King explained how he became a regular on 'The Sonny and Cher Comedy Hour' (King was known on the programme as

'Your Cultural Announcer', and at the time he was partnered with Murray Langston, who went on to become 'The Gong Show's' 'Unknown Comic', a zany character with a paper bag on his head). 'I was working for Western Union, making one hundred and twenty-five dollars a week. Murray was an operator for an answering service. We took sick leaves from our dull jobs and went to Europe to appear in military base performances together. When we returned, we dreaded having to go back to work on Monday. The Thursday before, our agent called and said he had this audition for us. "Terrific!" I said. I couldn't believe what I was hearing. "Whose show?" I asked. He said, "Sonny and Cher's". "C'mon you gotta be crazy! Their career is in worse shape than ours!" '

Despite their reservations, Freeman and Langston auditioned and were hired on the spot (even though Bearde and Blye thought they were the worst comedy team they'd ever seen; 'but we made 'em laugh').

'We were sitting in Schwab's in Hollywood when we got the call,' King smiled. 'It was like the rebirth of Lana Turner.'

King, Langston, Ted Ziegler, Billy Vann and Peter Cullen were hired to work with Sonny and Cher. Bob Mackie was brought in to design Cher's wardrobe. Everything was happening very quickly, and Cher had reason to be nervous. They didn't really seem to be prepared for this kind of attention and responsibility. But Bono assured her that they deserved this break. He had promised that he'd have them re-established in three years and he had managed to do it in two. This certainly solidified her faith in Sonny Bono.

'One day I said to him, "You know, I love you like a father, a mother, a brother, a sister. So far no one has come up with the word for the person you are to me. It's like you are a total *thing* for me. I learned, and you are my husband, my best friend, and the only person I completely trust." '

Clever use of animation and videotape would single out 'The Sonny and Cher Comedy Hour' as unique and interesting. Jimmy Durante was recruited to guest star on the series pilot.

Freddie Silverman felt that the pilot was a strong one but needed a number of modifications. The snappy dialogue between Sonny and Cher would have to be written with a bit more savvy; their delivery, though, was fine. Also, Cher would have a solo spot for her raw, soulful voice and Bob Mackie designs.

Now that the machinery was in motion and the careers of Sonny and Cher had been rejuvenated, Sonny Bono was not going to allow this opportunity for prime-time exposure to pass without having some kind of record on the market. Based on what was happening at CBS, he convinced John Musso to sign Cher as an MCA recording artist on the company's Kapp Records label. Sonny was signed to the label to produce Cher's first two singles, which he did. Both were commercial failures. ('You win some, you lose some,' said Bono.)

And then Snuff Garrett came into Cher's life.

Garrett had been in the music business for years, first as a disc jockey in his home state of Texas, then as a promotion man at Liberty Records (this was while Cher was signed to Liberty's Imperial subsidiary), and eventually in the Sixties as an independent producer. His many hit-song credits included six of Bobby Vee's best sellers (including 'Take Good Care of My Baby', 'The Night Has a Thousand Eyes', and 'Rubber Ball'), Gene McDaniel's 'A Hundred Pounds of Clay', all of Gary Lewis and the Playboys' million-sellers (including 'This Diamond Ring', 'Everybody Loves a Clown', 'Sure Gonna Miss Her', and 'Count Me In'), and Walter Brennan's 1962 gold record, 'Old Rivers'. By 1969, Garrett had produced twenty top-ten singles, eight for Snuff Garrett Productions (which he had formed with arranger–pianist Leon Russell). He parlayed his ambition into a successful publishing company and recording studio, and then when he was thirty and at his peak, he sold all of his interests to Warner Brothers for $2.25 million.

With that money, he purchased a mansion in Holmby Hills – the famous Colleen Moore estate – and after spending seven months decorating it, he planned to retire. Instead, he went on to produce four top-ten million-sellers for Cher (three of them number-one hits) and two top-ten singles for Sonny and Cher.

Garrett recalls that he and the Bonos happened to live next to each other in Holmby Hills, and that his name was mentioned to John Musso at MCA when they decided to try another producer on

Cher's releases. After an extensive meeting with the Bonos at their home, he decided to take on the challenge.

'That's exactly what it was, a challenge,' he said. 'Cher was a nonentity at that time. The two of them were not in good financial shape. They needed a hit badly.'

Garrett paid little attention to anything Cher had recorded up until this time at Imperial. None of it particularly interested him. He decided that he'd like Cher to record a story song though, so it does seem that he was influenced to some degree by the work she had done in the Sixties. 'I was looking for something on the lines of "Son of a Preacher Man", which Dusty Springfield did. To me, that was a song Cher could do.'

A week after their first meeting, Sonny and Cher invited Garrett and John Musso to opening night at a return engagement at the West Side Room in the Century Plaza Hotel. 'They were heckling each other and it was cute,' he recalled. 'But that was about it. It wasn't the rediscovery of Al Jolson or anything like that.'

A young writer, Bob Stone, heard about the search for a Cher single and met with Garrett at his office. 'This kid said, "I don't know exactly what you're looking for, but I'd like to give it a shot." I explained to him the kind of song I wanted and that night he went home and wrote a song and brought it back the next day. It was called "Gypsies and White Trash". We evaluated it. I wasn't too thrilled with the White Trash part, and in a day or two he brought it back to me as "Gypsies, Tramps and Thieves".

'I just knew that was going to be a hell of a song,' recalled Garrett. 'I couldn't wait to cut that baby. We used eight violins, two violas, two cellos, a full rhythm section, and a double piano. After I finished the track I wanted to add something different and so I called Amal Rich, a percussionist. He's got a warehouse of stuff and offered something I'd never heard of called a symlin. It's like a piano with the top torn off, only it's a string instrument you play with a mallet. We used that to kick the record off; it gave the sound I was looking for. When we had the track done, Cher put her mouth on top of it. The session was quick, real quick. What a voice she had by this time! I remember thinking this woman has a voice that can cut through a cement orchestra.'

'Gypsies, Tramps and Thieves' is an imaginative pop masterpice, and it typifies the kind of camp absurdity Cher would become known for in pop music over the next couple of years. The lyrics are a throwback to Cher's trampy image: she's the illegitimate daughter of a gypsy who herself grows up to become a gypsy with an illegitimate daughter. And the production has that orchestral feel that Spector had trademarked, except that now the arrangement (by Al Capps) is stunning in its clarity.

If timing is everything in show business, what happened next couldn't have been better planned. 'The Sonny and Cher Comedy Hour' made its debut on CBS on 1 August 1971. 'Gypsies, Tramps and Thieves' was issued a week later.

The first show garnered favourable reviews.

'Quite the most delightful new programme on the summer scene,' wrote New York Post critic Bob Williams. 'CBS is betting on it for January programme replacement, and it's a good bet. . . .'

'All right, Sonny and Cher are not Lunt and Fontanne,' wrote John O'Connor for the New York Times. 'And they can't resist the rather tacky gimmick of having Cher appear wearing the 733-carat Star of Queensland, reverently described in a press release as the world's largest black sapphire. But as a variety show, and relatively speaking, the show isn't bad.'

In the next five weeks, it became stronger and more purposeful; viewer reaction was enthusiastic.

'Gypsies, Tramps and Thieves' entered the Top 100 on 18 September 1971. In month and a half, the record was number one on Billboard's charts, and it stayed there for two weeks. It marked Cher's first appearance in the charts in four years. The record went on to sell millions.

'I think "Gypsies, Tramps and Thieves" is the best record I've ever done,' observes Snuff Garrett. 'I've been in the music business all my life and it surprised the hell out of me. I think it surprised Sonny, too, because we laid it down, they put it out, and the next thing we knew it was number one. When that sucker started rolling, it got up there real good. Sold somethin' like three million. Me, Cher, and Sonny, we made lots of money off that bad boy. . . .'

Silverman picked up the option for 'The Sonny and Cher Comedy

Hour'; it would return on Monday, 27 December 1971. Finally, Sonny and Cher's career was balanced and made sense.

After CBS announced that Sonny and Cher would return to the air in a regularly scheduled time slot, and while 'Gypsies, Tramps and Thieves' was showing its strength on the national record sales charts, John Musso signed the two of them to MCA Records as a recording act; Cher would also record as a solo. Snuff Garrett would produce both entities.

Sonny Bono wasn't eager to hand over production responsibilities to another producer, as he had been producing Sonny and Cher and solo Cher products for all of these years. Since he was so preoccupied with the details surrounding the new television series, though, it was easier for Musso to persuade him to delegate a bit of responsibility.

'John Musso called me and said he'd found this song on a Ray Charles album,' Garrett recalled, 'that it was very long, about five minutes, but that if we cut it down it could work for Sonny and Cher. He sent the tape over to my office and I liked it immediately. So did Sonny. So we recorded "All I Ever Need Is You", and it was released in October 1971.' By 13 November, the song was lodged in the top ten at number seven.

As far as Cher was concerned, these songs were standard commercial fare. She wasn't eager to record them, but because they were such runaway smashes, it was difficult for her to argue with Bono or Garrett.

Besides, from this moment on, she would always have money. During their first season on the air, Sonny and Cher were pulling 25 million viewers per episode, about 35 per cent of the viewing audience.

'With top-ten records and a successful show, you could not contain Sonny Bono,' said Snuff Garrett. '"See *that*! See *that*!" He kept bouncing about, telling everyone that they were rolling now.'

'I felt vindicated in a way,' Sonny said later. 'For years I believed in me and Cher, and the acceptance was appreciated – long overdue, too.'

Sonny was awed by his newfound fame. 'Notice how people approach,' he told a friend. 'First, there's recognition and then there's instant familiarity. Then, suddenly, they get embarrassed. See, they know me and Cher intimately. We've been guests in their homes, but they only get so close before they realize that they're talking to *stars*. Then it's "Christ, what's happening here? I don't have the *nerve* to talk to *Sonny Bono!*"'

Cher's attitude was a little less enthusiastic. 'People say, "Why can't you be *nice*? Why can't you be *you*?"' she complained. 'One day someone wanted to take my picture. I said, "Okay, I'll stand still, but I feel like I'm a national monument, like if a bird craps on me I'll know I'm okay."'

In the Sixties, there seemed to be no end to the layers of clothing Cher would wear: long, wide bell-bottoms, heavy coats and furs, leather boots. In the Seventies, Bob Mackie experimented to see just how much of that bulk he could remove. For the network to permit Cher to wear the risqué, slinky outfits she became famous for was remarkable considering the censorship problems CBS had had over the recently departed 'Smothers Brothers Show'. Some viewers were outraged by Cher's wardrobe – 'she actually showed her *bellybutton*' – and tuned in to see how she would continue to infuriate the nation. Mackie's designs for Cher were usually garish, all sparkle and flash, exposing inch after inch of skin.

She had become a stronger vocalist by this time, due no doubt to the extensive work on the road she and Sonny had become accustomed to. Whereas earlier it had had a big, booming sound, now her voice was a more controlled, resonant contralto. Sonny, on the other hand, still sounded, unfortunately, like Sonny. One critic said, 'Bono has the worst voice in the history of pop music.' But his personality compensated for any lack of vocal prowess.

The creation of the Sonny Bono persona on the television series was devilishly artful. Despite the fact that he was the brains behind most of the magic, to America he became the downtrodden, hapless buffoon. He was a sad-sack figure, a lovable oaf. His inability as a singer became part of his charisma. How *else* could a guy who comes off like that sound? Bono became a national joke.

A typical Sonny and Cher scenario:

They walk out onto the studio stage, sing an opening number, and begin their monologue. (Bono profusely thanks the audience for its applause, and suggests that the fans might want to applaud Cher as well. She folds her arms over her chest and glares at him, flipping her mane of hair from left to right . . . elegantly.)

SONNY (self-assuredly): 'Look folks, now don't worry about Cher's smarting off. 'Cause when she gets out of hand, I, like, give her a few belts when she gets home. In fact (turning to Cher), I'm surprised you're still popping off. Didn't you get enough last night?'

CHER (in a deep, flat, deadpan voice): 'I didn't get *any* last night.'

SONNY (stumbling over his words): 'Cher, you know, I thought our marriage was getting better all the time.'

CHER (looking right through him): 'Don't you think it's time your mother got a bed of her own?'

SONNY: 'Go ahead, folks, laugh. I know who's got the talent, the charm, who sings best. But I'm no fool. *I* know who's got the brains.'

CHER (fixing him with a long, baleful stare): 'I know too. So what have *you* got?'

If Sonny was a national joke, Cher herself was the ultimate laughing stock in many ways while she was a CBS television star. She never took herself that seriously and was always willing to make a fool of herself by appearing in the most bizarre costumes. 'Television was so goddamned drab,' she said, 'and that's the only reason I wanted to dress up.'

Vogue discovered Cher as a fashion plate, the perfect California girl, lean and tanned, glamorous and provocative. 'We think of her as the epitome of the American woman,' said a writer for *Vogue* at the time. 'She's brought back the halter, the strapless, the turban, the helmet. Possibly next spring she and Avedon will go to Paris and model the collections. Her own luxurious long hair is the envy of every woman.'

'There was nothing else like Cher on television,' Freeman King observed. 'In fact, when you think about it, there hasn't been anyone like Cher on television since Cher. They turned her into this gorgeous creature, this sex goddess. She was nothing like that in real life.'

Cher's Seventies persona was as much an act as her hippie Sixties look. Only this time, America bought it . . .

'I could never think of Cher as anything more than a jeans kind of girl,' said Harold Battiste. 'I never saw her dressed up like that unless she was in the public eye.'

Sonny and Cher acted out endless parodies: Snow White, Scheherazade, Macbeth, Sadie Thompson, The Three Musketeers, The Corsican Brothers. As *Rolling Stone* put it, 'The visuals compensate for the vague talents.'

Bono was just as astute: 'The adrenalin kind of makes up for the inadequacy and amateurism.'

Cher quickly learned the skills of a comedienne. If anyone was to argue that these were instincts that came naturally to Cher, they would only have to sit through one viewing of *Good Times* to understand that Sonny, not Cher, was the natural comic. Cher really had no presence until the series.

'It took her a while, but Cher did develop the greatest timing, and she used to floor us,' said Freeman King. 'Sonny and I were the worst cold readers in the world, incidentally. When we went to work on Mondays, the rest of the cast couldn't wait until we opened the script to start reading so they could laugh at us. But Cher was wonderful at cold reading.' (Because of her dyslexia, it's not likely that Cher was 'wonderful' when it came to reading an unfamiliar script. It's more likely that she was given a copy of the week's dialogue in advance and then would memorize the entire script, which is quite remarkable.)

'Cher has a lot of ability,' Chris Bearde said to writer Vicki Pellegrino, 'but she's an instrument who's only as good as the person playing her. She needs to be told what to do. In the right hands, she's a marvellous performer. But in the wrong hands, she's just a dull girl.

'I used to stand outside the camera's range and say, "Now get in there and shake your tits." She needs that. Sonny and Cher had to do five takes on everything, so we'd only tape the opening and closing segments in front of a live audience. Then we'd help them a lot in the editing room.'

Years later, Bearde recalled, 'Sometimes I had to lecture her right before the show. I'd have to tell her that if she doesn't want to have to go back out on the road again, she'd better do this right. People had been adulating her to death, but I know that chick. . . .There are times when she'd blow up. She'd slam the door in my face and then go to Sonny and say, "I slammed the door in Chris's face; I feel awful. What should I do?"'

Broad comic characters were written for Cher to personalize on the series, such as the tacky, gossipy 'Laverne' character in the leopard-print body stocking and oddball glasses, with the nagging, whining cackle of a voice.

'The first time I did the Laverne character, she was written as an old Jewish lady,' Cher once recalled. 'Somehow, I thought that that wasn't exactly what I felt like doing. So I changed it around and got her all dressed up. They liked it and made me do it every week.'

Her most memorable running gag, though, was the 'Vamp' segment, a series of short satirical spoofs about notorious historical female characters. The sketch would begin with an introduction, Cher outstretched on an old honky-tonk piano in one of her scandalous outfits singing, while Bono supposedly played a brief prologue that would end with '. . . she was a camp, a scamp, and a bit of a tramp. She was a V-A-M-P [provocative gaze into the camera] VAMP!'

Also popular with viewers was Sonny's 'Pizza Parlour' skit featuring Bono as the klutzy owner of a pizzeria and Cher as his flirtatious wife and waitress, Rosa; full-scale operettas based on legitimate operas; and a weekly segment in which past and present news headlines were treated in comical blackouts.

'I'm not ashamed of the Sonny and Cher show at all,' Cher has said. 'For a long time, it didn't matter to me. I never liked myself. I always thought I was a second-rater, a second-rate TV performer. At first all I wanted to be was famous; then I realized that fame had nothing to do with talent. I felt that I didn't do anything quite well enough, that I was one of those people who was famous but not very talented. So I said, okay, I'll be the Dinah Shore of the

Seventies, on TV all the time but nobody quite knows why. I was rich and famous and I had everything. I figured it was too much to ask to be talented, too.'

'I'm kind of like queen of a mediocre medium,' she said in 1975 in an interview with *Playboy*. 'Television is the kind of thing you can pay attention to if you wish, and if you don't, you can go clean out your drawers.'

Her unsparing self-assessment aside, Cher worked well under the battle conditions of weekly television. She worked hard to achieve that appearance of natural sophistication. Often she would be sick to her stomach, throwing up before a taping, uncertain whether she could live up to what America expected her to be. She was only twenty-six years old when the series went on the air. It's no secret that Cher's mystique and charisma carried that show, and that was a staggering responsibility.

'Cher developed these nervous habits that became an integral part of her personality,' said a friend. 'When she was nervous, you'd know it because she'd put her tongue in her cheek and then roll it back and forth across her teeth. Or she'd start scratching the palm of her hand with the fingers of that hand. Or she'd start flipping her hair. All of those were nervous habits that became part of her stage personality.'

'I was thinking I should be fulfilled, but I wasn't,' Cher complained. 'I wondered, "What the hell is wrong with me? Am I nuts?" And trying to make a nice face for everybody.'

It was while taping 'The Sonny and Cher Comedy Hour' that Cher realized that what she really wanted was to become an actress. It was a seed that would take a decade to germinate, but the quintessential television performer of the Seventies finally had an ambition. She wanted to act, and not in some carnival picture or cheap, undistinguished sexpot flick, but in a real movie. What she really wanted was to be Audrey Hepburn, but since she was Cher, she'd make do.

'I wasn't strong enough to turn my back and say "I really want to act and I'm giving it all up to be dedicated,"' she said years later in an interview with *Dramalogue*. 'I probably should have. But I didn't. I didn't choose to . . . yet.'

In May 1972, Cher was on the list of the ten best-dressed women in America. For her birthday, Sonny took her to the Villa Capri restaurant in Los Angeles for a quiet dinner that turned into a surprise birthday party. All of the immediate family was present: Cher's mother and her new husband, Hamilton Holt, Cher's sister, Georgeanne, Sonny's fourteen-year-old daughter from his first marriage, Christy, and even his ex-wife, Donna. It was an odd but festive group. A huge white cake studded with yellow roses was brought out. Cher blew out the one candle for luck.

She was making about $25,000 a week by this time. 'I want to be richer,' she said, 'so I don't ever have to worry about money. I'm not afraid to work for it if I have to.'

By the end of 1972 CBS had juggled 'The Sonny and Cher Comedy Hour' all over its weekly schedule, but the show held its own and placed consistently in the top-ten Nielsen ratings.

Cher's 1972 single releases were all produced by Snuff Garrett. After the success of 'Gypsies, Tramps and Thieves', Mo Austin was anxious to release an album, and the result was the Garrett-produced *Cher*, issued at the end of 1971. The first single was released in January 1972 – 'The Way of Love'.

Recalled Garrett, 'I had heard the song years earlier while I was in England. Cher loved it and we went in and did it rather quickly. It's a major production and if you listen to the song you'll hear that I had her sing half of the female lyric and half of the male lyric,' Garrett laughed. 'No one knew *what* to make of that, whether it was some kind of homosexual message or what. But, in actuality, Cher didn't even realize I had done that to the song. Hell, it was a couple of years before she called me and said, "Jesus Christ! Snuff, we messed up the lyrics to that song. I think it's a gay song now."

It wasn't a foul-up. I knew what I was doing; I just liked the way it sounded with the lyric switch.'

'The Way of Love' is a majestic ballad written by Al Stillman, Jack Dieval and Michel Revgauche that traces Jacques Brel's melody for 'If You Go Away'. The performance by Cher is considered one of her finest, and certainly it's one of her most controlled and self-assured efforts. With this one, Cher showed her full-circle growth as a singer. She maintained all the interesting full-bodied elements she had in the beginning of her career and finally rejected all the off-key, nasal, Sonny Bono influences that plagued much of her Sixties music.

The lyrics are ambiguous – either she's losing her lesbian lover, or her boyfriend is dumping her for another man. Either way, no one seemed to notice, and by 12 February the song was number seven.

Sonny and Cher had become two of the few distinctive personalities of the Seventies. Mike Frankovich wanted them to star in a film version of *The Sebastians*, which Alfred Lunt and Lynn Fontanne had excelled in on Broadway. Newspapers reported that the couple was negotiating a $1.5 million 'Barbra Streisand mega-deal with Caesar's Palace' in Las Vegas.

Around this time Sonny fired their manager, Joe deCarlo, who has said that once the television series became successful Bono no longer felt that he needed direction. Later, deCarlo would sue Sonny and Cher for $250,000 he claimed was owed him by the terms of a management contract they had signed with him in December 1965.

Producers Lee Guber and Shelley Gross made a deal with Bono for Sonny and Cher to appear in concert for the next ten weeks at their various music fairs. The contract called for a minimum of $1 million, and as much as $2.25 million. By this time Sonny and Cher were making at least $15,000 a night for club work. In a short time they had also become two of the highest-paid television stars in Hollywood.

'And then I started getting all of the ego-trip stuff between me and Sonny,' Snuff Garrett recalled. 'I don't like talking about it much.'

Success changed the little *paisano* Bono. He was always aggressive, instinctively ambitious, and shrewd when it came to the record business. But some of his friends say that once he became successful, he had so many axes to grind that he developed a mean streak, a superiority complex.

'He became quite the little egomaniac,' said a former associate. 'He treated his entourage, and even Cher, as if they were some kind of little army and he was the general or something.'

Snuff Garrett concurs. 'He had these jackets made up for everyone connected with Sonny and Cher, and you were ranked by the jacket you wore. His said something like "El Primo" on it. There were other Italian things on the jackets; I can't remember them all. After so many years, you got a different title and jacket. Actually, to me it was pretty funny. I would never wear mine. . . .'

(The black ski jackets Sonny had made for his troupe had his employees' names embroidered on them with titles such as 'Primadere' and 'Primadette' – Cher's said 'Prima Donna' – and strokes showing years of service.)

Bono and Harold Battiste had established a record label called Progress Records, a venture Battiste said he believed was a fifty-fifty partnership. One release by recording artist Mac Rebennack, alias Dr John, became a success and it seemed that the label might succeed. (It didn't.) The agreement between Bono and Battiste, though, was a verbal and not a written one.

Harold Battiste recalled in an interview with *Rolling Stone*: 'After I pressed to see the papers, I found that I was not a partner and that the company existed between Sonny and his two managers, Joe deCarlo and Harvey Kresge. It was a partnership between *them*, with me as a producer. I said, "No, man, this is not the way it's supposed to be; it's just not fair."

'Sonny was always able in these conditions to say, "Well, look, man, it's not *me* . . . it's *Joe*." It was always the manager or the lawyers who forced the situations on him that he really didn't want. But it always came out in his favour. I admired Sonny's ability to deal with all of these people and determine what was best for *him*.'

Battiste and Bono ended their business relationship, for the most part, at that point. However, their friendship has lasted throughout the years and is still a strong one today. 'What can I say?' comments Battiste. 'He's just a lovable guy. He's like a son to me, Sonny is.'

'Sonny was a little tyrant,' said a former employee, 'and he had a right to be. Hollywood treated Sonny Bono like dirt and they laughed at him and Cher. In this town, you don't get mad, you get even. Make no mistake, people at CBS Television were scared of Sonny Bono. He could convince Cher to walk off that show and that would've been disastrous. He was nasty to a lot of people. El Primo got his revenge. . . .'

It was said that Bono began to resent Snuff Garrett's success with Cher on the record charts. It was something he hadn't been able to do for her in years.

By the time they recorded Sonny's imaginative 'A Cowboy's Work Is Never Done', with Garrett producing, 'There wasn't a little bit of tension between me and Sonny,' noted the producer, 'there was a lot. You could cut it with a knife.'

'A Cowboy's Work Is Never Done' was released a month after 'The Way of Love', in February 1972. It would become Sonny and Cher's last hit record, peaking at number seven.

A 1972 album, *Foxy Lady*, was a success for Cher and spawned two single releases that didn't chart as well as expected: 'Living in a House Divided' and 'Don't Hide Your Love'.

Of 'House Divided', which stalled at twenty-two on the charts, Garrett recalled, 'I really worked my ass off on that record. I thought it would be much bigger for Cher than it was. I realize that it's not as tight as it could have been. It missed the boat somewhere.'

At the end of 1972, Sonny fired Snuff Garrett as Cher's producer. Garrett vividly recalled the incidents that led up to his dismissal: 'My wife Yolanda and I were on tour with Sonny and Cher. They had their own jet, a cook on the plane, and it was all real extravagant. It wasn't a business trip, though I do think we worked on the *Foxy Lady* album in Florida. Basically, it was a wonderful gesture on Sonny's part to take us along. Steve Martin was on that tour, so we had a terrific time.

'At one point, when we got to New Orleans, my wife wanted to go home because she missed our daughter. I had a lot of work to do anyway – Sonny and Cher weren't my only accounts – and I wanted to get back to the office. I went up to Sonny's room to tell him that Yolanda and I had made plane reservations to leave the next morning.

'When I got there, Cher wasn't in the room, but Sonny was there with all of his underlings around him, go-fers – you know, go for this and go for that. Anyway, I told him we were leaving and we had this big scene.'

'I've been meaning to pull rank on you anyway. Come into the bedroom,' Sonny said. Garrett followed him into the other room; the 'go-fers' were deadly quiet.

'You think you're the only record producer in the world, don't you? Well, you're not. I've produced a lot of hits myself, so you're not the big shot you think you are. Look, Cher's having a good time here with Yolanda, so you'll stay the rest of the tour.'

'We're catching the next plane out of here, Sonny,' Garrett said, standing his ground. 'Like it or not.'

'If you leave this hotel, I promise you, Snuff, you will never again cut Cher. And I mean it.'

Garrett concluded the story: 'I looked him straight in the eyes and I said, "That's your fucking loss, Sonny, not mine." And I walked out of there. Next day we left and I got fired.'

Snuff Garrett had brought Cher back into the top ten with two consecutive hit records, one that would be certified gold. He had also given Sonny and Cher their first two consecutive top-ten singles since 1967's 'The Beat Goes On'. He did all of this over the course of two years. Garrett was a resounding success as producer for the Bonos, and without him their recording experiences would be dismal ones.

First up would be the Sonny Bono-produced Sonny and Cher single 'Mama Was a Rock and Roll Singer (Poppa Used to Write All of Her Songs)'. 'It went to about ninety-three on the charts with a black parachute,' said Snuff Garrett with a snicker. Actually, the song didn't even crack the top one hundred. An album by the same name was a commercial disaster.

Each week on their series, Cher would lovingly perform a standard torch song in a lush setting with elaborate costuming. It was one of the highlights of the programme for many of her fans. Though she was in fine voice on the show, none of that essence was captured when Bono produced an album of standards for Cher called *Bittersweet White Light*.

The album included Cher's interpretations (or rather Sonny Bono's interpretation of Cher's interpretations) of Duke Ellington's 'I Got It Bad and That Ain't Good', George Gershwin's 'How Long Has This Been Going On?' and 'The Man I Love', and Harold Arlen's 'The Man That Got Away'. Sonny's background music production was rather clever; his excesses grew on you after a while. But Cher's voice was terribly abused; she savaged each and every song in a husky, off-key, nasal technique that was more Sonny than Cher. She had never sounded so bad.

'Good music requires full-time involvement,' Sonny told Digby Diehl in September 1972. 'If you're going to diversify into TV and acting, you can't be Neil Diamond and Burt Bacharach. Once I became a television performer, my head wasn't into the music any more. If the public buys you at a personality level, then they're accepting *you* and not the song. You don't need hits to keep current if the public has embraced your personality. . . .'

Meanwhile, Snuff Garrett continued his streak of chart successes. 'When I was cutting Cher, Sonny used to have to approve every song I cut,' he recalled. 'So I took him this wonderful Bobby Russell tune called "The Night the Lights Went Out in Georgia" [Russell also penned 'Little Green Apples'] before I got fired. I wanted to record it with Cher desperately because I knew it was a winner. "You'll never record that with Cher," he told me. "It's a bomb. A flop." "But Sonny . . ." He cut me off and that was the end of that.'

Garrett was also producing Liza Minnelli's *The Singer* album for Columbia at the time, and he suggested the song for that project, but the label had a more traditional image in mind for Minnelli. 'They wanted to make her a female Andy Williams, which was fine with me. This song was about a southern murder and wouldn't have worked for Minnelli.'

Vickie Lawrence, who was a regular on the Carol Burnett television series and Russell's fiancée at the time, ended up recording the song in a one-hour-and-forty-five-minute session. Just as Sonny predicted, the single release crashed and burned on takeoff. But six months after it was sent to radio stations, it began to climb the charts, and eventually it went to number one. It sold over a million copies and was Lawrence's first and only hit record.

'I was prouder than hell of that record,' Garrett said with a mischievous grin. 'That could've been Cher's number-one million-seller, but Sonny was so goddamned adamant about not letting her cut it.'

Cher said later that she had no idea that Sonny Bono had turned the song down on her behalf.

Cher was now twenty-six years old. Looking back over the last ten years of her life, she began to realize that not only had she abdicated to Sonny any involvement in her career, but he was also controlling her personal life. She had obeyed Sonny's wishes for years now; she'd never once defied him. She believed that Italians are chauvinistic by nature, that they are protective of their women. But, somehow, she could no longer reconcile herself to the cloistered life she led married to this man. Along with great stardom and fame came insulation from the outside world. All the trappings of their great success and wealth didn't seem to matter as much any more.

'There was always a sadness about Cher,' noted Freeman King. 'And she kept her distance – I don't know if it was her idea or Sonny's – like she thought if she got too close to anybody they'd want something from her. She seemed like a lonely person to me; she and Sonny didn't socialize with anybody on the show.'

Sonny routinely screened Cher's friends and associates, she complained. 'He thinks getting together with the girls is dumb,' Cher confided to friends. 'So I don't do too much of that. There are things he doesn't approve of, so I don't do them.

'I don't believe in very much,' she said meekly. 'I believe in Sonny a lot. And Chastity. Even she comes second because she could grow up and change the way she feels about me. But Sonny and I won't change. I believe he will always love me.'

'It seemed like only empty-headed people were around Cher all the time,' said a former associate. 'Never anyone smart, or anyone who could spark common sense in her. She was so in the dark about life, it was pathetic.'

Her feelings for Sonny were locked in love and conflict. Why was he so oddly indifferent to her unhappiness, she wondered? Why did he seem more concerned about his standing in the show business community than he did about her? There was a duplicity about her husband that worried her: onstage and in public he paid attention to her; offstage he seemed to ignore her.

'If you watched "The Sonny and Cher Comedy Hour", you assumed I was this wisecracking girl who ran our lives offstage, 'cause Sonny seemed so meek and easy going,' she told writer Tom Burke in 1984. 'Hah! In real life, he was this Sicilian dictator husband – I could say *nothing*! We were in the Nielsen top ten, we had all this money, everybody told me how lucky and happy I was – when actually I weighed ninety-three pounds, I was constantly sick, could not eat, could not sleep. I got suicidal. And I thought, "Either I'm going to leave Sonny, or I am going to jump out of a window."'

Before her birthday, she opened herself up to her husband. She told him that she was miserable and that something was wrong with their relationship. Sonny became furious. He told her she had no right to be so unhappy. They were finally achieving all their goals of fame and security. If anything, Cher was an ungrateful bitch. 'And I thought, Oh my God! I *am* ungrateful. I am just one ungrateful little bitch.'

In years to come, Cher would complain that Bono would screen the movies that she wanted to see (it took years before she finally saw A *Clockwork Orange* 'because he thought it was the wrong kind of movie for me'). She has said that rock and roll was taboo in their household (shades of Phil and Ronnie Spector!) and that only classical music was played. She wasn't allowed to play tennis or engage in any other activity that didn't interest her husband. For Cher, her life had become, as she put it, a 'stultifying existence'.

She knew realistically that she was carrying more than half the load of responsibility for their nightclub and television work, but still, had it not been for Sonny, 'I would have been in a closet someplace in East Guam. I never would have been out there.

'But I got pissed off about things that I wanted that weren't exactly outrageous and he just laid a definite *no* on.'

One of the aspects of Sonny's personality that attracted her to him in the first place was that he was so dedicated to taking care of her. Eventually, his eagerness to protect her started wearing thin.

Her friends say that Cher no longer believed that Sonny really loved her, that she believed he had fallen more in love with the commercialization of Sonny and Cher. But she still idolized Sonny. Some people whispered that she had him mixed up with God. When she began believing that she was only getting a simulated version of his love in return, she started to resent him. The thin line between love and hate was getting thinner every passing day.

Sonny simply couldn't understand Cher's misery. In his eyes, he had pulled an ordinary girl with little to offer from the depths of obscurity and pushed her – quite literally – into the spotlight. In two years she was an international sensation, and in eight years a phenomenon. So what's the gripe?

'He did everything for me,' Cher concurred. 'But the one thing he would not do was give me a moment's freedom. Not a moment's freedom.'

Sonny Bono made Cher a star. But it never occurred to him to make her his equal.

In October 1972, Sonny and Cher had just wrapped up a week-long engagement in Reno, Nevada, and were now appearing at the Sahara Hotel in Las Vegas. It was business as usual as far as Sonny was concerned: sound checks, interviews, performances, press receptions, and career strategy meetings. But inside Cher there raged a storm of emotion. She was exhausted, she had become anaemic, and she particularly hated Las Vegas. Audiences there were so unappreciative, for one thing. But there was also absolutely nothing to keep her busy in this city. All around her, holiday-makers gambled and enjoyed themselves, but after the show she would go to her room. She had seen these sights time and time again in Vegas, and she was bored.

Bored with Vegas, disgusted with Sonny, 'pissed off' at herself.

She asked her husband to take her to Europe. He had bragged that they now had a million dollars in the bank, tax paid. A couple of weeks in Europe would do her good, she thought. She'd certainly earned a holiday.

'Cher, we've got too much work to do! And you can't make any money in Europe anyway. Are you crazy?'

Tomorrow, maybe she'd go shopping. 'It was the only way I could get out unsupervised,' she said later. 'Just shopped my *ass* off. Then I took up needlepoint – my God, I needlepointed everything. I could have made a needlepoint *stove*, I was so unhappy.'

'Goddamn it!' she thought. 'I'm only twenty-six years old and these years have gone by so quickly. I just want to be a human being and go and *do* things!'

'If I can't have a vacation, Sonny, you can do the rest of these shows yourself. I'm leaving. . . .'

Did *she* say that?

It didn't sound like Cher. The words came from her mouth, but even she couldn't believe she'd actually uttered them. She also knew that Sonny didn't believe her.

'That night I thought about us all night,' Cher recalled. 'And the next day I kept thinking I'm going to do it. I *am* going to do it. It was so traumatic, saying goodbye to someone I loved more than anyone else in the world.

'I had horrible feelings of guilt. I had bad dreams. My skin broke out. I kept telling myself I was asking too much of Son, that it would be all right. It never was.'

'One night we were together and the next night it ended,' Sonny recalled later. 'And we were separated from that time on. Something had been building in her for years, I guess. I don't know; I'm not a psychiatrist.'

It would have been a lot more dramatic, in retrospect, if Cher could have just swooped up her belongings and swept away to San Francisco. Certainly that's how Audrey Hepburn would have done it. But she had no money. She asked Sonny for the plane fare to San Francisco and he gave it to her. Later he told her that he thought about throwing her off the balcony. He'd get seven years, they'd let him out on good behaviour, and then he'd get his own show. ('He had the greatest sense of humour,' she'd say years later. 'I had to laugh.')

Johnny Carson stepped in and replaced Sonny and Cher at the Sahara for the last two performances.

No one tried to stop Cher. Everyone must have known that whatever was happening in her head must have been serious because she'd never acted that way before. 'They figured it was so drastic they should just let me do whatever I had to do.'

The Sahara Hotel issued a press release explaining that the Sonny and Cher engagement was cut short because Cher had become ill; she had 'fallen victim to an ailment that had hospitalized her in the past – a spastic colon.'

The rumour started spreading that the real reason Cher left Sonny was because he had hit her in the heat of an argument, giving her a black eye. Gossip columnist James Bacon wrote: 'Waitresses and captains flatly announced to all customers that the Sicilian Sonny had given his Armenian wife a black eye, and she refused to appear in public with a shiner. Publicists, only doing their job, fed the trade press the story that the last night was cancelled because Cher was suffering from exhaustion. Which is the press agent name for a black eye.'

Cher's sister called her on the phone: 'Is it true that Sonny punched your teeth out?'

'The stories that I punched Cher are not true,' Sonny said angrily. 'I have never laid a hand on her in my life.'

Cher concurred. 'Sonny would never punch me. Never!'

She told James Bacon that 'I would have gone home to my mother, only I'm not too crazy about her either.'

(Any marital problems Sonny and Cher had were kept secret from Georgia. She has said she had no idea there was a problem between her daughter and her son-in-law until she saw Cher sing 'Didn't We?' on the series, 'and then I saw the whole thing in her eyes.')

Still, the thought of Sonny and Cher in a full-scale beat-'em-up seemed awfully tantalizing to the media. 'Sonny and Cher's Oozesome-Twosome act just does not convince everybody,' wrote *Rolling Stone*'s Chris Hodenfield. 'Many of my friends favour the belief that after work Sonny beats the shit out of her with a tyre iron.'

Once she got to San Francisco, Cher felt guilty. 'This isn't the way to do it,' she decided. 'I've got to go back and face it.'

When she returned, it was said that she started dating one of the musicians in the Sonny and Cher band.

'A *trombone player?*' Sonny said incredulously. 'She left me for a *trombone player?*'

Of course, Cher was not having a romance with a trombone player. She was simply reinforcing her independence.

'I was so happy to be free and there were so many things in our relationship that I thought were oppressive to me that I started going out immediately and having the time of my life,' she has said. 'I was really insensitive to Sonny's hurt feelings. But I kept thinking, "How can something that feels so good be so bad? It just can't. Whatever I'm doing, it's right."'

'She knew that it would *kill* Sonny, her dating one of the guys in his flunky organization,' said a former associate. 'But Sonny was too smart for that. He knew what she was doing; he didn't take it seriously.'

'Face it, she was twenty-six, she'd known the guy for like ten years,' Freeman King reasoned. 'Now she was the number-one lady in the country. People were saying, "Why the hell are you with this funny-looking guy when you could be with this good-looking fellow over here?" Suddenly, she woke up one morning and she said, "My God! What *am* I doing here?"'

Then they kissed and made up. Sort of. Sonny and Cher continued to live in the same house, but as far as Cher was concerned, they were separated. She would leave the house, unsupervised, whenever she pleased. She would lead her own life, and Sonny would have to adjust. The series continued as if nothing had ever happened.

During the 1972 season, 'The Sonny and Cher Comedy Hour' was in the top ten and in December of 1972, CBS gave it a more permanent time slot on Wednesday nights from eight to nine o'clock. It would remain in this time slot until its cancellation in 1974. Sonny and Cher often finished in eighth place for the week. For most of this period their public had no idea that the marriage was in serious trouble. After the well-publicized Las Vegas scene, the two enacted a public reconciliation with a vengeance. It is said that when on the road they would often stay in separate hotel rooms, and then slip back to a common room for appearance's sake if they were to be interviewed by a reporter.

In December 1972, Cher was featured in a stunning fashion layout, modelling bathing suits by Eres for a *Vogue* cover story. 'Cher is small-boned, lithe, so young,' wrote Phyllis Lee Levin. 'Her skin is sunbathed olive oil and expertly rosy with rouge. Her legendary fingernails are nearly an inch long and pink. Her hair is combed straight and immaculately, a silken black fringe spilled to the waist of her short raspberry velours dress. She continued her needlepoint, darting her eyes in my direction when she was especially interested in a question.' Sonny did all the talking, though, about how they were re-landscaping at the house and adding a tennis court, about how he'd just purchased three Mercedes, a jeep, and a Honda ATC 90 beach bike.

When Sonny and Cher were Oscar presenters on the 23 February 1973 Academy Awards show, fans noticed a marked difference in their offstage relationship. Said Mary Kaye Robinson, who attended the ceremony, 'When the two of them pulled up in the limousine, they got out and were all smiles for the television cameras and the fans. They walked down the red carpet holding hands. But when they got inside the theatre, Cher walked ahead of Sonny and kind of ignored him the whole night. They didn't really speak to each other until the moment they hit the stage, then *wham*! Sonny and Cher were back, laughing and joking. I thought the way they presented themselves to the public was masterful.'

If word got out that Sonny and Cher were not getting along, how would their ratings be affected? No one knew. 'America will *hate* you, Cher,' Sonny told her.

'You try touring forty days straight,' she snapped at a reporter backstage of Studio B at CBS; she seemed to be buckling under the pressure, '. . . and just . . . watch the whole world crumble before your very eyes. Like this morning, I had to get my nails done and so I got up at eight-thirty . . . you know, God, every hour of every day . . . I just don't know. . . .' Her voice trailed off.

Taping a weekly television series is exhausting work for even the strongest trouper. Sonny and Cher were usually at the studio no later than nine o'clock in the morning, and they rarely got home before midnight. Chastity would have to spend time at CBS just so that Cher could share special moments with her backstage between rehearsals and camera blockings. 'When we finished taping on Friday nights,' recalled Chris Bearde, 'you could usually pour Cher into a bottle and send her home that way. She was wasted. . . .'

'When we were through with the show, we'd have to go out on personal appearances, and the next day I'd go in and do some picture layout, and then five press interviews,' Cher once recalled of her pressure-cooker existence at CBS. 'For the first year of the show, I think I had fourteen days off. It made me *very* nervous.'

An interview with Claire Safran for *Redbook* magazine in February 1973 was particularly odd, coming from Cher at this time in her life. The article was entitled 'Sonny and Cher – Even When We Fight, We Love'. Safran reported that Cher began the interview session 'with the enthusiasm most of us show when we're going to the dentist.'

'I don't like to think that I *have* to sit through an interview,' Cher complained to Safran. 'Maybe I won't want to leave, but what if I do? It's like the way I felt about every other man before Sonny. They always made me feel like I was in a relationship I couldn't get out of. With Sonny, I never feel trapped.'

When asked how much of their onstage caustic television banter was reflected in their personal relationship, Cher responded, 'If Sonny and I are having a fight, I *never* say the things I say to him on TV. In fact, I usually don't say anything. If I'm mad, I sulk. If Sonny's mad, he screams. You go along not saying how you really feel, or what's really bothering you, and then it all comes to a head one day.'

That year Cher was included on Mr Blackwell's Ten Best-Dressed Women list. 'I was thrilled,' she said, 'until I saw who else was on the list. I mean, I don't think *Liza Minnelli* is so well dressed. I figure they just needed somebody in my category. I love to dress up and go to big parties. It's fun to see whose dress is prettiest. And usually mine is. It just turns out that way. . . .'

As for her future plans, Cher offered this cheerful sentiment: 'No one is sure what we'll be doing. I could walk out of this door and get killed. Then what would have been the use of planning?'

It was fairly obvious to anyone who knew Cher that she was working on automatic pilot by this time. She did over a hundred interviews in 1973 alone. 'And every goddamn body wants to know how Chastity is!'

TV Guide magazine sent Rowland Barber to Louisiana to interview Sonny and Cher for a July 1973 cover story. The couple took him to a private screening Bono had arranged of the bloody drama *Walking Tall*. Barber recalled that the manager opened the cinema after hours expressly for the Bonos. He said that whenever shooting or bludgeoning broke out on the screen, Cher buried her face in her hands.

'Is it over, Sonny, can I look now?'

'Not yet, Cher . . . okay . . . *now*.'

And this is a woman who wanted to see *A Clockwork Orange*?

'He's not a chauvinist,' Cher obediently told Barber of her spouse. 'But there are things he expects and gets from me because he is the man. Sonny has taught me so much. He turned me on to reading. My favourite book is still Pearl Buck's *Imperial Woman*. There are seventy-five movie parts I want to play, but that is *the* one. She starts her career as a seventeen-year-old concubine, then becomes the last empress of China. Maybe someday somebody'll take me seriously as an actress.' She paused and moaned, 'Well, I can dream, can't I?'

'People say, "How can you stand a whole summer on the road with all of the one-night gigs?"' Cher observed. 'Well, I *thrive* on it.'

That summer, Sonny auditioned for *The Godfather II*, but the part was given to another actor. He also hoped to secure a role in *Earthquake*, but he lost that as well. It did seem that Bono understood the ramifications of Cher's growing independence, that the time might come when she would exchange the security of their relationship and television series for her total freedom. He hoped to be prepared.

On her twenty-seventh birthday (20 May 1973), Cher was appearing in concert in San Antonio. Between the final two songs, stagehands brought out an enormous cake. Cher got misty-eyed as 10,000 people sang 'Happy Birthday'. But then a heckler up in the peanut gallery shouted, just as she was blowing out the candles, 'Hey, Cher! You're way over the hill.' He couldn't have known that he'd hit a raw nerve. Before Sonny could respond with a good-humoured barb, Cher startled him by reaching for the microphone and shouting back, 'Hey, you bozo, twenty-seven ain't over the hill.'

Then she got a standing ovation.

David Geffen and Sonny Bono are alike in many respects. They are both fiercely competitive businessmen whose consuming passion for the entertainment industry has made them very wealthy. One mountain is never enough; after it's been scaled, each begins creating new possibilities for the future. Excess is never enough; they are aggressively eccentric; the word *more* takes on new meaning with them. There are superficial comparisons: both are short, for one. Both have wrestled with life. In the battle for Cher, though, there would only be one winner.

Geffen was raised in a three-room apartment in Boro Park, Brooklyn; he slept in his parents' bedroom until his older brother moved out of the living room. Father was unemployed most of the time, while Mother ran her own enterprise out of their home, 'Chic Corsetry by Geffen'. 'The apartment was always filled with women with big tits,' he once recalled.

Like Cher, he lived on 'wits and instincts' as a youngster. He would sign his own poorly graded report cards; he lied to avoid military service.

While visiting his brother in Los Angeles, where the brother attended UCLA law school, Geffen was cast in a small role in a low-budget movie called *The Explosive Generation*. After he saw the movie, he had his nose fixed, returned to Brooklyn College, transferred to the University of Texas, and then flunked out. He moved to Los Angeles; by this time his brother was engaged to Phil Spector's first wife Annette's sister.

While Sonny and Cher were working for Spector at Philles Records, Geffen was one of Spector's 'go-fers'. 'Phil Spector was my idol. He was my God,' he has recalled. He had never been so dazzled by anyone and he, like Sonny Bono and at least a dozen other young show business novices, became one of the so-called 'Sons of Spector'. He immediately took on some of Phil's characteristics – most people who knew Geffen in the early Sixties remember him as being caustic and difficult.

After Spector, Geffen was employed for a time at CBS Television, where he was fired from two positions. He was then given a job in the mail room at the William Morris Agency, later admitting that he secured the position by lying and saying he was a UCLA graduate in theatre arts. When he heard that the personnel director had written to the school to verify Geffen's claim, he went to work early every morning for months, sorting out mail to search for the response. When it finally arrived, he took the UCLA letter to a printer, had the letterhead on the stationery duplicated, and rewrote the letter himself. He was nothing if not clever.

Through his connections in the record industry, Geffen eventually became a protégé of Ahmet Ertegun, the chairman of Atlantic who signed Sonny and Cher in 1965. Ertegun lent Geffen $50,000 to start his own management firm. Geffen parlayed his ambition and Ertegun's money into a successful career in show business. He managed Crosby, Stills and Nash and had them signed to Ertegun's label; he managed Laura Nyro, and the two became inseparable (Geffen said that Nyro was his greatest artist, and that when she broke up their romance, 'it was my first hurt'); he shared his home with Joni Mitchell for two years; eventually he moved into Julie Andrews's former residence with two suitcases and a bank account full of money.

Geffen went on to become co-founder of Hollywood's famed Roxy Theatre on the Sunset Strip. He established Asylum Records in 1971 and would manage the recording careers of Bob Dylan, Jackson Brown, Linda Ronstadt, The Eagles, and Traffic.

In its first year under Geffen's guidance, Asylum made more than $3 million. When the company merged with Elektra Records, Geffen became president of the entire operation and one of Warner Communications' largest stockholders. In 1973 *Newsweek* called him 'The Golden Boy', and in 1974 *Time* magazine said that he had 'the golden touch'. Today, David Geffen is the president of Geffen Records.

When Bette Midler performed at the Troubadour on Hollywood's Santa Monica Boulevard, Geffen attended the show with then-girlfriend Janet Margolin and Ahmet Ertegun. Sonny and Cher also attended the performance, and Geffen says that when he met Cher backstage he fell in love immediately. In September 1973, Neil Young played Geffen's Roxy nightclub; Geffen, Bob Dylan, and musician Robbie Robertson of The Band went to the show. Cher, sitting on the other side of the club alone, asked if she could join them. Geffen and Cher then had dinner and would be together for the next two years. Geffen was twenty-nine years old and single. Cher was twenty-seven and very married.

'For someone who's been in the music business most of her life, Cher is the most naive woman I think I've ever met,' Geffen told a friend. She had humour, stamina, and talent, and that attracted him. She also seemed full of insecurities and vulnerabilities, and that surprised him. She was, after all, Cher! Despite her long monologues about newly discovered freedom and independence, he knew that a little girl inside this bigger-than-life vamp needed to be cared for and protected.

The relationship between Cher and David Geffen became serious quickly. He wanted her to think of herself as being a strong-willed person, and she wanted that for herself more than anything else at this point.

When he began to ask her questions about her business affairs, it was clear that she knew *nothing* about *anything*. Geffen had been in show business long enough to know that Cher's lack of information and control over her own affairs was dangerous, and as he opened her eyes to 'the real world', she fell in love with him.

Geffen made her understand that she did have power; she was, after all, Cher of 'Sonny and . . .' and, in terms of potential for career advancement, the odds were in her favour. If her marriage broke up and the series were cancelled as a result, Sonny would probably be the one who would come up the loser.

'Good point,' Cher countered.

In October 1973, Sonny and Cher were appearing at the Sahara Hotel again. A year after her first confrontation with El Primo, Cher packed her bags and left him once more.

Some newspapers reported that she flew to Los Angeles to check into Cedars of Lebanon Hospital, where she would have her anaemic condition checked.

'I heard she took off in a huff,' Freeman King said. 'She and Sonny had a big blow-up. It was like World War III in Las Vegas. . . .'

Buddy Hackett took over for Sonny and Cher, and the Sahara management told Sonny that he and his wife would never work Las Vegas again unless they fulfilled their commitments to the Sahara. Eventually, the hotel would sue the Bonos for not completing their engagement. (They were being paid $65,000 a week to perform twice nightly.)

This time, Cher made it clear. The marriage was over.

There were still shows that remained to be taped for 'The Sonny and Cher Comedy Hour' and Bono told Chris Bearde that it didn't look as if they would be able to finish the season. (Said Bearde, 'I felt sick. I thought, My God, I'm losing the show not because of poor ratings but because my stars are getting divorced!')

Sonny Bono went to Palm Springs to try to determine his next move. 'It was like going to work and finding that your key doesn't fit the lock any more,' he said.

'The show's cast was in a panic,' said Freeman King. 'I remember asking the producers, "Hey, guys, what's up? What's all this about Cher walking out of a gig?" They said, "Oh, c'mon, you don't believe that stuff, do you? It's all publicity." Made me think that on the day we get the pink slip from the network we'd be told, "Hey, you're not out of a gig, this is just publicity. . . ."'

CBS brass flew from New York to Los Angeles to try to work out an arrangement that would enable Sonny and Cher to finish out the season. Finally, it was said that the Bonos were told they'd be sued if they didn't put their personal problems aside long enough to wrap up the series; the show was in the top ten and CBS wasn't going to let it slip through its corporate fingers without a fight. Sonny was eager to continue, but Cher had to be persuaded.

'You kinda felt like something was up when Cher started arriving at the studio in a different car when we did those last tapings,' recalled Freeman King. 'Fisher and Bearde called a cast meeting to tell us that after we wrapped up the season we probably wouldn't be back. We were all disappointed. It was like, "Hey, Bonos, we'll pray for you, but you are fucking up our lives here." I would've thought the network would have taken the position that the show could continue. I know that Sonny absolutely wanted it to go on. . . .'

'Continuing that show was the farthest thing from my mind,' concluded Cher years later. 'I finally decided that my life was more important. I never felt that I left Sonny for another man. I left him for a woman. Me.'

By the end of 1973, Cher's recording career had taken a turn for the worse. She hadn't had a hit record since Sonny Bono fired Snuff Garrett; none of the material her husband had produced for her was even remotely successful. Working with Cher was now difficult for Sonny; she wasn't as flexible as she once was, and the Phil Spector approach to recording was no longer a method Cher would tolerate. She'd do as many takes as she felt she wanted to do, and then she'd leave. There would be no more of this 'passing out in the studio nonsense'.

'She's become a real pain in the ass,' Bono complained to a studio engineer. The lack of communication was mirrored in the final result. Sonny's work with Cher at this point – like the *Bittersweet White Light* album – was cold and heartless.

'I got a call from Denis Pregnolato, who was Sonny and Cher's manager at that time, and real good people,' Snuff Garrett recalled. 'He asked me if I would consider working with Cher again. My first instinct was a firm "no way".

'But then I thought about how much I really like Cher. She's one of the cleverest people I know, and her sense of humour was, is, delightful. I also liked the fact that Cher was a quick learner. We'd pick out the songs we were going to cut, and I'd follow standard procedure by sending a demo of the song as it should be recorded to her home. But, knowing Cher, I always knew that she would never give that demo a second thought. She's never been the woodshedding type. When we'd finally get in the studio, she'd say, "Hey, play me that tape, will you?" I would, she'd learn the song on the spot, bam! bam! bam! and the record was finished. What a breeze. . . .

'So remembering all of that, I said, yeah, I'd work with her again. But only if Sonny isn't in the studio . . . no, correction, only if he's not in the *area*. I didn't want him around checkmarking every song and being El Primo. Those became the terms when Cher and I got back together.'

Lyricist Mary Dean was not aware of the fact that Garrett had not been working with Cher when she brought him a song she'd written called 'Half-Breed', a piece about the tormented daughter of a Cherokee mother and white father. She said she penned the song expressly for Cher. Garrett agreed. 'No one in the world could record this but Cher.' But Cher wasn't his artist then, 'so I put the song on a back shelf somehow knowing that one day I'd record it on her.'

After the contracts for their reunion were signed, Garrett played 'Half-Breed' for Cher. She felt it was an exploitive commercial venture, but she decided to record it anyway.

This time, at least, the decision was hers.

The song only took a couple of hours to record. 'I have a terrible voice,' Garrett recalled. 'And I was so excited about working with Cher again that I was singing along with the demo tape in my own inimitable style. She was listening to this on her earphones; she took them off, turned to me, and cracked, "Jesus Christ, Snuff! You have the worst voice I think I have ever heard. It sounds like *shit!*" I said, "Hell, Cher, if I could sing, I wouldn't need *you* here, 'cause I can do everything else."'

'Half-Breed' was released in August 1973, and by 6 October it was number one on *Billboard*'s charts. Snuff Garrett had done it again. The song is camp fun, playing off her tortured image beautifully. 'Half-Breed' topped the charts for two weeks and was certified a million-seller.

By this time, it was clear that Sonny and Cher's recording career as a team was over. The great rock romance of the Sixties had ended.

the last show

On Monday, 18 February 1974, Sonny and Cher arrived at CBS Television Studios in Hollywood to begin a week's rehearsal schedule before taping the twenty-fifth and last show of 'The Sonny and Cher Comedy Hour'. The concert segments of the programme would be taped before a live audience on Wednesday, and the comedy skits would be done privately on Friday.

The first day of rehearsal went smoothly despite the obvious tension in the air; nobody discussed the impending break-up, and unanswered questions about the show's fate were foremost on everyone's mind. Was there any possibility that the Bonos could reconcile before 15 April, the date CBS would make a decision about whether or not the series could be renewed for another season?

After rehearsing a sketch, Sonny would retreat to one corner of the studio, Cher to another. They hardly spoke.

After Tuesday's rehearsal, Bono filed for a legal separation from Cher in Los Angeles Superior Court, citing 'irreconcilable differences'. Plans for a multimillion-dollar Las Vegas run were iced.

'Couldn't he have waited until next week?' Cher complained. 'Why do that right now, in the middle of the last show? After all these years, he could have waited a week. *Christ!*'

Wednesday morning, Sonny and Cher arrived at CBS to pre-record the musical numbers they'd be performing on the show. It would be the first time they had seen each other since Sonny did 'this thing', as Cher called it.

Cher came down a hallway and turned a corner to find Sonny Bono coming out of his dressing room. He stopped and faced her. In what could have been a scene of painful recrimination, they hardly knew what to say to each other. She looked at him levelly, and he sized her up. Then the pain and hurt suspended itself for a moment; they began laughing. They had a good laugh standing there in the hallway.

What else was left to do but laugh?

It seemed absurd, but it was a profoundly affecting moment. It would earn a special place in their hearts and memories.

That night, 342 fans assembled in Studio 31 to watch them tape the concert portion of the show. It was official; all the newspapers had reported that Sonny had filed for a separation. An odd mix of excitement and sadness hung in the air. *TV Guide* sent Rowland Barber to report the 'event' for a cover story.

'Here comes the tap dance across the mine field,' said Chris Bearde backstage before walking out to face the audience and introduce Sonny and Cher. 'This is the hardest thing I've ever had to do.'

Bearde walked out onto the stage to polite applause. 'I know what you're asking yourselves,' he began. '"What's he [Bono] going to say *tonight*?" Well, I'm thinking exactly what you are. It's sad about some of the things that have been happening. Everybody has problems and everybody deserves the chance to work them out. What about Sonny and Cher's? They're going to be out here in a minute and you can decide for yourselves. You're going to see a lot of love on this stage. Thank you.'

Sonny and Cher were introduced, and the applause was manic. They performed a perfunctory version of 'Beautiful Sunday', which would be the show's opening number. After the obligatory comedy routine of put-downs, they performed 'I Got You Babe', which, appropriately enough, would be edited in as the programme's closing number. The performance was effortless; the crew remembered it as being one of the strongest of the season.

That evening Cher hosted a surprise birthday party for David Geffen in the Grand Trianon Room of the Beverly Wilshire Hotel in Beverly Hills. She had hired mariachis, jugglers, knife throwers, and fire-eaters. Barbra Streisand and Warren Beatty were on the guest list. Cher and Bob Dylan sang their rendition of 'All I Really Want to Do', and Geffen gave Cher an $8,000 diamond ring (which they both denied was an engagement ring).

'Wasn't last night, the concert taping, terrific?' Cher asked the

TV Guide reporter the next day. 'Before it started, I was nervous. And the audience was nervous. You'd think the show would be affected too, but no, it came together like it does every time we go on. Maybe even better.'

On Friday, the Bonos, their guest Joel Grey, and the rest of the company taped the comedy segments of the show, with twelve complicated costume and scene changes.

Freeman King recalled the taping of the last sketch: 'It was my "Cultural Reporter" segment. I was sitting in my big armchair in my tux getting ready for the camera work. Cher used to call me one-take Freeman, and it was customary that Sonny would do anything he could to make me blow my lines, just for laughs.

'In the middle of the take, Sonny crawled underneath my seat with a broom and started banging. He was in a great mood. Art Fisher, the director said, "What the hell is going on? I hear banging. Cut!" And I said, "Art, it's Bono and he's underneath my chair banging a broom on my butt trying to make me blow my lines." We started again and just as the camera was rolling Sonny said audibly, "Big break for you here, Freeman. Don't blow it."

'"*Cut!*"

'This went on for seven takes; I really think Son didn't want the day to end. Finally I turned to him and snapped, "Hey, Sonny, how's your marriage?" And it was like someone had thrown a grenade into the room. No one knew what to say. The subject had been carefully avoided all week. Sonny stood there blank-faced for a second, then he said, "Just like your acting, Freeman. Bad. *Real* bad!"

'The place broke up laughing. . . .'

The day was finished. Cher went off in one direction with a coterie of assistants. Sonny walked off in the opposite direction. Alone.

That night Sonny and Cher took off in their private jet for Houston, where they would perform four shows for 107,000 people at the Houston Livestock and Rodeo Show in the Astrodome. Breaking up with Sonny wasn't going to be simple, Cher realized. Most couples headed for divorce don't advertise it in the Astrodome. It was said that she didn't want to go but that David Geffen convinced her that if she refused, she would only be complicating what was already shaping up to be a legal war. He would stay in Los Angeles and help prepare Cher's response to her husband's request for a legal separation.

In Texas, Sonny and Cher would stay at the same hotel, but in separate rooms. Sonny had met another woman, a fashion model named Connie Foreman, and after this engagement he would go on a holiday with her.

Meanwhile, Cher and David Geffen attended the Grammy Awards together. 'When Cher walked in with that guy, it was riotous,' said a fan who attended the ceremony. 'She wore a white gown with a bare midriff, and she had a butterfly in her hair, and another one coming out of her tits. The two of them made a great couple, smiling a lot, holding hands, and acting very much like they'd been together for years.'

For the next couple of years, Cher would be stalked by the scandal of what she was about to do to Sonny Bono. Her life was a clean slate now, and she was ready for the creation of something new. But first, it would be out with the old. She would respond to Bono's charge of 'irreconcilable differences' on 27 February.

Or, as one friend put it, 'Five days before Cher addressed Sonny's legal action, the Sonny and Cher show ended, and Art Fisher told the stagehands to strip the stage bare. "*Everything goes*," he said. Cher must've thought he was talking to her. . . .'

part two

'CHER'S NAGASAKI'

'I could not be a person under the El Primo regime. I thought I had nine-tenths of the pie, and I kept wondering why the other tenth was eating at me. And then I realized that it was nine-tenths of Sonny's pie. . . .'

– Cher

So she had a bigger heart than smarts, so what?

Sonny Bono had the controlling interest in every aspect of Sonny and Cher's multimillion-dollar enterprise. Cher suspected this all along; in fact, she had insisted that she not be involved in their business affairs. She trusted her husband.

But now, leaving him made sense. If she'd been more savvy, if she'd had any experience at all, she would have calculated a separation in advance; she would have had an attorney investigate her affairs before the marriage was over. But in 1973, she was wrestling with contradictory emotions, simultaneous joy and heartbreak.

Cher had no idea what the ramifications would be, the size of the can of worms she was about to open, when she decided to break up not only her marriage, but 'Sonny and Cher' as well, when she risked both their careers and pulled what Sonny referred to as 'Cher's Nagasaki'.

On 27 February 1974, Cher sued her husband for divorce and charged that he had been holding her in 'involuntary servitude', that he had 'unlawfully dominated and controlled my business interests and career'.

Sonny was said to be stunned. His friends say he never expected Cher to take their separation any further; what he expected was that she would come to her senses when he filed his action, that she would plead for a reconciliation, that she would realize that without Sonny, there would be no Cher. But he hadn't counted on David Geffen's influence on his estranged wife.

Prior to this, Sonny and Cher were both represented by the same attorney, Irwin O. Spiegel. Back in October 1973, when Cher left Sonny a second time during the Las Vegas engagement, she reminded him of an agreement she thought they had: if their relationship became uncomfortable, he would move out of the mansion and she would live there with Chastity. 'Sonny, you're going to have to move out when we get home,' she told him, 'because you're really making me feel bad in my own home and on the road. It's a drag and I do not like it.' Sonny told her that he'd never leave that house. (He probably remembered that Cher told him the exact same thing a few years back when they almost lost the mansion.)

Cher called Spiegel and asked him to remind Sonny of the agreement. She said that he called her back and told her that Bono had hung up on him, and he suggested that Cher move out.

'You're *kidding*? You *do*? Well, all right, I guess I will.'

'I didn't know that once you moved out, you couldn't get back in,' she said later. 'No one told me that.'

When Cher left the home, twenty-four-year-old Connie Foreman, a statuesque redhead Sonny had employed as a secretary, was said to have moved in. Foreman was supposedly earning $600 a week. She and Bono made all the gossip columns when they arrived at Nicky Blair's restaurant in Los Angeles one evening in his black Porsche Carrera to have dinner. The way the newspapers had it, Sonny had to have his girlfriend smuggled out through the kitchen after photographers had been alerted of their date and began holding a vigil outside the restaurant.

Cher moved into a rented five-bedroom beach house in Malibu, where she stayed with Chastity, her sister, Georgeanne, and David Geffen. The house cost $4,000 a month. Bono was giving Cher about $7,500 a month, and she said that that amount did not cover all her expenses. She couldn't cash any cheques she'd sign without the additional signature of Sonny Bono or their attorney.

'It had been ten years of work for me and I couldn't get any of the money I thought was half mine,' Cher complained, totally nonplussed. 'I didn't want any more than half. I said, "There's a *lot* of money there, so you take half and let me have half, and let's cool it." "No, no, *no!*" he said.'

Cher asked David Geffen to help her unravel this mess. In court documents filed months later, Sonny charged that Geffen and Cher called a meeting with a William Morris Agency representative to announce that Cher would now be a solo artist, that Sonny and Cher were finished as a marriage and an act, that CBS should be informed immediately and all concerned should begin thinking in terms of 'The Cher Show'.

Bono also charged that David Geffen encouraged Cher to ask for a new split of any future royalties from new recordings by Sonny and Cher: 75 per cent to Cher and 25 per cent to Sonny.

Meanwhile, the trade newspapers reported that Geffen began negotiating a solo deal for Cher at Warner Brothers.

David then suggested that Cher see a new attorney and have all the legal work involving Sonny and Cher's business affairs examined. After going over the stacks of documents, the new lawyer asked Cher if she realized that she was actually an *employee* of a company called Cher Enterprises, owned by Sonny Bono, and that as an employee she was entitled to one three-week paid vacation a year.

'I started reading what I had signed, and I got really pissed off. That made me angrier than anything else. My head for business is nil. I just didn't care. All I wanted was to work, sing, and be stupid.

'I knew that we owned half the show, and I thought Cher Enterprises was just a company that you had because people are always forming companies – I really didn't even know why. We had a payroll, the cheques said "Cher Enterprises", and I thought that's where the money gets deposited, and then it goes back out again.'

In her action, Cher asked that her marriage to Bono be dissolved, and then in an accompanying civil action, she charged that her contract with Bono's company constituted 'involuntary servitude' or slavery, in direct violation of the Constitution's Thirteenth Amendment. Her contract with Cher Enterprises prohibited her from working for any other company until 1977, it provided no compensation to her should she not be able to perform for any reason, and it gave Sonny a claim on her future earnings should Sonny and Cher be dissolved as a working entity. Cher's new lawyer found that Bono owned 950 shares of Cher Enterprises stock and their attorney, Spiegel, held fifty shares; Cher had none.

Also, any income Sonny made as a result of his efforts as a songwriter and producer would be considered 'separate and apart' from money generated by Cher Enterprises. Cher, on the other hand, was not permitted to perform any services outside of her work for Sonny's company.

She said in her legal action that she signed such an agreement because she 'lacked sophistication in business matters'. She explained privately that she would have signed anything that had Sonny's or their attorney's name on it. 'I mean, who has *time* to read? And who would understand it anyway?'

Later, she would accuse Sonny of entering into a recording agreement with MCA on 1 February 1974, that would extend their existing contract with that label until 13 December 1976. She said that she was never consulted about such a renegotiation.

She demanded 'restitution of 50 per cent of the sums paid to defendant Spiegel from 1 January 1972', and nullification of the contract with Cher Enterprises.

Sonny tried to explain that the agreement had been completely misinterpreted, that it was designed to protect the Bonos as a couple from frittering away their money as they had when they went broke in 1969. 'Cher knew darned well that the agreement was written to give us both the kinds of safeguards we were looking for. We wanted to get whatever insurance we could so that if something should go wrong, as it did previously, we would have annuities this time.'

'If anything, Cher set herself up for this whole scenario,' said a former associate. 'She had no common sense, no understanding of human nature. She was a person who couldn't have a normal perspective about anything that involved a man who made her a star before she was twenty. She idealized Sonny. But ideally your husband doesn't put you in a position of disadvantage, or in a position of not being an equal partner when you're doing equal work. Now she didn't know if Sonny ever really loved her, especially when in black and white it didn't show up love.'

'This country deified Cher. She became this huge S-T-A-R,' said Sonny years later. 'She hired a savvy lawyer who went public on her behalf and claimed that I held Cher in involuntary servitude. 'You only have to know Cher to understand how ridiculous that is. But the public wanted to believe it. They turned against me with the help of the press. Cher was never an involuntary *anything*. But the public didn't want to know that. Nor did the public want to know that I'd been had.'

'I was not prepared to be cast in the role of the villain,' Sonny told a reporter, 'the hanger-on who had victimized the talented one. Suddenly, after eleven years in the business, doors slammed in my face. I was that guy who had been married to Cher.'

'Sonny is a real human being, but America thinks of him as totally perfect,' Cher told another. 'They think *I'm* wicked.'

'He was really angry,' she told Andy Warhol. 'He said, "You know, you really screwed up everything. I could have made all this money and, you know, it's your fault that I can't, so I should be the one who keeps what's left." I said, "That seems logical, but when I met you you were a truck driver and I was doing nothing, and *we* were nothing. Now we have all this money and all these things, and you should take half and I should take half."'

Sonny Bono struck back at his wife with a lawsuit that demanded half of the $14 million he had estimated they would have earned if Cher had not cancelled the future of Sonny and Cher as a recording and entertainment act.

'Sonny protected Cher from all the trials and ordeals I had gone through when I was trying to make a go of it in the movies,' said Cher's mother, Georgia. 'In his enthusiasm and with his terrific drive, he didn't realize he was working Cher so hard. He forgot that she was no longer sixteen, that she was an adult capable of making her own decisions. . . .'

Cher's father, John Sarkisian, offered his assessment as well: 'I don't know anyone who knows Cher well. I don't. Her mother didn't. And I don't think Sonny did either. I'd say this: she would never have made it without Sonny Bono. People kept saying that if it weren't for Cher, he'd be nothing. She got to hearing it so much, I think she finally believed it. . . .'

Cher's drama with Sonny was enacted before a whole country of interested bystanders, and the fact that the Battling Bonos were so loquacious with the press made their combative divorce loom even larger. Soon, it seemed as if everything that happened in Cher's personal life was a matter of national interest. It was a fascination that would last for years. The media invented an image for her to live up to and, needless to say, she did. She was glamorous, wealthy and controversial, and she could have any man she wanted.

Her well-publicized exploits would be covered with great imagination in tabloids and magazines with names like *TV Radio Talk*, *Screen Stars*, *Movie Stars*, *Movie World*, *Movieland*, *Photoplay*, and, of course, *The National Enquirer*. Their covers would scream sensational and tantalizing headlines: 'Cher's Dark Secrets About Her Sex Life', 'Cher: "PLEASE SONNY, Don't Beat Me!"', 'Why Cher Traded One Lover for Another', or 'Cher and the Way She Toys With Sex'. Even Chastity got into the act, with magazine covers that wondered, 'Can Chastity Survive Cher's Nightmare?'

'They call me the Queen of the Newsstands,' Cher complained. 'There are not enough hours in the day for me to do all the things they say I do, and with all the people they say I do them with. They had me walking down the beach in Acapulco with Jim Brown, and they pasted two photos of us together. They've done the same thing with me and Paul Newman, Robert Redford, and Elvis Presley, and I had never met any of them. They had Elvis paying for my house and giving me alimony. I called his wife, Priscilla, and said, "Look, if he really means it, here's my number."'

Later, in an interview with *Playboy*, Cher said: 'I have this sex-siren image, but, really, I couldn't give a shit about that. I am so uninterested right now in all the Robert Redfords, Elvis Presleys, and anyone else's husband that I really don't care. I feel it's almost like being a bank clerk. I go and do my job, and that's my job, the sex queen stuff.'

Fuelled by the idea that Cher was now the embodiment of sex, avarice, and every modern evil, it was only natural that 'Dark Lady' would become another million-selling single and number-one record for Cher in March 1974. 'Dark Lady' tells the story of a woman who goes to a fortune teller to find out why her marriage is falling apart. The mysterious 'dark lady' suggests that the woman leave town immediately and forget about her husband. Later that night, the woman recognizes the fortune teller's perfume in her sheets, realizes that she's been had, and goes back to the fortune teller's home, where she finds her husband. She then murders both of them.

'I always tried to find songs for Cher that would get her in a different, bizarre situation every time,' Snuff Garrett laughed. John Durrell penned 'Dark Lady', Garrett explained, and just as he was going to record it with Cher, he decided that in the end the protagonist should shoot the soothsayer. In the original composition, there was no murder. Durrell was in Kyoto, Japan, by the time Garrett tried to track him down to rewrite the lyric.

'The connection was so muffled when we finally made contact, he could barely understand me on the phone as I shouted "Kill her; kill her." "What?" he said. "I can't hear you."

'"*Kill her*! In the third verse, *kill her*!"

'Eventually I got the point across and in twenty-four hours he telegraphed three different endings to the song and I chose the one where the main character kills both the fortune teller *and* her husband. Cher loved that.'

After 'Dark Lady' came 'Train of Thought' (in which Cher's boyfriend commits suicide and she's so torn up about it that she, too, commits suicide in order to 'stop this train of thought').

'There was a lot of excitement in the studio when we cut that one,' recalled Garrett. 'But when Cher recorded, it was always a big event, lots of people hanging around. I also cut a song with Cher called "I Saw a Man (and He Danced With His Wife)" (in which Cher's boyfriend turns out to be married, and in the end he leaves his wife for her). I was trying to do a Glenn Miller orchestration on that one and never got it right. Still makes me crazy today to hear it.'

Garrett said that Mo Austin at MCA decided to release 'Train of Thought' after 'Dark Lady'. He, though, believed that the follow-up should've been 'I Saw a Man'. 'It was just a gut instinct I had,' he recalled.

'My wife and I were out having dinner one night when we ran into Richard Perry, the producer. "Hell of a song you got there on Cher, that 'Train of Thought' thing," he told me. I told him I wish the hell I felt that way 'cause I thought it was a stiff. And it was. And then when they put out "I Saw a Man", that was a stiff too.

It's always time, place, and instinct in the record business. Screw up the order of things and you blow the whole ball game.'

It took nine weeks for 'Dark Lady' to top the charts. It would also be Cher's last number-one record to date, and her last top-ten release until 1979. Snuff Garrett and Cher would not work together again until 1977. Friends say that David Geffen wanted Cher to express herself with stronger material, and so he pulled her from MCA, signed her to Warner Brothers, and replaced Garrett – with none other than Phil Spector.

Cher never performed her Snuff Garrett hit singles in her night-club act, and she has said that she doesn't like any of them and won't sing them again. Garrett noted with a grin, 'Its *beneath* her to have a hit. I don't care if she ever sings them again or not; that's her business. You see, I am not an esoteric producer. To me, a product is a product for the masses; you make it commercial; you make it sell. They told me to assist in a major resurgence in Cher's recording career, and I did. If that was a shortcoming, I'm certainly not going to apologize for it.

'When an artist begins to grow, he sometimes questions the material that made him famous, and that's the case with Cher,' he concluded. (Garrett prizes an eight-by-ten glossy of Cher on which she wrote: 'To Snuff – You bastard! What am I gonna do with you? Cher.' 'The more hits I gave her, the more of this stuff she had to record, so she called me a bastard,' Snuff recalled with a chuckle.)

'My only regret is that Sonny and I were always at odds because we should have done more Cher material, and more Sonny and Cher songs,' Garrett concluded. 'We lost a lot of money because of egos. Cher was very stylistic and promotion conscious. You never had to create an image for Cher. Cher was, *is*, an image.'

The studio reunion of Cher with Phil Spector wasn't as memorable as her fans had hoped it would be. It had been over ten years since she and Spector had worked together, when she had been a background singer on his 'Wall of Sound' creations at Gold Star Studios. She'd come a long way since 'Ringo I Love You' by Bonnie Jo Mason, the Spector tax write-off.

Phil Spector's career had started to slide in the mid-Sixties when Berry Gordy Jr began to monopolize the pop charts with black entertainment from Detroit's Motown Records. When Spector produced 'River Deep Mountain High' by Ike and Tina Turner and it didn't become a major seller, he became disenchanted with the recording industry. He believed that the song should have been a resounding success, that the industry had somehow turned against him. He went into semiretirement after a few years. In the Seventies, Spector resurfaced as coproducer of the Beatles' *Let It Be* album (which set a record by generating $25 million in just two weeks, selling more than 3,700,000 copies in that short period of time), George Harrison's *All Things Must Pass* album, and John Lennon's *Imagine* album and 'Power to the People' single.

In 1975, Phil Spector produced a maudlin record for Cher called 'A Woman's Story', 'one of the biggest disappointments of the Seventies', as *Creem* magazine put it. The flip side of the single was a crafty reinterpretation of The Ronettes' 'Baby I Love You', which Cher performed as a sulking ballad. It was a flop.

The next year, Spector teamed Cher with Harry Nilsson for a folkish version of Holland, Dozier and Holland's Martha and the Vandellas chestnut '(A Love Like Yours) Don't Come Knocking Every Day'. It, too, went nowhere.

Record industry insiders began whispering that David Geffen and his former mentor Spector disagreed on concepts for Cher's Warner releases. It was said that Geffen had somehow used his tremendous influence in the record industry to thwart the success of both Spector singles.

This doesn't seem likely. Neither single needed any assistance from Geffen to become a runaway commercial failure.

The legal action between Sonny and Cher, and Cher's refusal to continue with 'The Sonny and Cher Comedy Hour', caused more than a panic at CBS. When the programme aired its final episode for the season in May 1974, it had won a 38 per cent share of the viewing audience. It was the eighth most popular show on television. In terms of advertising dollars, the series was top drawer, generating hundreds of thousands of dollars.

Said Chris Bearde to *Variety*, 'Nobody wants the show to go off. Yet at the same time, it's a ticklish situation between two people who are going to be divorced, whether the public will buy a "divorce show" or not. Strange as it may seem, all options are open at the moment.'

Bearde was referring to a statement Cher had made that had the decision been left to her, the last episode of the series would have had a divorce format: Sonny and Cher would state their case before America, explain their marital woes, and then go on with the show. 'Sonny probably would have gone for it,' she said. 'It would have been honest.'

A statement from one of the show's major sponsors, Revlon read: 'If the American public accepts them, we'll be delighted. If the American public doesn't, we won't be so delighted.'

Cher had already made it clear that regardless of how much Sonny would like her to, she would not continue with the series. In April 1974, she and Geffen alerted the network that she had not changed her mind. Freddie Silverman had no choice but to cancel the option.

No one was more disappointed than Sonny Bono. He told friends that he was able to deal with the cancellation of his marriage to Cher better than he was the cancellation of the series. He had worked years for the kind of respect and recognition that programme allowed, and now it was over. He wasn't naive; the next few years would be tough, and he knew it.

So the legal drama continued. . . .

Sonny publicly called David Geffen 'a little antagonizer'. He charged Geffen with interfering in Cher's and his businesses and he filed an amendment to his original action against Cher, this one demanding $13 million from Geffen. He was incensed by Geffen's seemingly proprietary interest in Cher's career and accused him of 'contractual interference' and 'conspiring to destroy Sonny and Cher's business'. He implied in interviews that David Geffen was a gigolo living off Cher's fame and fortune.

According to Sonny's court documents, Cher was spending $6,000 a month on clothing, $600 a month on fingernail care, and $900 a month on psychiatric care.

Cher informed Sonny that she wanted to move back to the Holmby Hills estate and that if he wouldn't leave, she would move in anyway and stay in a separate bedroom. Bono reacted by filing a temporary restraining order to prevent her from moving back into his home, saying that her presence 'would be interfering with my privacy'.

The Bono mansion was an opulent place to live, and it's no wonder that neither Sonny nor Cher wanted to give it up. Designer Ron Wilson had decorated the home with eighteenth-century furniture acquired in France, Belgium and Italy, Portuguese and Oriental handmade rugs, hand-painted sky graphics on the ceiling, and Louis XV panelled walls.

Architectural Digest featured the garish estate in its May 1974 issue in a photographic layout, with the following description of their master bedroom:

'The master suite is lavished with eighteenth-century print in cotton by Brunschwig & Fils. French porcelain lamps sit beside the French shell-carved Italian Renaissance bed ornamented with an eighteenth-century cartouche. Windows with floral wreath-carved arches and Duppioni lace under drapery flank a Louis XV marble mantel surmounted by a bronze fire box. Accompanying the Louis XV commode with a nineteenth-century Venetian mirror are a Chinese export jardiniere on lacquered stand, eighteenth-century French bronze and painting on black mesh screens, and a nineteenth-century French chair. Carpet by Stark.'

And that was just the room they slept in.

From the official court records, Bono said, 'I am informed and believe that she [Cher] entered into a lease of the Malibu premises for the purpose of living there with an adult male, and also with our child, Chastity Bono. I believe that the adult male has been and still is residing out at the Malibu place with Cher and our daughter.

'I do not believe that there is any possibility of an amicable joint occupancy of the Carolwood residence now. My wife has already stated that she found working with me to be emotionally humiliating and physically upsetting. Therefore I do not see how, with those circumstances, she now feels that she can amicably live under the same roof with me.'

Allowing Cher back into the mansion would, said Bono, be 'both emotionally and physically upsetting to our daughter and would also interfere with my necessary work and day-to-day living.'

Before Santa Monica Superior Court Judge Richard Wells, Cher said that the reason she left the mansion in the first place was because 'a non-family' member of their entourage had been encouraged to move in. She was homesick for the house, she said, and Chastity missed her friends.

Sonny said that he had pleaded with Cher not to take their daughter and move to Malibu, and that in the months after her relocation, Cher would come and go from the Carolwood estate whenever she pleased 'and in this manner she disturbed me and my own personal use and enjoyment of the Carolwood estate.' He added that he and Cher had agreed to sell the home anyway because it was no longer practical for them to maintain it.

The judge did not come to a decision that day. As the Bonos left the courtroom they, in true Sonny and Cher fashion, flung their arms around each other and kissed.

'Does this mean a reconciliation?' one of the reporters asked Cher.

'I think not. It's just that Sonny and I find it very difficult to be angry with each other, truly angry, now that we are separated.'

Cher added that she did plan to marry David Geffen as soon as 'these hassles' ended.

Earlier in the week, ABC announced that it had signed Sonny Bono to star in his own variety show. When asked why she didn't have a similar deal, Cher responded, 'I guess you can say I'm just a late bloomer.'

Sonny piped in, 'But when she does get her own show, I'd really like to produce it.'

(The real reason Cher didn't have her own series was because her contract with Sonny Bono prevented her from working on one.)

And then they were whisked off in separate limousines to their respective homes – Sonny to Holmby Hills, Cher to Malibu.

'One thing you can say about Sonny and Cher,' wrote a newspaper reporter. 'They give the press and the public quite a good show. Surely divorce has never been so jolly.'

Privately, though, the jollies were wearing thin.

Sonny eventually agreed to sell the mansion to Cher for half the amount at which it was valued. Cher had not paid him by July, Sonny claimed later, and so he remained in the house with Connie Foreman.

On the evening of 8 July 1974, Sonny was working in a recording studio when he received a frantic phone call from Foreman telling him that Cher, her secretary, Chastity, and David Geffen had commandeered the residence. They had, she said, two private security guards with them. In what Sonny later called 'a guerrilla action', they moved Bono's belongings out and theirs in.

'Sonny was absolutely frantic about this,' said a former associate. 'He was crying and, well, he was on the verge of some kind of breakdown.'

'*This* was a new Cher,' Joe deCarlo, former manager of Sonny and Cher, later noted. 'One who speaks. One who doesn't say "How high?" when Sonny says "Jump!" One who says, "Up your ass!"'

Back in court, Sonny said that he had telephoned Cher that evening to ask if she had a court order allowing her entrance to the house. He alleged that Geffen picked up an extension and yelled at him.

'I was informed that there was a policeman at the house and that he had a gun. I didn't know if that meant I was going to get shot if I tried to walk in the house. Before all this happened, Chastity warned me, "Daddy, be careful, Mommy says she is going to get the police and they're going to throw you out." I think that's bad. When a child says that, I think that's bad. . . .'

(Later, Cher would say that 'Chastity hated David, and I found out later that he didn't think much of her either. So that was no good.')

This final confrontation brought home all of the separation and misunderstanding, hostilities and recriminations. That night, Sonny and Connie checked into the Beverly Hills Hotel and David and Cher lived, and continued to live, 'openly and notoriously', as Sonny put it, in Holmby Hills.

Cher explained that emotional evening by saying that she had a memorandum agreement signed by Sonny Bono promising that he would be out of the house by 1 July. When that day arrived, Cher explained, he told her that he needed one more week to facilitate the move. By 8 July, Cher said, she assumed her estranged husband had vacated the house and so she moved back in.

When Sonny and Cher presented their respective cases in the divorce hearing before Superior Court Judge Goscee O. Farley in Santa Monica Superior Court, Cher was accompanied by her two attorneys and David Geffen. It seemed a bit unusual for a woman suing her husband for divorce to appear in court with her boyfriend.

Later, the judge would decree that Cher be given $25,000 monthly alimony for a six-month period and $1,500 monthly child support for Chastity.

Custody of their daughter would be a battle that both parents waged for some time. 'Sonny wants to have her for half the time, but I don't think she should be split in half,' Cher said at the time. 'There are some things I just can't be pushed into doing. We're going to have a *big* argument about that.'

Later, Cher would say in an interview with writer Tom Burke, 'Sonny did try to take her from me once – tried to prove that I was an unfit mother. The grounds were things like I once took Chas to Hugh Hefner's place to see the animals he has; nobody else was even there except for Pam Grier, the actress. Another ground was that I was living with David.'

For the time being, Cher was granted physical custody of the child, but legal custody was awarded both parents. Bono was given a schedule of visitation rights. Later, these restrictions were rescinded.

'Cher and David Geffen tried to put that weekends-only visitation nonsense on me,' he said. 'I would like to believe that David was the one who was difficult about it. I was getting ready to do my television show and would be working weekends. So I went to court again, had my say, and things loosened up. When Geffen was gone, Cher couldn't have been nicer.'

Settlement of the Bonos' property would drag on for years. Cher asked for an additional $195,000 so that she could purchase a condominium in Aspen, Colorado, but the judge ruled against her request.

She wasn't in court when the judge awarded her alimony; she learned the news from David Geffen when he phoned her at her exercise class, and later, again, at her massage. 'Are you a happy lady today?' he asked. 'You walked home with all the marbles. You got everything – twenty-five thousand a month, custody. Sonny just gets weekends. And there's injunctive relief; they can't spend your money. Sonny went out today to book a Sonny and Cher Show! *Do you believe that?*'

Geffen also outlined some of the deals he had pending for Cher, which included $600,000 for a month-long Las Vegas engagement, a $1 million personal concert tour, a television special for CBS, and a weekly series for that same network.

'More than anyone he could remember in recent history, Sonny hated David Geffen,' said a source. 'He was saying to himself, "Look, I took her in when she was nothing and I made her a star. *I* made her rich, and now she's going to spend it on some other guy, make *him* her whole life and I'm on the outside looking in? That's bullshit!"'

Years later, Sonny said, 'There were times when I wanted to kill David Geffen. I think it was a very bad period for Cher too. The shock to men in divorce is to find out that you don't own what you thought you owned. Now amplify that to an act, and then to a business, and you'll know why I wanted to kill David Geffen.'

'Sonny said to me, "You know, you were my best student," and I said, "Yes, I know,"' Cher recalled. 'And then he said, "Sometimes it's like a quick draw, you know, when the quick draw teaches the young draw and one day they have to come to the big shoot-out." We laughed. I am sad it's over. But I could not be a *person* under that regime, under the El Primo regime.'

It had been a tough, emotional summer for everyone. Sonny became bitter, Geffen became a chain smoker, and Cher gained weight and her face broke out in blemishes. (Cher had always had trouble with her skin, but while working on the series she suffered make-up poisoning, 'an allergic reaction to wearing all that shit on my face'.)

That summer cost David Geffen $38,000 in his own legal defence. 'It's not that I want to do it. I'm not looking to be a personal manager,' he told Julie Baumgold for an *Esquire* cover story called 'The Winning of Cher' (February 1975). 'But this is the woman I love. It's not a client. She needs help right now.'

During her interview with Geffen, Baumgold recalled that 'between normal business calls are frantic divorce bulletin calls that leave Geffen looking stricken, announcing things like "Sonny's at the house". Geffen's concern in the divorce seems to be keeping Sonny away from Cher.' Geffen purchased the condominium for Cher that Sonny refused her, for $212,000.

Cher convinced David to buy a Corniche Rolls Royce with wire wheels; they skied in Aspen; they enjoyed lavish dinners with Diana Vreeland; they hosted marvellous parties. She lovingly referred to him as 'Mr Beige', because he was so conservative. He bought her diamond necklaces. *Esquire* painted this picture: 'Cher's tongue is deep inside Geffen's mouth. Her thick braids swing forward onto his neck. She straightens up and smooths her leotard into her famously flat midriff. "Feel my ass," she says to Geffen. "Hard as a rock."'

Whereas David Geffen was once a low-profile entertainment mogul, when Cher came into his life he became part of a media 'event'. Pick up any magazine, and there they were: Cher and David, dodging reporters, coming and going from courthouses all over Southern California, Cher all smiles, David looking menaced.

But the couple did have extravagant fun, as well. Shopping sprees for shoes with Diana Ross and her husband, Robert Silberstein, were always major productions. Limousine chauffeurs would be sent out for pizzas and hero sandwiches for the quartet to munch on as they'd make themselves at home in Manhattan shoe stores, trying on shoes and boots of every imaginable size, shape and colour. At one store, Geffen suggested that Cher charge the sale on her credit card because if she did the entire amount could be deducted as one of her business expenses. Cher retorted, 'Well, you can call me Mrs *Bono* then,' an observer recalled. Geffen paid for the shoes – $1,750.

When Cher, Geffen, Bette Midler, Elton John, Ross and Silberstein went en masse to see a performance of *Grease* on Broadway, the result was hysteria. When the party left the theatre for a breath of fresh air during intermission, half the patrons followed dutifully into the street. 'The people were pouring down from the balconies,' Geffen recalled. 'The second act was thirty minutes late beacuse of the madness.'

Later that evening, the group went dancing at LeJardin, a New York hot spot, and then Midler suggested that they finish the evening in a gay bar, the Limelight.

'When that group walked into that gay bar, it was received with all the religiousity of a "close encounters" landing,' said a patron. 'All these divas, and in silver sequins and spangles. The guys were throwing themselves at their feet, touching and feeling them to make certain the whole thing wasn't a holy apparition.'

The media embraced Cher as a symbol of liberation for millions of women. 'She is the most together woman of the Seventies,' Rona Barrett declared. She had had enough, and she wasn't going to take it any more.

Sonny Bono didn't like what had happened to his creation. 'She has put herself beyond human reach,' he told Joseph Bell for *Good Housekeeping*. 'She's escalated into some kind of superstardom. The one thing Cher always wanted was to be rich. Sure, I managed her life for her, but as far as I knew, we were in full harmony.

'Everybody wants to hang that sad, despondent label on me; I guess because I didn't come out of this thing throwing parties. That wasn't my style before and it isn't now. Right away, Cher and I had roles placed on us. She was the newly liberated woman and I was the despondent, rejected man. I *was* for a while.

'I always thought Cher could step back into reality,' he concluded. 'But now I wonder, when I keep hearing about how this oppressed woman broke out into freedom. Cher was *always* free; she always did what she wanted to.'

'the sonny comedy revue'

The ABC network's 'Sonny Comedy Revue' premiered on 22 September 1974. The final show went on air three months later, on 29 December.

'I was hopeful that Sonny's show would make it,' recalled Freeman King (the entire company from 'The Sonny and Cher Comedy Hour' was recruited for Bono's solo outing, except for the tall, glamorous Dark Lady). 'Sonny had a lot of balls, he really did. He wanted this show to succeed in the worst way. They were all saying that he was the brains and she was the talent, that he *had* no talent. That hurt.'

Sonny told friends that while it was true that he taught Cher everything she knows, he didn't teach her everything *he* knew.

'I told Sonny, "Look man, I have never been on a show that didn't make it,"' remembered King. 'And he said, "Yeah, Freeman, but you've only been on one show, mine with Cher." I said, "Yeah, but that one made it, didn't it?"'

Sonny's guests on his debut show were The Jackson Five, Howard Cosell, and Sally Struthers. Cher's spirit loomed over the hour like a ghost from Sonny's past, and there were numerous references to her. Bono continued to play the Chaplinesque 'little man' always beset with troubles and always the underdog – but somehow it wasn't as comical as it had been.

'It was the exact same premise, but without Cher,' said Chris Bearde. 'And that's saying a lot. Sonny and all of us, including Teri Garr, who joined the cast, were fifty per cent. Cher alone was the other half. Man can't live by 50 per cent ratings alone; you gotta have the whole apple.'

The critical reaction to a Sonny without Cher was hostile. Reporter Kay Gardella wrote: '[Cosell and Bono] offer great hope to all the talentless people in the world. It has always been our contention that [Bono] has absolutely no talent.'

On the first episode, Bono performed his first and only MCA solo release 'The Last Show', which he wrote in reference to his failed marriage. It's an agonizing record to listen to, mostly because of Bono's 'voice', but his performance of it on national television was a triumph of heart, if not of artistry. 'Sonny was real torn up after he taped that segment,' said an associate.

Guests on future shows included Jerry Lewis, Hank Aaron, Joey Heatherton, Dyan Cannon, and Twiggy.

'They've got a funny way of letting you know you've been cancelled,' Freeman King recalled with a chuckle. 'You get to work one morning and the nameplate on your parking space is gone. You say to yourself, "Christ! I've been parking here for six weeks, haven't I?"

'One day Sonny came into the studio and he looked at me and he said, "Hey! My nameplate is gone." It was kind of pitiful.'

The cast met with Chris Bearde and Allan Blye and were told that the series had been cancelled. Sonny said, 'That explains it!'

'It was like one of the skits on the show,' King remembered. 'Steve Landesberg has a joke about that. He says that in Germany if you have a show and it gets cancelled, they call you at four in the morning and shout at you over the phone, "It's over! It's over!" But in America they just let someone else park in your space.'

Sonny was heartbroken about the cancellation. He had hoped that he could prove his ability without Cher, but American audiences wouldn't go for it. Somehow, he couldn't help but think that his ex-wife had engineered the whole scenario, even though he knew that that was impossible.

Cher told reporters that she was 'sick' about Sonny's failure in front of the nation. 'What happened to him was real unfair,' she said. 'He wanted to work, but he didn't want to do what they had him doing. He wanted new material and a new concept. I think it was a giant obstacle to have a female guest star every week that was actually a disguised Cher. They kept Sonny under the weight of Sonny and Cher and he couldn't get a new start.'

Friends say that Cher was privately mortified about Bono's disastrous attempt at individuality because she wondered what her chances were if his were so hopeless.

It was said that Bono's relationship with Connie Foreman ended and that he began calling on Cher, asking if they could see each other occasionally. Cher insisted that a future for the two of them was impossible in view of all that had happened. She did, though, consent to a few harmless dinners. 'Sonny still loved Cher,' said one source. 'She never believed it, but he never stopped.'

'After Cher and I split, I went through many women,' Bono said to friends. 'I found that bed-bouncing depressed me; it only accentuated my loneliness. I was fighting for my sense of self-worth, my confidence, my manliness.'

drugs in them thar hills

Meanwhile, Cher was enjoying her freedom. David Geffen treated her like a queen, but somehow she just couldn't accept his care and attention. She had felt so imprisoned by Sonny that now she felt as if she wanted to hang a sign on the front door: 'Free to Date'. The romance with Geffen was stymied because of Cher's eagerness to meet new people, try new things. On 23 September 1974, she discovered one of the reasons Sonny had prohibited her from socializing with rock-and-roll musicians. She was fully aware of her naiveté, but she has said that she really felt like 'Little Aunt Fanny' when she attended a party in Hollywood at which one man died from a drug overdose and she saved another man's life.

Cher had gone to the Troubadour to see a performance by The Average White Band, a rhythm-and-blues/rock group that would soon be popularized by a million-selling single, 'Pick Up the Pieces'. After the show, she and about two dozen friends were invited to an impromptu party at the Hollywood Hills home of Ken Moss, a native New Yorker and Wall Street financial whiz.

According to Lieutenant George Rock of the North Hollywood division of the Los Angeles Police Department, Moss passed around a small bottle of white powder that subsequent investigations proved to be heroin. An inquiry disclosed that party guests were led to believe that the powder was cocaine. Robbie McIntosh, a twenty-eight-year-old drummer with the band, took what his wife described as 'a giant sniff' of the powder. She told police that she went to the bathroom and returned to find 'everyone – or almost everyone – collapsing all over the floor. Their eyes were bulging from their heads. . . .'

Cher later recalled, 'This guy passed stuff around, and he said,

"Do you want some?" and I said, "No," and I was sitting there and ten minutes later everybody was out of it.'

In the midst of what must have been a horrible panic, Cher took hold of Alan Gorrie, the band's lead singer and bass player, and drove him to the Holmby Hills mansion, where she proceeded to make him throw up the ingested chemical by sticking her finger down his throat.

'I called my doctor for two of the guys,' she told writer David Standish a few months later, 'because I really didn't know what to do. It was strange; all I could get was my gynaecologist because he was on call. I told him I had gone to this party and that this is what had happened. And he told me to get one guy to a hospital right away and to walk the other around and not let him fall asleep. Once he got the dry heaves, he would be fine, the doctor said.'

Cher applied ice packs to Gorrie to keep him awake and he survived the ordeal. McIntosh died in his wife's arms. (The coroner's report said that the cause of death was 'acute morphine-heroin intoxication due to an overdose inhaled nasally.')

A police investigation followed. 'Cher leveled with us completely,' said Lieutenant Rock. 'She gave us chapter and verse on what happened and the role she played in saving Alan Gorrie's life.' The police made it clear to the press that Cher did not sniff any of the heroin.

When investigators went to Moss's home to question him about the ordeal, they discovered that he had fled, and suspected that he went to British Honduras.

'What was I *doing* there? I was at a party, *that*'s what,' Cher said later. 'Afterward, David said to me, "How could you go to a place where you didn't know everybody?" And I thought, what a ridiculous thing. Has it come to this in America, where you have to know everybody before you can go someplace?'

'[pause] and cher'

In October 1974, Cher, David Geffen and George Schlatter, producer of Cher's upcoming CBS television series, discussed possibilities and concepts for the show over an elegant dinner at Antonio's Mexican restaurant in Los Angeles.

'I think our show should be called "[pause] and Cher"' Schlatter suggested.

'Maybe you could walk out with a midget?' Geffen offered.

'I've been doing *that* for twelve years,' Cher deadpanned. 'Maybe a very tall man, and I just look up and say, "You don't know what a *relief* this is for the neck muscles."'

For the next few months, Cher would be the subject of a major media blitz to establish herself as a solo performer in the minds of the American television audience. Her solo series would debut at the beginning of 1975.

In December 1974 Cher was featured in a lavish *Vogue* fashion layout entitled '60 Years of Cher'. Bob Mackie designed 'one-time-only costumes' for the regal Cher to interpret historical periods from the Twenties to the Seventies. It was a stunning colour tribute to Cher's flair and mystique. 'Nothing happened with Cher until she got in front of the camera and lights,' said Bob Mackie. 'Then – *magic*! She was a reincarnation from each period.'

When David Geffen arranged a solo recording deal for her at Warner Brothers, the first album release was produced by pop-music veteran Jimmy Webb. It was called *Stars* and Cher worked intensely on the project, hoping to reaffirm her new individual identity. The album was a commercial failure.

Of Cher's performance on it, Robert Hilburn of the *Los Angeles Times* noted, 'She is a bit like a pitching machine that gets the ball over home plate, but seems incapable of striking anybody out. She, in short, follows the flow of the material well enough, but fails to add any insight to the lyrics or vitality to the spirit of the songs.'

Most of Cher's fans dismissed the album's failure by charging that Webb didn't give to the project the time and attention it deserved. But in the end, Cher took the brunt of critical reaction. 'The issue is whether one now starts faulting Webb for his failure to extract any new statement or depth from Cher or one finally begins to accept the limitations of her talent,' wrote Hilburn. 'She has no one but herself to blame for the emptiness of her new album. Without a dramatic reversal, Cher's monument of public attention may get bigger, but the mediocrity of her work will remain at its foundation.'

Warner Brothers was stung by the negative reaction to *Stars*. 'It's not what we expected,' said Margaret Stevens, a former promotion staff member for the label. 'But the problem with Cher was that she was such a media image, but not a music personality. Her personal life was too high-profile and no one could take her seriously as a recording artist . . . no matter how strong the product, a bias had developed.'

On 6 January 1975, Cher, Geffen, her secretary Paulette Eghiazarian and Bob Mackie arrived at Studio 31 on the CBS television lot to tape the first instalment of Cher's new series. From that day on, Cher's life would never be the same.

'Cher was a nervous wreck,' said a former associate. '"What if I can't cut it? What if I'm no good?" She went from 110 pounds down to 104 because she couldn't eat. She called Lucille Ball on the phone and started boohooing. "What if people hate my guts because of what they think I did to Sonny?" Lucy told her to get herself together. "You think no one has ever been through this before? You just go out there and work your tail off and become a star, damn it!"'

To *TV Guide*'s Rowland Barber, who has been tracking Sonny's and Cher's lives and careers for years, Cher decided to express dramatic humility: 'I'm so afraid of that first walk out. Here I am. Alone. Naked to the world. What do you think, world? Do you still love me? Do you forgive me?'

Perhaps those thoughts did cross her mind for a passing moment, and it's true that she was concerned about how her public would perceive her now that her husband was not in the picture. She was too independently motivated now, though, to wonder whether America would 'forgive' her. She was smart, too. A chip off the old Bono block, she knew exactly which buttons to press to appease a sceptical audience.

Years later, when she felt that the test was over, she would share this vitriolic sentiment: 'My behaviour is very, quote, masculine because I do exactly what I want. I don't give a shit who knows it, or who cares. As long as I'm happy doing it, everybody can kiss my ass. . . .'

Director Art Fisher, who had worked with Cher on the series with Sonny, introduced her as she composed herself, slicking back her hair and smoothing down her white sequinned sheath. She began to walk out on to a ramp that jutted a quarter of the way into the audience. She stood there a moment, alone; the applause was strong and enthusiastic, led by her mother, sister and daughter. She was the queen of the moment and the entire room was fixed on her as she inched her way to solo stardom.

'All kinds of things were going through my mind during that opening,' she recalled later. 'Those childhood dreams kept shooting at me: "I'm going to be somebody famous. I'm going to be a star." For some reason, the first time I saw Diana Ross onstage all alone flashed in my mind. And now it was me instead of Diana. It was just me and the piano and I was so nervous I didn't know how my voice got out. Then the full track came up and suddenly I felt good. Real good.'

Her opening song was 'Let Me Entertain You'. After the number she had to do the obligatory monologue, this time relating to the audience the way Sonny used to. It was a terrifying thought, probably complicated by the fact that her dyslexia made reading any cue cards very difficult.

Before the show, she confessed to George Schlatter that she was especially nervous about the monologue. He called her a 'twerp' and told her that she was the star of this show and had no choice but to face the audience. She has said that she was so angry about his seemingly unsympathetic approach to her dilemma that she forgot to be nervous. She memorized the monologue Digby Wolfe had written.

'Please let me remember the words,' she fretted to herself while standing on the ramp. 'And watch it, Cher, don't speak too quickly. And don't be too sincere. Don't be somebody you're not; don't be Mary Tyler Moore. . . .'

'For those of you who haven't noticed, I've been gone,' she began tentatively. 'For those of you who have, I'm back.'

When she finished her routine and walked off into the wings, she found Geffen, her secretary, Schlatter, Mackie, and her guest Bette Midler in a corner crying. 'They were crying like babies because they wanted so much for Cher to be good, and she was,' a fan who was there remembered. Even Cher had to catch her breath at the magnitude of what she had just done, but she had a delayed reaction: she burst into tears in her bubble bath that evening.

Then she went to bed and had this nightmare: 'CBS opened this Pandora's box and out came all these chicks in transparent dresses, shaking it down the street. And CBS couldn't get them back into the box. . . .'

It was a difficult week. After taping the first show of her series, which would be run as a special (with Midler, Flip Wilson and Elton John), Cher was called to testify at the grand jury investigation of what had happened at the Ken Moss party in Hollywood. She testified for forty minutes.

In her testimony, she said that Ken Moss told his guests that the powder they were given was cocaine. He handed the glass vial to McIntosh, who sniffed some of the contents. '[McIntosh] took two hits, [one] in each nostril,' she testified, 'and passed the bottle to Alan Gorrie, and then the bottle got passed around the table.'

A short time later, McIntosh passed out. 'He looked like he was asleep,' she said. 'Everybody thought also that he had been drinking and was just tired and passed out.' A while later, she said, McIntosh's 'fingernails were blue and his face was kind of grey. I mean, he looked like he was dead.'

She also testified that Moss tried to calm down his guests, telling them, in her words, 'Man, I have been through this a hundred times. It'll be cool. We'll pour water on him. He'll be fine in the morning.' She added that Moss called her an 'over-reacter' because of her concern, that he admitted his guests were really given heroin 'and were lucky to get it.'

Five days later, on 9 February, Cher's network special went on air; the regular run of Cher instalments would be shown on Sunday evenings, replacing the ill-fated family programme 'Apple's Way' opposite 'The Wonderful World of Disney'. Sonny called to wish her luck.

On her own show, Cher's 'Laverne' character returned, and other new portrayals were written for her, including a takeoff on Johnny Carsons's matinée lady TV pitchwoman, 'Donna Jean Brodine'. In each show, Cher was shown returning to a sparse apartment after another dull evening out with a deadbeat date. She would disconsolately slip into a bulky pair of pyjamas, explaining that 'If you don't fly, you don't need a parachute.' Then she would flop into bed with this line: 'If this bed could talk, it would say, "Where is everybody?"'

'That was the *real* Cher,' George Schlatter said 'We were trying to let people discover the nameless, vulnerable kind of quality beneath that somewhat brassy exterior.'

A monologue on one of the early shows: 'All you turkeys out there, lay back, mellow out, stay cool, and we'll hang out for the next hour. And if you're hip enough, we'll really freak out together.'

Just an ordinary chick . . . sort of.

'When I first started the show CBS said, "You cannot say turkey and you cannot say far out – you can't say that stuff." I come out and say that dumb little bunch of shit at the beginning of the show so that people know there's a *person* behind all those costumes, a person who's having a good time singing and dressing up.'

During a question-and-answer session, one member of the audience asked Cher if Sonny would ever guest star on her show. She impulsively announced that he would, next year on the first show of the new season.

'I saw it on television the same way everyone else did,' Sonny said at the time. 'Nobody checked with me. It's the sort of uninhibited sensational thing Cher has been doing lately.'

Originally, it was said that Cher wanted Sonny to guest on three of her shows, at $7,500 an appearance. Bono said he would only work with Cher if he could appear on six programmes at $12,500 each. 'They told him to take a hike,' said a friend. 'He really could not believe that Cher did this series without asking him to produce it for her. He thought for sure she'd at least ask.'

The first regular show of Cher's series went on air on 16 February. On 20 February 1975, Cher was linked by the press to the drug death of McIntosh when Ken Moss was finally indicted for murder. The grand jury ruled that Robbie McIntosh's death resulted from ingesting heroin allegedly provided by Moss.

The Los Angeles Police Department had publicly credited Cher with saving Alan Gorrie's life. 'But the next thing I knew, I read in the papers, "Cher busted at Hollywood drug party". And I don't even *do* drugs,' Cher said later to writer Eugenie Ross Lemming. 'I always find myself fucking up, but my mistakes seem so magnified. It's like I'm a joke in this town . . . something to talk about, a topic of conversation at a cocktail party.'

(In January 1976, Kenneth Moss was sentenced to four months in Los Angeles County Jail after pleading guilty to the charge of involuntary manslaughter in the McIntosh case. Superior Judge Vernon G. Foster imposed the jail term on the condition that Moss be placed on four years' probation. The main thrust of the Moss defence was that McIntosh was a heroin user and that he had provided the fatal drug that night, not Moss. A private investigator testified that an East Los Angeles car dealer told him that McIntosh had purchased heroin from someone else about the same date the fatal overdose occurred. But the defence could not produce the car dealer, and the alleged drug dealer was shot to death in July 1975. Judge Foster said at the conclusion of the hearing that witnesses, including Cher, convinced him that it was Moss who had provided the fatal drug to McIntosh.)

CBS brass were frantic about what they saw as very unfavourable publicity for Cher just as her show was getting off the ground. Most industry insiders felt that her time slot opposite 'The Wonderful World of Disney' was ludicrous positioning on the network's part anyway. 'Young people are going to be watching this woman's show,' said one reporter. 'Their parents read the newspapers. The network has a big problem with Cher. . . .'

It seemed that CBS wanted Cher as a network star, but once they had her, they didn't know what to do with her. When they discovered that Cher was less than conventional, they panicked. It was reported that network officials asked her please to be more careful about the types of people she socialized with. 'You can be sure *that* went in one ear and out the other,' said a friend.

'You gotta face it, Cher went completely *crazy* when she and Sonny separated,' Freeman King said with a smile. 'She got into all kinds of outrageousness. She ran out and started doing things that made headlines for years to come. She was so naive, you couldn't believe it. Just a little child at heart, trusting, loving, totally unaware. . . .'

Sonny Bono then filed another lawsuit against Cher, asking for another $10 million in damages and charging that she should not have been able to enter into the $2.5 million recording deal with Warner Brothers after refusing to record with him at MCA.

Cher's romance with Geffen began to deteriorate after he finally straightened out her affairs and began concentrating on other business ventures. It was reported that when Cher and Geffen went to New York so that he could attend meetings involving Carly Simon's career, Cher complained about having to sit alone at the Plaza while he mingled with the city's movers and shakers. A ten-day vacation was planned but cancelled at the last minute when Bob Dylan demanded Geffen's attention. One newspaper reported that Cher went on alone and was joined later by Geffen, who arrived bearing diamond earrings as a peace offering.

'Sonny has his own show, and what have I got?' she complained before the deal was struck for her CBS series. 'Nothing but a lousy album [the Jimmy Webb collection]. There are no offers coming in.'

Cher was so determined to emerge from her battle with Sonny Bono an independent woman she turned Geffen down when he proposed. It was obvious that the romance was finished when Cher started making statements to the press about 'him': 'Maybe I'll marry him; maybe I won't. Maybe I'll just do business with him. And maybe I'll never see him again. What I do is my business and it'll be my decision. I'm my own boss. The worst thing a woman can do is allow herself to become subservient to the power structure of the chauvinistic world she lives in. . . . I want *details* now; my days of blind faith are over.'

'She was a hurt puppy,' said a former associate. 'She loved David, I'm sure of it. He was very good to her in every way. But the timing was wrong.'

'I never met anyone kinder or more amiable,' she has said of Geffen. 'But with David it was a pay-or-play deal.' Ten years after her break-up with Geffen, Cher would say, 'I still love David. Very much. I was a fool for not marrying him.'

But back then, after the break-up, Cher expressed lingering feelings for her husband. 'I think it's over with David, but I don't know,' she said. 'I can't be sure. I thought it was over with Sonny but I still love him more than I ever dreamed I would at this stage. I've always said that after all we had together I could never stop loving Sonny, but I never thought I'd miss him so much.'

It seemed to many observers that David Geffen had been used and then discarded. He had spent untold sums of money on Cher's behalf, involved himself in the Bonos' scandalous divorce, outlined the new record deal at Warner Brothers, and assisted in negotiating the television series for CBS. He had replaced Sonny Bono as the mastermind behind Cher's career, and he claimed publicly to love her even though Bono maintained that he was only exploiting Cher's weaknesses for his own personal gain.

David Geffen also fostered a sense of independence in Cher, which, in the end, gave her strength to stand alone.

But not for very long.

After taping the fourth show of her new season, she and her secretary flew to New York on a business trip. While there, Cher tracked down Sonny Bono in Denver, where he was appearing in concert, to ask him how he would feel about resurrecting the old 'Sonny and Cher Comedy Hour'.

In May 1975 Sonny Bono premiered his new solo act at Harrah's nightclub in Lake Tahoe, Nevada. He was optimistic about the new show, and was now sporting a dark, exotic twenty-one-year-old girlfriend, Susie Coehlo. An actress and model, Susie was born in

England and was part Indian, her parents hailing from Bombay and Madras. With Susie on her arm, Bono told reporters in Lake Tahoe, 'Cher just didn't want to be married any more. Women's lib or something like that. . . .'

Sonny Bono was still a commercially viable property. *People* magazine ran a cover story earlier in the month with the brashly assured headline, 'Cher Always Calls Me When She's in Trouble'.

'The separation was inevitable,' he said, now much more level-headed than mean-minded. 'When you marry a seventeen-year-old, I suppose you've got to know that somewhere along the line she's going to ask herself if there isn't a part of life she missed, and then maybe decide to catch it before it's too late.'

He said that he and Cher had wanted another child, and that they thought she was pregnant a few years back, but it turned out to be a false alarm. 'We were very disappointed.'

Bono talked of his anxiety over having to re-establish himself in the entertainment industry, but added that his security cushion of wealth made the struggle easier, 'and I'm not driven by fear or panic, just a desire to work'.

'I'm not bitter,' Bono said later in a pragmatic mood. 'Bitterness makes for losers. I was had once. I'll never make *that* mistake again.'

In his solo performance, Sonny was supported by a full orchestra and two background vocalists (Edna Wright and Darlene Love, sisters who had recorded for Phil Spector when Bono was employed by Philles Records). He received mixed reviews on his first touring act without Cher at his side. Co-headlining with Tim Conway at Harrah's, Sonny opened the show with the self-deprecating humour for which he'd become known: 'Welcome to the "What the Hell is Sonny Bono Going to Do by Himself?" Show.'

'By himself, Sonny Bono doesn't do much,' countered one reviewer. 'But what he does do is fairly entertaining. When he wasn't lamenting Cher's absence in film clips or desperately trying to win over the audience by showing films of Chastity, Bono showed promise as an entertainer. He performed contemporary fare such as "Boogie on Reggae Woman" and "Never Can Say Goodbye". . . .'

Bono went on to open for Dionne Warwick at the Riviera Hotel in Las Vegas.

While on the road, Sonny began hinting to close friends that Cher had been in touch and that they might have a television reunion. No one, of course, believed such lunacy could ever happen. 'David Geffen took a brilliant show [Cher's] and shot it into decline,' he said triumphantly. 'There's just one Cher, and I guess she's finding out that there's just one Sonny.'

In her conversations with Sonny, Cher explained that she was in over her head with the solo show; it was more than she could handle. She especially felt awkward about having to assist the producers in writing scripts, choosing music, and selecting guests. 'And that opening monologue is just *not* me,' she moaned. 'I'm not having fun any more!'

The divorce would continue as planned; it still wasn't finalized.

Getting Sonny Bono out of her life had been an emotional nightmare. Now she was inviting him back in.

'I told Cher, "As long as I know you, I will never cease to be amazed by you,"' Sonny recalled later. 'Then I said, "Well, why not?" Doing a show together made a lot of sense because I wasn't having any fun by myself either. I knew the terrible demands of Cher doing a single; I saw her going down. They were trying to make a producer out of her. She is an intuitive performer and terribly insecure if she's made to do anything else. Even her singing was affected.'

Cher was tired of playing hopscotch with the CBS programming censor. 'They said my wardrobe was becoming too revealing. I told them that was bullshit. It's like you can have tits everywhere, but you can't show them from the side or underneath because if you do you're doing something filthy. They were freaking out because they wanted Cher but not *that* much. . . .'

'She wears clothes like no one else,' Bob Mackie has said of Cher. 'When the camera's on her, she knows instinctively what to do, how to look, how to walk. It's an inner magic she projects.

'Her bare look was a trademark at first. After all, she had a beautiful midriff. Why not show it to her advantage? My favourite design, and I'm sure it's Cher's, is the beaded dress that made the cover of *Time* in 1975. People still talk about it. . . .'

It wasn't so much what Cher wore on television as it was the way she was photographed; the camera would *linger* on her body, panning up and down her frame, stopping at key points. An interesting alternative to Minnie Mouse on the competitive station, to say the least.

On one particular show, Raquel Welch was Cher's special guest star. The two women performed a duet, and the network threatened to edit the performance from the final broadcast because the censors felt it was too suggestive. George Schlatter insisted on Cher's behalf that the song not be cut, and so it wasn't. Instead, Raquel Welch's solo of 'Feel Like Making Love' was deleted from the programme.

When the show went on air and Welch saw what had happened, she was livid. She insisted that she'd spent many hours working on the song and that there was no reason for it not to have been included. When she called the network she was told that it was Cher's idea to cut the song.

So Welch called Cher.

'Raquel, I swear to God on my daughter's life, I had *nothing* to do with it.'

Welch hung up on Cher.

Cher called the network and was told that the song had been cut because 'she performed it in a sexy manner and placed her hand on parts of her anatomy'. Furious, she tracked down Freddie Silverman and explained to him what had happened and how she had lost a friend because of it. She demanded that Silverman call Welch and apologize, which he did. It was said that Raquel Welch didn't believe that Cher was innocent, and that she refused to speak to Cher for some time after the incident.

'This kind of crap has got to stop,' Cher demanded.

'All I know is that I got in trouble for showing my bellybutton, and then when I finally did go off the air every time I turned around all I saw were Cheryl Ladd's boobs,' she later said.

Each episode of Cher's show cost nearly $250,000 to produce; it always ran about $20,000 over the allocated budget, and $10,000 of that was to pay for all of that Bob Mackie magic. 'We dreamed up great stuff for shock value,' he said.

Mr Blackwell wasn't impressed. Cher was ranked number five on his infamous Ten Worst-Dressed Women list in 1975. He likened her look to 'a Hawaiian Bar Mitzvah'.

Meanwhile, Cher's series, which started out in the top ten the first three weeks it aired, began to limp along in the ratings. In the third week of April 1975, the show placed twenty-two in the Nielsen tabulation. In September 1975, the show was moved from its spot opposite Disney to a more appropriate slot on Sundays at 8 p.m.; Steve Martin and Teri Garr remained as regulars. It didn't help the ratings, though. Sonny didn't make it without Cher, and now it seemed as if Cher wasn't going to make it without Sonny.

When *Time* magazine featured Cher on its cover, the article did little for Cher's image. 'She has some more stretching to do before she and her show can reach its full potential,' wrote Richard Schickel. 'Her comic range is nothing for Lily Tomlin to worry about. The monologues are often monosyllabic, the sketches are as thin as her own profile. There is also a feeling that she will not entirely prove herself until she dares a show that lacks such heavy artillery [costumes and guest stars]. She also seems to need the security of incredibly lavish productions.'

The 1975 cover was magnificent, even if the story had a biting edge. Cher, deeply tanned, wore Mackie's favourite seethrough gown, with silver bugle bead trim and white feathers. She was all sombre sex and vampish pout with, as Bette Midler would put it, 'nipples to the wind'.

'Cher has a way to go before her private life is a model of common sense,' said the writer. 'She owns over a thousand gowns and five hundred pairs of shoes. Over her massive hearth is a big neon CHER. Her social life strikes many as excessive. "Nobody in this town lives like *that* any more," sniffs an anonymous critic who was not too proud to accept the invitation. "Four hundred guests assembled and Cher made a sweeping entrance down a spiral staircase. . . ."'

The reporter closed with the story Cher's fans refer to as 'the one about her gut.' Sonny Bono was visiting Chastity at the Holmby Hills mansion when he heard that Cher was going to sell the home – this after all the brouhaha about who would live there. At the time, Cher was having a three-hour tricolour manicure. Sonny

Cherilyn Sarkisian at age 17. No one messed with her; she'd shred you with her tongue...LOVE CHILD ENTERPRISES

Sonny and Cher in 1963; Sonny Bono was 28, Cher was 17. "When I found out how old he was and that he had a wife and daughter, I didn't want him around," said Cher's mother of Bono. LOVE CHILD ENTERPRISES

Sonny and Cher's first film, Good Times, *was shot in their home in 1967; William Friedkin made his directorial debut. Here, Sonny is outwitted in a game of checkers by an unlikely opponent. Cher seems unimpressed.* 21ST CENTURY PUBLISHING

Cher wanted nothing to do with Good Times *and her reluctance to do the movie was worked into the script.* 21ST CENTURY PUBLISHING

Another scene from Good Times. *Said Cher, "Hippies thought we were square. Squares thought we were hippies. Sonny and Cher were down the toilet...."*

Cher in transition from sixties hippie to seventies glamour girl. This shot was taken in early 1969. J. RANDY TARABORRELLI COLLECTION

Sonny and Cher, all glossed up by 1970. 21ST CENTURY PUBLISHING

By 1971, the transition was complete. This revealing outfit was typical of the Bob Mackie costumery Cher became known for wearing on "The Sonny and Cher Comedy Hour." J. RANDY TARABORRELLI COLLECTION

Cher, prime time and wholesome. DANIEL F. ROMO COLLECTION

A break in taping in 1972. "There was a sadness about Cher. She kept her distance and seemed like a lonely person. She and Sonny didn't socialize with anybody on the show," said series regular Freeman King. DANIEL F. ROMO COLLECTION

Sonny and Cher in a skit from the TV series. DANIEL F. ROMO COLLECTION

A Cher publicity session, circa 1975. CINEMA COLLECTORS

Most people agreed that Cher's relationship with Gregg Allman, a rock musician and heroin addict, made no sense at all. She married Allman three days after her divorce from Bono was finalized. Nine days later, she filed to dissolve the marriage. PHOTO TRENDS

After a number of separations and reconciliations, a family shot from 1976: Gregg Allman, holding the new baby, Elijah Blue, Cher, and Chastity. J. RANDY TARABORRELLI COLLECTION

Cher contemplates a scene on the set of Mask. *J. RANDY TARABORRELLI COLLECTION*

Cher, outrageous as ever at the 1986 Academy Awards presentation. "As you can see," she quipped, "I did receive my Academy handbook on how to dress as a serious actress." RUSSELL TURIAK

attacked: 'See, Cher, that's you. You got your dream, and now you're done with it.'

Cher shook her head. 'You don't understand,' she said matter-of-factly. 'I felt secure here in this great, strong house. But now, man, I got the house inside *here*.'

And with her free hand, she pointed to her gut.

gregg allman – full-moon lover

'It was a full moon, man,' Cher said of the night she met Gregg Allman. 'And I always get in trouble when there's a full moon.'

Gregory Le Noire Allman first laid eyes on Cher back in 1965 in the Whiskey à Go Go nightclub in Los Angeles. Allman and brother Duane were playing in the house band. Cher, in a black leather dress, walked into the club with Sonny, 'smoking a cigar and being a big shot', Allman recalled. He turned to Duane and said, 'Isn't that the most beautiful woman you ever saw? Man, I hope to God that someday I've got whatever it takes to deserve a woman like that.'

Ten years later, in 1975, Allman was officially introduced to the woman in black when his rock group The Allman Brothers appeared at the Troubadour on a bill with Etta James. In a couple of months, he moved into the Holmby Hill estate as Cher's new lover.

When Cher was invited to see The Allman Brothers show, she wasn't very familiar with their music; she was more interested in seeing Etta James. She attended the show with Georgeanne and a few friends. Someone came up to her table and told her that Gregg Allman would like to meet her, and she agreed to see him. Allman, nervous at the prospect of meeting *the* Cher, came over to the table and, as Cher once recalled, 'grumbled a couple of unintelligible words'. Later that evening he sent a note over to her expressing how thrilled he was to meet her, and asking if they might go out on a date sometime in the near future.

One afternoon, Cher was relaxing at the Malibu beach house with her sister when Allman called on the telephone. He asked her out, and even though Cher had never been on a date with someone she didn't know well, she decided to accept his invitation. He took the lead and carried the offer one step farther and asked her to accompany him on a vacation to Bermuda. She was non-committal.

Years later, Cher would recall, 'The date was a fiasco. Here's this big blond country boy pawing me in his car. I put him down, but it didn't stop him. We went to a dark nightclub and he started sucking my fingers. "I'm not that kind of girl," I said, and I knew it was the dumbest thing. After dinner, we went to a friend's house. At one point I noticed he had his boots off, so I took the opportunity to split. He followed me out the door barefoot asking when he could see me again. "If you're really interested in seeing me, stop playing these silly macho roles," I told him.'

Driving home, Cher was confused and apprehensive about her future as a single dating woman. She was really out of practice, she thought.

The next day, Allman called to tell her that he had never before been on such a horrible date, that he had had a terrible time, and that no woman had ever treated him so poorly. Cher agreed. The evening was not much fun. He suggested that they try again, and though she couldn't imagine why she would want to see him, she relented and agreed. She called Georgeanne, who proceeded to give her helpful suggestions on how to behave when dating: 'Let the guy do all the talking, and then pretend to be interested. Don't be too forceful. . . .'

Allman and Cher went dancing and had a reasonably good time. In the car on the way home, the silence was deafening. The two really had nothing in common ('Our backgrounds couldn't have been more different if one of us had come from Mars'). Allman, trying to be social, began to make small talk. But Cher was impatient with the one-sided conversation. 'You know what?' she cut him off in mid sentence. 'I really hate fuckin' small talk and you are boring the *shit* out of me.'

So much for her sister's advice.

Allman began to laugh; he had never met a woman so tough-willed and sharp-witted. Cher was genuinely indifferent to his status as a rock star, and that was a refreshing change. Cher would say later that before she came into his life, Allman believed that women had two purposes on God's planet – to make the bed and to make it *in* the bed. In Cher, he had met his match.

Gregg Allman was born in 1947; he was twenty-eight – a year

and a half younger than she was – when he and Cher began dating. He was born in Nashville, and in 1958 he, his brother, and his mother moved to Macon, Georgia, after his father was murdered by a hitchhiker.

Gregg and Duane and some friends formed The Allman Brothers in the late Sixties; by the time Gregg met Cher the group had five gold and three platinum albums to its credit. His brother Duane was killed in a motorcycle accident in 1971 in Macon. Gregg was shattered by the tragedy, and friends say he never quite recovered from the loss. A year later, the band's bassist, Berry Oakley, was killed in another motorcycle accident a block away from where Duane had been killed.

By his own admission, Gregg Allman buckled under the pressure of his role as a rock star and of the personal tragedies that tormented him. He became a heroin addict. 'There are guys out there who're gonna hit anybody with a guitar strapped around his arm. The guy says, "Hey baby, you wanna buy? Just poke some of this into your arm or up your nose and it'll feel better,"' he once said. 'There was a cat in my body, with his air used up and his claws out. Then, bam, the old spike goes in and you can almost see the cat go to sleep at the bottom of your foot. But you know he'll awaken and try to get out again.'

'Gregg's addiction was a shame and a waste,' said one musician. 'Most people don't know that Gregg was first in his class two years in a row at Castle Heights Military Academy in Lebanon [Tennessee]. He also played linebacker on the football team, and he lifted weights. He was a champ, but he had a lot of tragedy in his life that he couldn't handle. That, and the pressures of his image as a rock and roller. . . .'

For a while, Jenny Arness, daughter of actor James Arness, dated Allman. When she committed suicide, she supposedly left a note saying that the reason she was killing herself was because Gregg had become romantically involved with Cher. Cher, who said that she had never met Arness, insisted that the woman sent letters to three other boyfriends telling each that he was the reason she was taking her life. She said it had been two years since Allman and Arness had broken up.

'I haven't sung a lot of happy songs,' Allman once said.

While Cher was reeling from the emotional upheaval of her separation from her husband and from Geffen, and from the trauma of the Moss scandal, she flew to Macon to visit Gregg. While there, she stayed in one of his penthouses at the Hilton Hotel. One evening, the couple enjoyed themselves in a backwoods honky-tonk bar called Uncle Sam's Roadhouse, where Razz Bailey and the Aquarians were appearing. Cher and Allman joined in an impromptu performance of 'Proud Mary'.

Rock and roll had been good to Allman and he was quite wealthy for a while (money slipped through his fingers like water), though he hardly looked it. He wasn't suave or debonair; he was a far cry from the sophistication of a David Geffen or even a Sonny Bono. Allman had a paunchy shape and his hair was a shoulder-length dirty blond. He had a spotted beard. He looked as if he needed a good bath and shave – in that acceptable rock-and-roll sort of way. He did own an Excalibur, a 1941 Ford Coupé, and a Cadillac El Dorado. Divorced twice, he complained that both women 'had nothing in mind but fame and money. They see you signing autographs and making all that bread as a rock-and-roll star, but they don't realize that you're a piece of meat with blood and guts and feelings.'

Cher had a wonderful time with Allman in Macon, where he wined and dined her with expensive meals and champagne. Her romance with the rock star was well-publicized, and further antagonized Cher's CBS Television superiors. Gregg simply did not seem like a suitable mate for *their* Cher. Many of Cher's friends agreed. Of course, as far as she was concerned the best response to this kind of disapproval was to become more 'unconscionable'. She solidified the love affair with a vengeance. Gregg was charming and intelligent despite his problem with narcotics, she insisted. He respected her independence. In fact, he encouraged it and she liked that about him. She was certain that she was strong enough to help him, perhaps even cure him.

All of that plus the fact that she had never experienced passion the way she did when she was with Gregg. When they made love, she felt as if she'd never before been with a man. 'Too hot to slow down' is how she would put it later. The fact that he was 'forbidden fruit', so to speak, that he was someone she secretly felt she probably shouldn't be with, made him even more appealing. Their lovemaking was intense in a way she had never imagined possible.

So if his drug addiction was to be a problem, she'd take the risk. It was as bad a decision as Cher ever made.

On Friday 27 June 1975, Superior Court Judge Mario Clince granted Cher a divorce from Sonny in a Santa Monica courtroom, after deliberating for five minutes. Cher, wearing a huge, floppy straw hat, grey sweater and flowered dress, confined her responses mostly to yes and no as she answered a series of questions from her attorney and the judge. When Clince asked if she and Sonny might reconcile, or possibly benefit from counselling, her response was 'No, no, no, *no!*'

She walked briskly to and from the courtroom, working her way through the gathered reporters, answering no questions. The only statement the media was able to pick up was words of appreciation to the bailiff who walked her to a waiting limousine. Sonny did not appear in court that day.

Three days after the divorce decree, Cher and Gregg Allman impulsively flew to Las Vegas to be married at Caesar's Palace. The wedding took place before twelve friends and relatives in attorney Mickey Rudin's suite; the best man was former Sonny and Cher manager Joe deCarlo; sister Georgeanne was maid of honour. Cher wore a floor-length, two-piece, ice-blue satin gown with a camisole top and white lace appliqué. Allman was dressed in a white suit with white scarf.

He recalled in an interview two years later: 'One Sunday morning, I woke up and she said, "I got this Lear jet and Nevada ain't too far away. Why don't we get married?" And I said, "I don't know if I'm ready to get into this but, okay, let's do it." I was sorry that I had done it. We came home from the wedding, got off the jet, and I was gone for two days. [There was no honeymoon because Cher had to be back at CBS on Monday to work on her series.] I ain't puttin' her down or anything like that; she was just as sorry that we'd done it.'

The reaction from Cher's television producer was, 'Well, I guess that blows the guest shot with Sonny.' (Ironically, Allman was a guest on Cher's repeat show on Sunday, 19 June, hours before they left for Vegas.)

In Nashville, Allman's sixty-four-year-old grandmother told the press that she approved of Cher, 'but it would be nice if she started wearing more clothes.'

It only took four days for Cher to realize that she'd made a terrible mistake in marrying Allman. His problem with drugs was much more complicated than she had realized, and the relationship was made even more difficult because Gregg wasn't able to come to terms with the tremendous media coverage he was subject to as a result of marrying a mainstream diva.

On 9 July, nine days after the wedding, Cher filed to dissolve the marriage and told reporters that the whole affair was a mistake 'and it's better to admit one's mistakes as soon as possible'.

'I wasn't surprised when they got married,' said Cher's mother, Georgia, 'but the divorce certainly surprised me.'

'A lot of people didn't want to see her marry me,' Allman tearfully told reporters. 'So they planted lies and rumours about me. Cher worried that the publicity might affect her audience. I love that lady. I wouldn't mess up her life for anything.'

James Bacon said in his Hollywood column that if Cher married again, 'she should tell her friends not to throw Minute Rice,' and satirist Irving Schatz added, 'It sure is dull . . . Cher hasn't been married or divorced all week.'

'I loved him by the time I found out how serious his problems were,' Cher said of Allman years later. 'And then I tried to save him.'

But Cher's friends felt that she should have known that in trying to cope with Gregg she woud be dealing with an addictive disease involving chemicals as powerful as they are cunning. She had her father to look to as an example after all. Allman was also a heavy drinker. He was distant and uncommunicative most of the time, as if any real feelings he may have had were stifled by narcotics. Cher was used to fencing with red-blooded, healthy hotheads; Allman was an entirely different personality, and privately she told friends he was quite sloppy around the house.

'I didn't want to be controlled, and Gregg wasn't a threat,' she said later, again proving to have great hindsight if not foresight. 'He couldn't control me because he couldn't even control himself.'

For the first time, it was she who was the strong one in a relationship. But now she had to wonder if it was worth it.

The Nielsen ratings for Cher's television series took a nose dive after she married Gregg Allman. She was not living up to the general public's wholesome ideals of what a star of her calibre should and should not do. As a substitute for the amiable Sonny Bono, the scruffy, recalcitrant Allman seemed an unsuitable choice. When Bono appeared on 'The Six Million Dollar Man' with girlfriend Susie Coehlo in an episode called 'The Song and Dance Man', the show came in sixth in the ratings; it had been scheduled to appear opposite Cher, who clocked in at a cool thirty-nine.

When Cher telephoned Gregg, now in Macon, Georgia, to tell him she was filing for divorce, 'he was so high he didn't even understand me,' she said. Three days later, when he was sober, he realized how much he loved Cher and that the ball was in his court. He flew to Buffalo to consult a husband-wife psychiatric team that specialized in treating drug addicts. Besides his addiction and drinking, there were other problems: he didn't like most of Cher's friends, particularly David Geffen, and Sonny Bono made him feel insecure. He also felt uncomfortable in the Bono mansion (he and Chastity, though, became great friends).

On 14 July, a week after Cher filed for divorce, Sonny appeared on 'The Tonight Show' with guest host George Segal, Bob Hope, Elliott Gould, and Goldie Hawn. Cher popped out from backstage as a surprise guest. She and her ex-husband bantered just as they always had in public, and later that night she, Sonny, and his girlfriend Susie had dinner at the fashionable Bistro restaurant in Beverly Hills. It was as unlikely a trio as anyone had expected to find there; the gossip columnists buzzed about it for days afterward. Cher insisted that she and Sonny, and even Susie, were 'just friends'.

'I'm producing a variety show, but living a soap opera,' complained her television producer, George Schlatter. 'It's like residing on the wall of a volcano. Her personal problems take too much attention from her work. She doesn't need any more publicity; the world knows more now than it needs to.'

The madness had reached the stage where, quipped Schlatter, 'the lawyers are costing a lot more than her gowns'.

A public backlash against Cher wasn't restricted to American audiences. When her series was shown in Britain, a reporter for the *Observer* wrote tht she spent $5,000 a week on manicures, drove one of three Ferraris when not using her Rolls Royce or Mercedes, had 600 pairs of shoes and 1,000 beaded dresses . . . and yet she's miserable and isn't it a pity?

'I sure as hell wouldn't like anyone like that,' Cher complained. 'Thank God she doesn't resemble anyone I know. Why do they do that to me? First I wanted to throw the paper in the trash, or burn it. Then I just sat there and cried.'

After Gregg had consulted psychiatrists, he became determined to make the marriage work and to kick his drug habit. One of the doctors called Cher in Los Angeles and told her that he had never seen anyone try so hard to break an addiction, that Gregg was sincere, and that if she really loved him she should be by his side during this turning point in his treatment.

Now she was really torn by conflicting emotions. She wanted her marriage to be a success, but she didn't believe her husband cared enough about her to change his destructive life style so drastically. She needed advice, and she didn't know where to turn. So she turned to Sonny.

He had always been there for her in the past, and no matter how difficult her life with him had been she somehow felt she could trust him. Sonny was sympathetic to his ex-wife's problem, and he suggested that if Cher really loved Gregg she should go to Buffalo. What did she have to lose, Sonny asked? If he couldn't straighten himself out, at least she could say she'd tried to support him. If she didn't go she would always wonder if she could have helped.

'Take the next plane to New York, Cher,' Sonny advised.

On 16 July, Cher took a commercial flight to Cleveland, where she met Gregg, who was performing there that evening with The Allman Brothers. Together, after the show, they took a private jet to Buffalo. They spent the next couple of days at the home of a Buffalo doctor, trying to work out their problems.

'I couldn't believe the change in Gregg when I saw him,' Cher later told writer Leo Janos for a story in Ladies Home Journal. 'I think it was seeing him in Buffalo that made me realize that I truly loved him. It was like seeing him for the first time. I had seen glimpses of the real Gregg, but in Buffalo he was completely rid of the narcotics in his system. He was so warm and wonderful, I forgot about divorce.'

Cher talked about Allman's warm side: 'We lie in bed laughing and crying – especially crying. Once I was resting my head on Gregg's chest. The late-night television movie had a very sad ending and I was trying to keep my head from shaking because I didn't want him to know I was crying. I peeked at him from the corner of my eye and tears were streaming down his cheeks, too.'

It was said that the press found the two of them weeping together in a restaurant and interrupted their emotional discussion with questions and requests for posed pictures. 'He wasn't used to seventy-five thousand reporters and cameramen showing up everywhere we went,' Cher said later.

Cher returned to Los Angeles on 20 July to go back into rehearsal for the series; Gregg stayed in Buffalo. The television show always seemed to be an obstruction in the relationship.

On 1 August 1975, she dropped the divorce action.

A week later she found herself back in New York, this time in Manhattan. Her skin had broken out so severely, as a result of make-up poisoning and all the emotional turmoil of the past couple of weeks, that taping of the series had to be suspended. A Los Angeles doctor burned her face trying to treat the condition, and she told friends, 'Now I really look like shit. I don't know what to do.' Someone recommended a doctor in New York.

While she was there, her husband called from Buffalo and suggested that he fly to Manhattan to be with her. 'No, you can't,' she cried. 'I look so horrible. I don't want you to see me like this.'

'When are you going to understand that I don't give a damn what you look like?' Gregg asked her. He joined her that afternoon.

But a couple of days later he had to leave on a four-month tour with the group. The timing was completely off. Cher wanted to be with him, but she was committed to CBS and had to return to Los Angeles. She knew that Allman's leaving Buffalo was premature; that he needed constant supervision, much more treatment. She was right; the tour was a rough one and it wouldn't be long before Gregg was back on drugs.

In retrospect, Cher would remember times when she should have known Gregg was still addicted, but didn't see the signs: 'Like he would often complain that he was cold at bedtime and put on a T-shirt. Later I realized he was probably trying to hide needle marks from me. He would become very irresponsible. He'd say he had to go out for an hour, and return two or three days later.'

When the Allmans reconciled, they attempted to present a composed, controlled facade, but Cher's friends whispered behind her back that she'd often return home at night from a tough day at the studio only to find her husband a hopeless, miserable lump.

Most of her memories of life as Allman's woman are unhappy ones. She shared this with *Cosmopolitan* in 1984: 'Christ! There were some people over at the house; in the den, I had this gorgeous coffee table, antique painted glass set in lovely old wood – and these *people* were doing lines of coke on my fucking coffee table! I was so pissed off! "Don't you guys have any respect for anything? Get that fucking stuff off my table and don't do it in my house." I will *not* deal with people on drugs because when they're junkies they're not *people* any more.'

Allman said later that he felt as if he didn't really belong in Cher's life. And his fans certainly felt that she didn't belong in his. Allman *was* a rock star, after all; he had an image to uphold. 'One thing he was supposed to be was sleazy,' said a fan of The Allman Brothers, 'and that was hard to do being married to a glitzy cabaret singer.'

Fans of Gregg's band blamed Cher for breaking up the act, even though he has insisted that the group was having internal problems before Cher came into his life. It was said that her presence was as destructive to The Allman Brothers as Yoko Ono's was to the Beatles.

Actually, though, The Allman Brothers were finished when

Gregg was heavily criticized as being a stool pigeon after testifying at a grand jury hearing against his friend and manager Scooter Herring. Published reports claimed that Herring had once saved Allman's life with half a gramme of cocaine daily. Gregg testified against him in return for immunity. Herring was convicted and received a seventy-five-year sentence, which, after judicial review, was later overturned. According to reports, the federal judge fumed, 'The person who ought to be prosecuted is Mr Allman.'

'Gregg makes a great villain because he's taken drugs,' Cher said in his defence. 'They acted as if he had turned his road manager into a drug dealer when it was really the other way around.'

Allman added pitifully, 'I've been the fall guy for this whole thing.'

Cher was an oversized personality by this time, and the press couldn't have found an easier target. Mean-minded cynicism marked nearly every news report of the couple's alleged activities. It was erroneously reported that the Allmans were enjoying a dinner in a posh Italian restaurant when Gregg suddenly nodded off into his spaghetti.

When Cher's network picked up the story and reported it on its news programme without verifying its accuracy with her, she was furious. Of course, this *seemed* like something Allman might do, but he hadn't done it. Cher called CBS brass and threatened to sue. Not only had Allman never passed out in public while they were together, she insisted, the two of them had never been to the restaurant mentioned in the report.

Another story, this one derisively reported by Diane Bennett, a former columnist for the *Hollywood Reporter*, had it that the Allmans were performing at a benefit when Gregg passed out over his drum set.

'He's an *organ* player! Weren't you there?' Cher ripped into Bennett later. The reporter explained that she was not at the benefit, but that she had gotten the information from a reliable source. 'And you didn't even check it out?'

'I was furious. I wanted her *ass!*'

All of this adverse publicity, combined with the scandal of the drug death in the Hollywood Hills as well as strong opposition from ABC programming, ruined any chance Cher's series had for longevity. Her private life had become so much bigger than anything she could possibly do on television. Most people began to believe that this Cher character was some kind of idiot. 'I *am* an idiot,' Cher said, 'but not a *total* idiot.'

On 4 December 1975, at a press conference in the Beverly Wilshire Hotel, Sonny and Cher announced that they would be reuniting for another television series. James Bacon reported that the media circus 'had more press agents present than the last ten meetings of the Publicists' Guild'.

When Cher called Sonny long distance, New York to Denver, a year before to suggest a television reconciliation, her show was a ratings winner. By December 1975, it was thirty-fourth in popularity. A month earlier, the two of them had reached a complicated agreement that would allow 'The Sonny and Cher Show' to premiere in Cher's old time slot, Sundays at 8 p.m., beginning 1 February 1976.

The press conference was attended by 150 news people; CBS's vice president Perry Lafferty and attorneys for the divorced couple outlined terms of the agreement. Two weeks of round-the-clock negotiations had ironed out most of Sonny and Cher's legal woes. As outlined by Sonny's lawyers Marvin Mitchelson and Irwin Spiegel, and Cher's Sanford Mendelson, in a twenty-page document, their multimillion-dollar mutual lawsuits would be dropped. Cher had agreed to perform 101 personal appearances with Bono over the next three years; he was guaranteed $1.5 million from those concerts (if Cher missed a date, she would have to post a bond for $500,000; if she didn't make any of the appearances, she would have to pay him the 1.5 million in cash). She said later that she wasn't compensating her ex-husband for anything he may have gone through emotionally but because she agreed that when she left him she broke up the act, which effectively cancelled out his career.

This out-of-court settlement ended Cher's suit to invalidate the 1972 contract with Cher Enterprises. Many observers now believed that the charge of 'involuntary servitude' was something that David Geffen inspired. Now, Cher decided the money she'd received up until this point was fair. She also had the Bono mansion, for which she'd paid Sonny only $450,000 in September 1974 (the house was worth well over a million dollars).

The settlement agreement was initialled page by page, signed by Salvatore P. Bono, Cher Bono Allman, and their attorneys.

On 1 February 1976, Sonny and Cher would go into court to finally, and peacefully, divide what was left of $2 million in community property.

'When we punch out after a hard day's work, she'll go to her house and I'll go to mine,' said Sonny, who seemed particularly ill at ease in front of the inquiring press at the news conference.

It was said that Gregg Allman was not at all happy about the fact that Cher obviously still had a strong emotional investment in 'Sonny and Cher' as well as in Sonny Bono. 'What is this *hold* that guy has on you?' he was said to have charged. 'What the hell does he have?'

Cher had to ask herself the same question. Meanwhile, her marriage to Allman was falling apart again. 'A lot of it has to do with my work,' she admitted to *People* magazine for a cover story called, appropriately enough, 'The Cher and Gregg Soap Opera'. 'Gregg would say, "You're a big star, but you're not that much fun to be around any more because you're *not* around!"'

When the pressure mounted, Allman surprised everyone by filing for divorce. He said if he hadn't, she would have.

When asked at the news conference how the professional reconciliation with her ex-husband would affect her marriage, Mrs Allman snapped, 'You all read the papers – you know what's going on.'

The media now referred to her as '1975's Ricochet Bride'.

Mego International Toy Company, makers of Batman, Robin and Star Trek dolls, launched twelve-and-a-half-inch plastic versions of Sonny and Cher, 'complete with Cher's notorious navel and wardrobe of thirty-two Bob Mackie originals,' reported *Time* magazine. There was no Gregg doll.

Just when it seemed as if her marriage was finally over, Cher discovered that she was pregnant with Allman's child. The plot to this soap opera was thickening. She was concerned about the fact that the baby was conceived while her husband was addicted to drugs, and wondered if this would have a damaging effect on the child. After seeing a specialist, she was confident that the baby would be fine. But now she was alone in that huge house, with Chastity, but without the father of her unborn child. He was back in Macon.

She had to admit that despite everything, she still loved Gregg. 'A lot of people wonder what I see in him,' she told a reporter. 'He's a country boy, a rock star. I'm the big-city girl — real sophisticated. I don't know how you explain the chemistry of falling in love, but I really do love that guy. It may turn out to be impossible for us to get along living together, but that won't mean I'll stop loving him. I don't take relationships lightly. I stayed with Sonny long after I knew our marriage had had it. I'm not flighty and irresponsible.'

If anything, Cher was stronger and more self-assured than ever before. Most people would have buckled under this kind of pressure, but Cher seemed determined to have the baby. She told friends that she hoped Gregg would be at her side when the child was born, but that she wouldn't take him back unless he promised to rid himself of drugs once and for all. 'He knows the conditions,' she said.

'I was thinking the other day that nothing that's happened this year has been so terrible that I just couldn't handle it,' she told Leo Janos. 'In fact, I think there's only one thing I couldn't handle at this point — if something should happen to Chastity. Other than that, I can cope.'

She began thinking about names for the baby. If it were a boy, she'd name him Elijah Blue. A girl would be called Skye Blue.

The media were sceptical of Cher's composure during this difficult period in her life and of the upcoming reunion with her ex-husband on network television while pregnant with her estranged spouse's baby. The popular Cher joke of the year was 'She named her first baby Chastity. This one's going to be called Publicity.'

hellos and goodbyes

The last show of Cher's solo series went on air on 4 January 1976.

No one was quite sure what to expect from the forthcoming 'Sonny and Cher Show'. Certainly, Hollywood could accept a pregnant woman whose current husband was a drug addict, singing and clowning on prime-time televsion with her ex-husband, the so-called 'slave master'. But how would middle America deal with such a blatant display of 'show-biz decadence'?

CBS decided that the best way to address the problem and controversy at hand was to laugh the whole dilemma off as just the sort of thing that happens to two crazy kids in Tinsel Town. Nick Vanoff, veteran producer of ABC's 'Hollywood Palace' programme, was recruited as new producer for the reunion show. He told Cleveland Amory at the time, 'The publicity works in both directions. I believe there is a tremendous interest in them. If we begin with a strong show, I think the big audience will stay with us. The situation with Cher and Sonny has been silly, wacky, crazy fun. I want to get in on the fun.'

'There's just been one insulting comment on Cher and me being back together,' Sonny complained. 'Johnny Carson says we've done it only for the money. What the hell is *he* doing? Sure, we work for the money. I can't deny that. But professional integrity is our first concern.'

Privately, Sonny Bono was certain that Cher's well-publicized antics over the last couple of years had all but ruined the Sonny and Cher image of wholesomeness. He was sure that there would be no way to rekindle that flame of innocence that made their ribbing and banter so much fun; the audience would never accept the same kind of good-natured criticism from a couple who had just made a public spectacle of their divorce.

But he was eager to appear on the programme with Cher just the same because he felt that it would, once and for all, vindicate him of his ex-wife's accusation that he was an ogre. 'When Cher bombed on her own and I was called in, that proved my overall importance to the act,' he said much later. 'It also told the public just how involuntary Cher's "servitude" had been if she was so willing to work with me again.'

'She wanted to do the show because she felt guilty,' said a former associate. 'She felt that, somehow, she had handled the whole thing with Sonny the wrong way. She'd been influenced to deal with it in ways that weren't her nature. She owed Sonny a lot, even if he was so difficult to live with . . . that's why she did the show and eventually another concert tour.'

'Now, *that's* explosive,' quipped George Schlatter, who, it was decided, would not produce the reunion series. 'There could be some difficulty in keeping it together. There are some volatile personalities involved. Maybe it'll wind up on "Wide World of Sports". In fact, it could replace "Monday Night Football"!'.

On 1 February 1976, Sonny and Cher were together again and America held its breath.

With the highly rated '60 Minutes' as a strong lead-in, 'The Sonny and Cher Show' was the most anticipated prime-time programme in years, and is still considered by television historians as one of the top ten most-watched shows in TV history (right up there with 'Who Killed JR?').

On the set, their names were cleverly designed in two matching chrome logos. The ampersand was shaped by two crossed fingers, presumably for luck.

'Ladies and gentlemen,' a voice triumphantly announced, 'together again for the first time [drum roll], Sonny and Cher!' The studio audience stood and cheered as the divorced couple walked out on to the stage.

It truly was a memorable sight, Sonny and Cher sharing this common adventure, beaming and holding hands, their mutual bitterness now seemingly tempered by time and experience. Finally, it seemed as if they were equal soul mates, and that was terrifically heartening.

'Anyone who saw that opening show who even had any remote connection to Sonny and Cher will never forget the instant they appeared onstage again for the first time after the divorce,' said Thomas Griffith, a devoted Cher fan. 'It was the most famous divorce in recent memory, and there they were together again, and happy.'

When examining this reunion, it really must be taken with a dash of cynicism, though, because Sonny and Cher are not perfect robots; they are hot-blooded human beings who had just been through an explosive divorce. It would be naive to imagine that there was no hostility between them. But, as always, the two of them certainly knew how to put on a show and, if nothing more, the reconciliation was certainly entertaining.

'I don't know if any of you have heard about it, but, see . . .' Sonny began, his personable old self, 'Cher and I aren't married any more.'

Someone in the back of the studio let loose a long, mournful 'Awww . . .'

Sonny shot back incredulously, 'You mean you *haven't heard*!'

He sized up Cher, whose pregnancy was just beginning to become apparent. Circling around her, he said, 'Well, Cher [shaking his head in amazement], when you do something, you *really* do it, don't you?'

'We're still in love,' Cher asked, 'aren't we?'

'Sure! From the nose up!' he shot back.

'To tell you the truth,' Sonny added in his 'but seriously, folks' tone, 'working without you hasn't been many laughs.'

Cher took on the stance: arms folded in front of her, frame resting on one leg. She swung her trademark mane from left to right. 'I know,' she deadpanned. 'I saw your show.'

They were back.

The first episode was rated seven in the Nielsens. The second was nine. But rather than find a sense of dignity or meaning in Sonny and Cher's portrait of happiness, when the novelty wore off, the viewers turned off. The third instalment was rated thirty-eighth for the week.

'I guess the whole affair was pretty amazing,' Cher recalled a couple of years later. 'I don't think anyone had ever done this. I went back to a man I had been divorced from, and I was pregnant by another man who had been divorcing me. All of America watched it unfold on TV. In the history of this country, that's probably never happened.'

In May, after the final episodes of the series were taped, Cher took her daughter Chastity to Hawaii for a holiday. She hadn't been feeling well and decided she deserved some time off to try to sort out her feelings for Gregg. She was seven months pregnant and there was no sign of a reconciliation with Allman. What about Sonny? 'What more could he give me in marriage that he isn't giving me now? I have his affection, support, partnership in work,' she said. 'I have it all.'

While in Hawaii, she began experiencing problems with the pregnancy. She remembered her two prior miscarriages and became frightened. The doctors determined that she was suffering from an irritated uterus. This was the problem that had caused her to lose the other babies. She called Gregg in Macon, frantic. He flew to Hawaii immediately to be by her side. This was the Gregg Allman she loved; he was sensitive and caring, both for her needs and for Chastity's. Cher was in intensive care for a week, and when she was released, she, Gregg and Chastity stayed in a private villa in Oahu for five weeks. 'Those were the happiest five weeks of my life,' she has said.

She and Allman got back together again. 'Gregg's going to get screwed up from time to time, and so am I,' she told the panting press.

'No, Cher,' he disagreed. 'I honestly think all of that is over. It seems we have reached a good plateau.'

On 10 July 1976, Cher gave birth to a blond, blue-eyed spitting image of her husband. They named the seven-pound, six-ounce baby boy Elijah Blue.

Allman, who participated in Cher's pre-childbirth Lamaze classes and assisted in the baby's delivery, said, 'Watching him being born was incredible. It affects you far more than anything you ever saw on film. Cher didn't break into a bead of sweat. She had him in an hour and fourteen minutes. I'd like her to be pregnant all the time. She's so happy then.'

After the baby was born, Cher went to New York to have her breasts lifted and firmed up. 'They were like watermelons,' she told friends. To date, she has had this type of cosmetic surgery done three times.

CBS changed 'The Sonny and Cher Show' time slot twice, and the programme still could not sustain the audience. It was cancelled on 29 August 1977. Now Cher would concentrate on her marriage and family. Her 'new life' was, naturally, the subject of intense scrutiny by the news media.

'Our whole world was shot to rat shit,' Cher complained to a reporter who asked how she and Allman had been dealing with his drug addiction. 'I ought to write a soap opera.'

After the series was cancelled, the Allmans continued their relationship as entertainment's most bizarre coupling. He had enrolled in a very intense methadone programme at a private health facility and announced that he was no longer dependent on any kind of drug. 'What keeps me straight now is my beautiful butterfly Cher. She helped me out of it. There is a cure for heroin. It just takes somebody loving enough.'

Allman now weighed 200 pounds (he was down to 125 when on drugs). Photographs of him (looking quite ghastly), Cher, Chastity, and the new baby, Elijah, began surfacing in all the popular consumer magazines. Accompanying interviews detailed their newly discovered bliss. For the first time since their wedding, they insisted, Allman had 'stopped drinking and stopped doing any kind of drugs'.

'I've always loved Gregg,' Cher confided, 'but until now, I never thought it would last. For the first time, I feel like married people.'

'We've had some heavy settling-in pains,' Allman said, downplaying the magnitude of their problems.

Meanwhile, Cher also admitted that the on-again/off-again relationship with her mother was off again. 'She doesn't think Georgeanne [who was now an actress with a recurring role on the 'General Hospital' soap opera] and I give her enough time. Probably we don't,' Cher reasoned. 'But there isn't enough time for everything. . . .'

At about this time, Cher's mother, Georgia, began dating Craig Spencer, a Washington antiques dealer twenty-one years her junior (and two years younger than Cher). Georgia Holt had temporarily resumed her singing career and said in interviews, 'Now that Cher and I have something in common, she has welcomed me into her world.'

Holt told the press that in recent years she had sold her piano and car to pay her rent. 'Even now people think I'm rich because I look rich or because I've been married to rich men or because my daughter is rich. But I am barely hanging on by my fingernails. I'm still looking for a pot.'

Her new boyfriend piped in, 'I think Georgia has a better voice than Cher's. And I think Cher could have done a lot more for her mother than she has.'

Ten years later, Cher would tell Phil Donahue: 'I've gone through periods of being comfortable with my mother, but sometimes I'm not comfortable with her. My mother and I have had a very, very stormy relationship and it still continues to be that way.'

Just as Gregg was coming to terms with his sobriety, he began to feel the pressure intrinsic to being married to Cher. It seemed that the public expected him to become the perfect mate, and that if he was perfect, the marriage would be ideal as well. Now he had to be witty and handsome as well as 'cured' of his addiction; and his clothes had to match his wife's for photos that would appear on the covers of magazines like *People* with stories like 'Cher and Gregg: She Helps Him Stay Off Heroin' (8 September 1975).

In May 1977, Sonny and Cher embarked on their first concert tour since the divorce, as per their settlement agreement. It was an odd entourage that took off in a Lear jet to the Westbury Music Fair in Long Island: Sonny and Susie, Cher and Gregg, Chastity and Elijah, servants, managers and attorneys. It was said that the Allmans did not stay at the same hotel as Bono and his girlfriend.

A Sonny and Cher single was produced by Bono and David Foster for Warner Brothers to promote the tour. It was a disco-inspired disaster entitled, interestingly enough, 'You're Not Right for Me'.

'Inexplicably, the show is mostly Bono's,' wrote a critic in his review of their new act for *Daily Variety*. 'He repeats his pop idol parody that he did in his single outing two years ago, bringing a woman onstage for an interminable amount of time. When they're on together, he's almost always out front. There's so much talent being wasted here. . . .'

'Cher had her hands too full with Gregg to worry about the show,' said a musician. 'He was one unhappy dude and making her miserable. When they had days off and time to spend together, they seemed as if they were very much in love. Actually, Sonny and Gregg also got along fairly well.'

Cher and Allman had been working on an album for Warner Brothers that would team their talents and be called *Two the Hard Way*. Cher enjoyed recording the album; she was inspired by the hard-edged rock sound – but the critics were not. 'The best thing about the album is the cover,' said one music reviewer. 'Both Cher and Allman are airbrushed into glamour. The music is another story, and it's a short story called "God Help Us All".'

On 6 November 1977, Cher and her husband left for a twenty-nine-day promotional tour of Europe. 'The tour was a pain in the ass,' she recalled to friends later.

It was said that Gregg had begun drinking again, that the more he drank the more he hated himself, and the more he hated himself the more he drank. It was slow, tortured suicide that Cher couldn't bear to watch. He was out of control.

When the couple returned to Los Angeles, Cher told Gregg that she was 'tired and pissed off'.

'She just told me it was over,' he said. 'I never wanted to hurt that lady. I loved her. There was no future for us because she has that constant paranoia of [me] going back to alcohol.'

Cher was crushed by the way Allman had let her down, by the way the marriage ended. When she first met this man she was lonely, but her perception of herself, her self-esteem, was at a peak. She believed that she was 'the most screwed-up woman in the world' when she and Sonny were together and she was proud of the way she'd redeemed herself. And if she had done that for herself, surely, she believed, she could help Gregg Allman solve his problems. 'He was the only man with whom I have truly been in love,' she told reporters. 'I will always love Gregg.'

Cher probably could have done without Sonny Bono's assessment of the melodrama, but he offered it anyway. 'Allman had no chance from the beginning,' he concluded. 'He came into a situation with no money, no power, and a drug problem. And there was Cher with a battery of people who gave him an allowance. There was no way he was ever going to feel like a man. He was monitored and mothered.

'Furthermore, he had to compete with Cher egotistically because she was a hot television property. He seemed to me to be a very nice guy, but confused; a great musician too, which doesn't mean anything if you're strung out. He was very nice to Chastity, and that's what really mattered.'

Today, Cher admits that Allman has never given her any child support, and never sees his son. 'Elijah is available to see Gregg, but Gregg doesn't want to see him. I am amazed at these fathers who just have kids and forget about them. My father was the same way. I try not to bring up Elijah's father, but when the subject comes up I have to be honest with him. Some of us are unlucky when it comes to fathers; life is tough. Chastity has a good father, I did not. Elijah does not. Those are the breaks. . . .'

'I just didn't have the juice any more,' Cher said when the marriage broke up. 'I wouldn't have gone through it all except that nobody ever made me feel as happy as Gregg did. God, he's wonderful. I just don't understand why he can't see it. He's the kindest, most gentle, loving husband and father. But then he forgets everything and it all goes right to shit. . . .'

On Thursday, 16 December 1976, Sonny and Cher did their first joint concert in three years, at the Inglewood Forum in Los Angeles, as part of an annual KHJ Christmas benefit. Later in the month, Cher was again paired with Snuff Garrett, for a Warner Brothers album that would be issued in February 1977, entitled *Cherished*.

'Is that what it was called?' Garrett asked facetiously. 'I hardly remember it. It's a nonentity to me.'

He recalled, 'The way it happened was that Cher had not had a hit record since my "Dark Lady" and that was in 1974. I was getting ready to go to Texas for the holidays and I got a call from Warners asking me if I would consider doing another Cher album. It surprised the hell out of me; I had no earthly idea as to why they would call me after all those years, 'cept that I always came to the studio on time. I told them that I thought it was too late to reclaim that commercial sound we had with "Half-Breed" and the rest of them. But a couple of weeks later, we were in the studio.

'Cher wasn't into this album at all,' he remembered. 'She was beginning to want to sing rock and roll, and they wouldn't let her. "This isn't my *bag* any more," she complained about the songs we chose. "I want to *rock* out."

'We had a single release called "Pirate" that was a great song, but it didn't sell two copies. Had it been issued during the run of hits, it would've been platinum. Another single, "War Paint, Soft Feathers" was more of that "Half-Breed" stuff, and it bombed out.

'Her attitude about the whole thing was "I'm committed to Warners to do this album, and I'll do it, but I ain't gonna like it."'

She had reached a turning point in her life. Though there would be an occasional television special (like one she did with Dolly Parton and Rod Stewart), she was no longer a regular on prime time. She kissed her recording career goodbye. Soon she would get a California court to allow her to drop the names Bono and Allman legally. Both were best forgotten. Now she would be just 'Cher', a single parent raising two children.

When the relationship with Allman ended, she dated for a while but found the experiences difficult. 'Men are afraid of me. Nobody asks me out,' she complained. 'I hate to go to parties anyway. I hate Beverly Hills, and Beverly Hills ladies, too. They hold parties so they can dress up, impress each other, or get laid.'

In an interview with *Los Angeles Times* reporter Roderick Mann, who wrote that Cher looked like a cross between a Tibetan high priestess and a gypsy fortune teller on the day they met, Cher moaned, 'Sue Mengers, the agent, tried to fix me up with someone just the other day. "You'll love him," she said. "He's a big studio executive, terribly attractive." Well, you wanna know something? I hated him, I couldn't stand him. He kept calling me afterward and sending me things, but I thought he was abysmal. It isn't easy meeting people, is it?'

the demon

The heavy-metal outfit Kiss, consisting of bassist Gene Simmons, guitarist Paul Stanley, drummer Peter Criss, and lead guitarist Ace Frehley, was formed in 1972. The New York-based band made its debut in a small Manhattan club called the Daisy; only their girlfriends and a jukebox repairman attended the performance. To attract an audience and develop an identity for themselves, the band members came up with an imaginative and, at the time, very unusual gimmick: using make-up and costumes they emerged as horrifying spectacles. Simmons became a fire-breathing, vampirish ghoul, Stanley a pouting-lipped sex symbol, Frehley a silver-eyed space creature, and Criss a cat, complete with whiskers.

It was a terrific idea, and at a concert in the Crystal Ballroom of the Diplomat Hotel in Times Square, they were spotted by Bill Aucoin, a former television director who would go on to become the group's manager and sign them to a recording contract at Casablanca Records. Their debut album was issued in February 1974; their second, *Hotter Than Hell*, at the end of that year; and their third, *Dressed to Kill*, in early 1975. *Kiss Alive*, their fourth album, sold more than 2 million copies by January 1977 and established the band as one of the major forces in popular rock. Their cult following was fiercely loyal.

In concert, Kiss was a pyrotechnical wonder. Simmons, known for his long, lapping tongue, became famous also for his fire-breathing antics. In 1978, Casablanca issued solo albums by each group member, and all four sold over a million copies (although all but Stanley's were critically assailed by a music press that had grown leery of Kiss's multimillion-dollar merchandising and exploitation campaigns, which included starring in their own comic book – touted as being printed in ink 'mixed with blood').

Gene Simmons was the most theatrical member of the group, a towering presence in twelve-inch-high platform boots, each shaped like a demon's mouth, complete with bladed teeth. His ability as a bassist was praised by publications like *Rolling Stone*; one critic called him 'the best fire-and-blood spitting bassist who will, hopefully, ever live'. Simmons, who, along with Stanley, still fronts the Kiss band today – but without the make-up gimmick – was a style-conscious, shrewd businessman who understood that heroic rock figureheads had an image to protect. His popular image as a womanizer was, it has been said, well-deserved. But chances are he hadn't really bedded '365 virgins in 1974', as one fan reported.

Part of the group's gimmick was that the members were never seen offstage without their make-up. To protect their identities, they would wear handkerchiefs tied to the lower half of their faces when they were in public. It was all very bizarre, but as a promotional tool, it worked.

Cher has said that she first met Gene Simmons at a fund-raiser for California's Governor Jerry Brown. A friend came up to her and asked, 'Would you like to meet Gene Simmons?' Cher responded eagerly, 'Oh, yeah, I'd love to. I've seen *all* of her movies. . . .'

Her first few dates with Gene were as melodramatic as the ones she had with Allman at the beginning of their relationship. 'The first time I met Gene he wanted me to go back to his place, but I said no, come to mine. We sat up until six-thirty in the morning, just talking. He was amazed that I didn't ask him to take me to bed. He couldn't believe it. "You'd *better* believe it," I told him. "You'll turn old and grey before I ask you to do that."'

The date was uneventful. Simmons flew back to New York and, calling long distance the next day, apologized to Cher and said he hoped that she hadn't been offended by his lack of humility. She said that she never expected to hear from him again. As weeks went by, he began sending her flowers and telegrammes describing his undying love for her.

'Then he said on the phone, "I have something neat to tell you,"' Cher remembers. '"I think I love you." And that was the beginning of our relationship. He was telling me he loved me before we had even kissed. It made those the hottest telephone conversations in history.'

To Cher, this guy was a breath of fresh and much-needed clean air. Despite his image, Gene Simmons does not drink, smoke or take drugs. He's a former schoolteacher, a man with great common sense and good humour. His offstage persona was as far removed from his public persona as Cher's was from hers. In that respect, they really were kindred spirits.

Her romance with Simmons was odd, though. Cher never pretended that he was a major source of passion in her life. 'It's not important that I don't feel madly in love with Gene,' she told friends. 'I can *count* on him.'

She never really thought that Gene, who is four years younger than her, was particularly attractive – he's a hulking six-footer with a ruddy face, deep dark eyes, and thick black hair. But he provided her with a sense of stability and security that she ached for after the tumultuous relationship with her ex-husband.

Of course, the public had adopted the attitude by this time that anything Cher did made absolutely no sense at all, so when she and Gene, in full demon make-up, appeared on the covers of magazines, it all somehow seemed oddly 'normal'.

'I can't help what people think of him because of what he does onstage,' Cher said of Simmons. 'I know my fans think, "Oh my gosh, Cher is getting crazier. She went from one weird musician to someone totally out of it." But Gene treats me better than I've ever been treated. He's perfect.'

She, Simmons, Chastity and Elijah appeared on the newsstand shelves in poses reminiscent of those struck when Allman was a family member and, predictably, with similar reflections by Cher. 'You know,' she said wistfully in one interview, 'we're a *real* family. . . .'

'Really, what Cher has always wanted from the time she was a child was a so-called "real" family,' said a former associate. 'To her, the ideal of family life was the traditional man and woman working together, living and loving in harmony. She may not have loved Gene, but she loved the idea of loving him.'

Her personal life was safe for the time being, but her professional one was a crashing bore. She could not relate to any of the contemporary music she was being asked to sing by eager songwriters and producers. Her mind was set on hard rock music during a period when disco was just beginning to generate excitement in the record industry.

She was a celebrity, but she'd begun to think that maybe she'd like to be an artist as well. The idea of Cher as an *artist* was incongruous even to her, but still, she began to feel that creating a meaningful legacy for herself was important, even necessary. 'I was never really good,' she decided in another sharp-eyed observation. 'I was just something different and I got to be famous by being different.'

She remembered how much she had enjoyed studying drama with Jeff Corey when she was sixteen, just as she was becoming acquainted with Sonny Bono. Corey had directed his own professional workshop since 1951. He has always been a shadowy figure on the cinema scene, admired as a serious actor in the Forties and remembered as one of those who took the Fifth Amendment before the House Un-American Activities Committee. He wasn't able to secure any work after the hearings, and so he started the actors' workshop.

Corey's students had included James Coburn, Robert Blake, Richard Chamberlain, Anthony Quinn, and Jane Fonda. 'Engage in your own intuition, use your frames of reference, and give something that is uniquely yours,' he told his students. 'Put something rich into your performance rather than some external result that hasn't got your face. Simplicity is the cherished quality.'

'Freedom is not given to anyone,' he had said. 'You have to *take* it.' My God, she probably thought. If she had made some of her own choices earlier in life, maybe she really could have been an *artist* by now. Better a late start, though, than none at all. Corey's words now had real meaning.

She began knocking on doors. 'I finally got sick of what I was doing,' she said later. 'I went to every director and producer here [in New York] in 1976, 1977 and 1978 and I couldn't get arrested. Nobody was willing to take the risk. There's no such thing as an overnight star sensation – people everywhere are busting their asses but you're not great until someone says, "Oh my God, you *are* brilliant!" People don't have a lot of imagination in this business. Nobody would take the time to see if I was talented because it costs too much money and takes too much effort.'

She was considered for the lead role in a remake of *A Star Is Born*, and it seemed like a winning idea. She could certainly relate to the fibre of the script, a story of life in the fast lane of rock and roll. Talk about 'frame of reference'. But when Barbra Streisand expressed interest in the role, Cher was tossed aside.

'Inasmuch as they did a takeoff on my life, it wasn't much fun to see someone else do the part,' she complained to Chicago reporter Gene Siskel. 'I thought the movie was terrible.'

When she heard that Mike Nichols was directing *The Fortune*, she asked him for a role. He didn't believe she had any talent and turned her down.

She was considered for Jessica Lange's role in *King Kong*, but that didn't work out, and later she would turn down a part in a silly basketball spoof called *The Fish That Saved Pittsburgh*. ('I thought, you just can't be any good with *all* the odds stacked against you.')

She realized that opposition to her goal would be vehement. She would continue trying, though. Meanwhile, she had bills to pay, a house to maintain, and children to support. She would have to go back into the recording studio, but she wouldn't like it.

And everyone would know it.

'take me home'

When Cher signed a recording contract with Casablanca Records, the label Simmons's group, Kiss, recorded for, in March 1978, she told company president Neil Bogart that she wanted to sing as much hard-edged rock music as possible. Bogart, the former president of Buddah Records, was king of the Sixties bubblegum music movement. He had more recently transformed Donna Summer from an obscure cabaret singer to a major disco star, thanks to a sexy dance song produced by Giorgio Maroder called 'Love to Love You Baby'. (She moaned and groaned in orgasmic ecstasy for at least ten minutes.) He knew a disco star when he saw one, and Cher was the embodiment of all that was disco – she was flashy, glitzy, and an already proven success as a media image.

He told her that he'd like to establish her in the dance market and then, when she was once again before the public eye as a recording artist on the charts, perhaps they could experiment with her rock concept.

Cher balked at the suggestion. To her, and to a lot of other people at this time, disco music was energetic fluff. It had no 'integrity'. 'Neil, I want to rock *out*,' she insisted.

Not yet, Cher. . . .

(It's ironic that the late Neil Bogart would go on to do for Joan Jett precisely what Cher had asked him to do for her. He took the former Runaways vocalist and made her an important and at one point even dominant force in a rock world ruled by men when her 'I Love Rock and Roll' anthem sold a million copies for Bogart's Boardwalk Records label in 1981.)

Charles Koppelman, of the Entertainment Company production house, was recruited by Bogart as executive producer on Cher's album. Producer Ron Dante was asked to produce six songs for her.

He did, and she hated all six. Bogart wasn't that impressed either.

'You see,' she groaned. 'This isn't going to work. I *hate* this crap.'

Paul Jabara, who had experienced great success with Donna Summer, was asked to work with her, but had to pass because of a prior commitment to Summer.

A young producer and songwriter named Bob Esty was carving out his own niche in popular music with his collaboration with Paul Jabara on Donna Summer's 'Last Dance'. Released in April 1978, the song from the motion picture *Thank God It's Friday* went on to win Grammy Awards for 'Best Rhythm-and-Blues Song' and 'Best Female R&B Vocal Performance'. In 1978, 'Last Dance' was winner of the Academy Award for 'Best Song From a Motion Picture'.

Bogart was thrilled with this success because it legitimized Donna Summer to a broad pop market. Before this, she had been considered strictly a disco star. But 'Last Dance' was commercial enough for vigorous attention by AM top-forty stations, and it changed Summer's status in the industry. The same thing could happen to Cher, Bogart theorized.

'Listen to this record,' Bogart told her. 'This is *you*. This record has *you* written all over it. We need to get you a "Last Dance".' Bogart explained to Cher that disco was an 8-billion-dollar-a-year industry and that even the Rolling Stones were doing dance music at this time ('Miss You' from the *Some Girls* album), as was Rod Stewart ('Do You Think I'm Sexy?' from his *Blondes Have More Fun* collection). So she agreed to meet with Bob Esty.

Esty had just finished putting the final touches to Barbra Streisand's bid for disco fame, 'The Main Event', on Columbia Records. (The song was the theme to a movie of the same name, and Esty cowrote and coproduced it with Paul Jabara.)

'I had broken my leg in New York, so the first time I met Cher at the Beverly Hills Hotel, I hobbled in on crutches,' Esty remembered. 'I was going for the sympathy vote. . . .'

Neil Bogart asked Esty to write a song he thought would best exemplify Cher's persona for the dance market. Along with his partner Michelle Aller, Esty wrote 'Take Me Home'.

'The concept we had for Cher was that she was a take-charge kind of person,' he said, 'and she would not find it at all strange simply to ask a guy up front to take her on home and have sex with her. To us, that was Cher.'

When he played the song for her on the piano, Cher told Esty that she liked the composition; she also made it clear that this kind of music 'bugged the shit out of her'.

Esty said that he had second thoughts about working with Cher after the initial meeting. 'I thought that maybe I shouldn't get involved if she's so against it,' he recalled. 'When I did "The Main Event" I thought that Streisand was singing something she didn't want to sing. That's always a problem. But I was talked into Streisand's session, and into Cher's as well – ultimately, I'm glad I was.

'I also wasn't quite sure of Cher as a vocalist, in the sense that she was not a normal voice,' he continued. 'Whereas with Donna and Barbra I knew exactly what to expect, with Cher I couldn't tell where her range was. I found that there are qualities in her voice that are unmistakably unique to her and appealing as well. What I wanted to do was bring out the appealing aspects and play down the elements I thought were unattractive, like her vibrato. By the time I got to her, Cher had vocal habits that were tough to break. . . .'

Recording time for 'Take Me Home' was booked at Studio 55 in Los Angeles.

When Cher told her and Gene Simmons's friends – the 'extended family' – what she was about to record, they were horrified. Their disdain for disco music was exactly what Cher was afraid of. She was told that disco was bastardized black music cutting into their own record sales and ultimately shaking the foundations of their careers.

'She wanted to prove to Gene's friends that she could do rock and roll,' said Esty. 'She reminded me of someone at a picnic with ants in his pants, never satisfied. But in my mind, Cher could never be Chrissie Hynde or Joan Jett because rock and roll is related to serious dues-paying and most of Cher's dues were protected by Sonny. Her public image was as a Bob Mackie wonder-doll and that wouldn't change no matter how many rock stars she got involved with.'

Esty said that the saving grace for the project came, ironically enough, from Gene Simmons. He told her that his friends really didn't care what she sang, and that he wanted her to be a success. He was very supportive of Bogart's plans for her because he, more than most of his friends, understood the value of strategic marketing.

'But Cher told Gene she wanted to be like his outfit. And then she wanted to be the Doobie Brothers. And then she wanted to be Toto . . . and then. . . .'

On the first day in the studio with 'Take Me Home', Cher discovered that Esty had cut the entire instrumental track in the wrong key. 'It was a wonderful way to start the session,' he laughed, 'especially one she was so eager to do.'

The track was quickly recut in Cher's key.

In the studio with Cher: 'I found tht she tends to oversing a song when she first learns it. With Streisand on "The Main Event" I had to teach her every single phrase because, stylistically speaking, that kind of music was not what she'd been accustomed to. Donna, on the other hand, was a disco star who could come in, sing the song through twice, say "thank you", and go shopping. Cher was listening to rock at home and singing disco in the studio. I asked her to mimic my phraseology and she was resistant to that, so it was difficult at first.

'I thought she would be a lot funnier than she was,' Esty added. 'And livelier too. She's very moody, and that's the most difficult thing about her. She's not the easiest person to spend the afternoon with. She's like Barbra in the respect that unless you get into a conversational role with her, you could be in a lot of trouble.'

He said that it had taken him a while to adjust to Cher's moodiness and that, at first, he was sure she was angry with him for some reason: 'Naturally I assumed that it was something I was doing wrong. Or that there was something wrong in the control room. She was never excited and always seemed sort of miserable. . . .'

Esty and Cher spent hours trying to record 'Take Me Home', and Cher had become so exasperated with the session that at one point she asked Esty to leave the studio. She thought that he was being too demanding and difficult. She would be supervised only by Charles Koppelman. 'But that didn't work out at all,' Esty said. 'She was frustrated because we were asking for certain phrasings, asking her to hold notes longer than she was used to holding them. It had been a while since she had recorded, and breaking her voice back in wasn't easy for her.'

He added that she was able to sing for only a short time before her voice became hoarse and unrecordable.

'She's basically real insecure about her voice,' he noted. 'She would work hard, then listen to a playback of what she'd recorded and be totally disgusted with herself. She could hear all of these imperfections and it pissed her off. She was co-operative in the respect that she'd do the song over and over until she was fed up. Ultimately we got the performance from her we wanted. . . .'

When the song was finally finished, Esty played the tape for Neil Bogart, and both were pleased with it. It would be released as a single immediately, and Bogart allocated a budget for an album. It was a small budget, though, because Casablanca Records had already invested so much into Cher, footing the bill for the six Ron Dante tracks she had originally recorded and the high cost of recording 'Take Me Home'.

Two of the Dante productions would find a place on the final album release, including 'My Song', a composition Cher wrote inspired by Gregg Allman. The lyric line tells of her problems with Allman, how they found it difficult to communicate, and how he'll never get to know his son. She would perform the song in her act, with films of Elijah Blue rolling as a backdrop (the movies were shot by Sonny Bono).

'Gregg was pissed off at first,' she recalled later, 'because he thought I was talking specifically about him – like he's off the edge. But that didn't really occur to me. When I wrote that, I thought that the *relationship* was what was too far gone.'

'When we went into the studio to do the *Take Me Home* album, that's when we really started having fun,' Esty remembered.

Mark Bego, in an article on Cher for *After Dark* magazine, observed the singer with her producer in the studio: 'Cher banters and kids with the young soft-spoken curly-haired producer Bob Esty and his boys at the control board before strapping on earphones in an isolated sound booth and belting out the tongue-twisting lyrics to a disco number called "Happy Was the Day We Met". She relentlessly repeats the song, working with Esty to perfect each phrase. During playbacks, Cher swigs from her bottle of Miller Lite beer and keeps the atmosphere light by quipping over her microphone: "Why does it take three Californians to change a light bulb?" And then answers: "Because it takes one to turn the bulb and two to appreciate the experience."'

'Gene came by a couple of times and the two of them seemed to get along well,' Bob Esty remembered. 'He's a funny guy. There's a song on the album called "Get Down (Guitar Groupie)" because Cher said that if she weren't famous she'd be the character in the song, chasing after a rock band like a groupie. As for the rest of the album, I like the song she wrote for Gregory, I'm not crazy about the Ron Dante stuff, and except for "Take Me Home", I think the rest of the material is just filler. It didn't matter, though, because we knew that unless Casablanca really screwed up royally, we'd have a hit with "Take Me Home".'

The song was issued in February 1979 and stayed on the best-selling record charts for nearly five months. 'It was a triumph, that's for certain,' said Esty proudly. The record became a tremendous disco success, and a pop hit as well. It peaked at number eight on the national top ten, Cher's first top-ten single since 1974; it is her last hit to date.

Cher's reincarnation as a disco princess was taken with a grain of salt by the entertainment community. Said one publicist: 'If the market went in the direction of German Shepherd Rock, Cher would adapt with matching costumes, accessories, and boyfriend.'

On the cover of the *Take Me Home* album Cher is pictured in brass-plated armour – an antler-like headpiece, gold cape, and gold armlets; gold-plated pieces capped her breasts, much of which were seen through cutouts in the plating (the point of each plate was engraved with a nipple). On the back cover, in a standing pose, Cher wore the same Viking-type outfit but a wing-shaped bikini bottom was now visible. The concept was Simmons's.

'When we got back the proofs on the cover photograph, Cher was furious because the make-up was the wrong colour,' said a former employee in Casablanca's art department. 'So we had to airbrush the whole thing and paint in her entire body and face in a skin-toned shade. It was a shame because Cher doesn't need to be airbrushed, but there was no time to do the session over again.'

When Barbra Streisand's 'The Main Event', issued in June 1979, peaked at number three on the charts and sold a million copies, Bob Esty was called back to produce the follow-up to Take Me Home. Bogart again asked him to dream up a concept that would inspire, or at least interest, Cher. Esty decided that an album detailing Cher's fishbowl existence – her high-profile life and the dichotomy between the way she is perceived and the way she perceived herself – would be something she could sink her teeth into.

Cher thought that the concept was a good one, and they agreed that the album would be called Mirror Image. The front jacket, they decided, would bear a photograph depicting Cher's glamorous image; the inner sleeve would be designed with headlines and blurbs from popular gossip tabloids detailing Cher's exploits and her sensational life style; the back-cover photograph would be of a 'laid-back' Cher, scrubbed clean, simple, unassuming, and inundated with stacks of fan magazines with her picture on the cover, paparazzi photographs and posters. She would have an exasperated 'get-me-out-of-here' look on her face.

Esty certainly had enough material to work with for a concept such as this. 'Barbra would never have done this,' he said of Streisand. 'She has no sense of humour about herself at all. But Cher does, and I found that delightful.'

He wrote ten songs and demos were recorded on each by himself and Michelle Aller, but by the time they were finished, Cher was on the road touring with her nightclub act. Scheduling recording dates was almost impossible. 'We had to fly all over the country to track her down,' he noted. 'Her whole thing was that she was making big bucks in Vegas and who needs this recording stuff, she was tired, it's not the music she wants to do, etc. . . .'

The album started out as originally conceptualized. 'Outrageous' was a song about Cher's extravagant costumes and the fact that she's a biker at heart but has to put on this amazing drag show to make a living. 'Hell on Wheels' was recorded because Cher admitted to being a roller-skating fanatic. (She would rent an entire roller-skating rink for her family and friends every Monday night – Chastity once asked if Mother could rent Disneyland for her private use.) 'Mirror Image' was a song about her celebrity and all of the publicity she'd generated. 'Shopping' was about her habitual 'one in every colour' shopping sprees.

'But then Cher blew it,' Esty recalled in an annoyed tone. 'It was going too smoothly so she had to throw a monkey wrench into it. She decided that, yes, she *was* going to sneak some rock and roll into the album. We all cringed. "Here she goes again," we thought.

'"Boys and Girls" was written by some rock band she heard through Gene Simmons, so we had to cut that even though it had nothing to do with the format we had agreed on. Then Tom Snow had "Holdin' Out for Love", and she said she had to cut that, so we did. Then she begged David Paich of Toto to come into the project and give her some credibility as an artist. They had worked with Sonny and Cher on the road years before. So they wrote a song called "Prisoner" and we had to do that. Can't argue with the Toto boys. By this time, my concept was shot to hell. It was a real sad experience for me.'

Esty said that he felt Cher really didn't want to record the album after all, and to make matters more interesting for herself she decided to involve her friends in the project. 'Maybe they would like her album and then they would like her,' Esty surmised. 'She wanted *desperately* to be liked by these people. Before I knew what was happening, the album was called *Prisoner*.'

Prisoner was released at the end of 1979. On the cover, a nude Cher is bound by chains in a sadomasochistic pose, her handcuffed hands joined together to cover genitalia. More mixed signals from a performer looking for integrity.

Wrote one critic: 'To say that it should be thrown to patrons of her Las Vegas show is giving it more credibility than it deserves.'

'When I saw that cover, I *screamed*,' Esty remembered, laughing. 'And we thought *Take Me Home*'s cover was shocking. At least that was funny. . . .'

By the time this album was issued, Casablanca Records had been sold to the Polygram Corporation, and Neil Bogart was leaving the label. Without him at its helm, there was no reason for Cher to be signed to the company. The album crashed with a thud, as did the ill-fated single written by Tom Snow, 'Holdin' Out for Love'.

Cher taped a video for 'Hell on Wheels', and it's considered to be one of the first modern music videos. But there was no outlet for it. 'She was ahead of the craze by years,' said Esty. 'They had a video but no one knew what the hell to do with it, so they showed it to the secretaries in the office at Casablanca.'

'I know that the only reason Cher worked with me was because they told her she had to,' Bob Esty concluded pragmatically. 'I can't say I ever got a fix on her, as much time as we spent together. She's real complex. A blocked wall exists today between us, probably because of *Prisoner*. Nobody likes to have a stiff album. And she hasn't had any success at all in the recording market since "Take Me Home". Despite that, if I know Cher, she probably wishes that she hadn't been talked into it,' Esty concluded with a tone of resignation.

'If I know Cher, she probably wishes "Take Me Home" was recorded by Donna Summer. Now, *that's* like Cher. . . .'

Cher's affair with Gene Simmons continued through 1979, a year she spent working in nightclubs like Caesar's Palace in Las Vegas. It was work she had always despised, but it paid the bills, so she made the best of it.

She purchased a $250,000, four-bedroom log cabin in Aspen, where she and Gene would spend quiet weekends. At one point, he flew in from Europe just to spend a romantic evening with her. Kiss maintained as heavy a tour schedule as Cher did, and jetting about from one time zone to another just to share quiet, private moments became a necessity.

Cher fumed when she was turned away by Manhattan's elegant Dakota, where John Lennon and Yoko Ono lived. (She was denied residency because the owners didn't want any more rock singers living there, 'and they were sorry they had let John and Yoko move in'.) Cher was now living in an exotic Malibu home (*Architectural Digest* reported in June 1979: 'In the living room relics from the past – ammonites from the Carboniferous period and a dynastic

Egyptian polychromed attendant form an evocative mantelpiece still life, flanked by large bird of paradise trees. It is where the trivia of the world can be forgotten and there is a welcome air of tranquillity'), but she decided to sell the house for $1.3 million and begin building an Egyptian-style palace.

To her fans, Gene Simmons was Cher's 'Oh, what the hell' relationship. He mattered, but then again, he didn't. Cher said that she was sure he was sleeping with other women while they were involved, but that this didn't bother her because 'I have a very masculine attitude toward dating.'

'I'd always been afraid to talk about this relationship with Cher,' Gene said. 'I thought it would be the death knell of Kiss. From a publicity standpoint, this is not the most popular thing we could do. The fans who buy our records think it's horrible. But I'm crazy about Cher, nuts about her, she's my first love.'

Cher told friends about the wonderful weekend she and Simmons spent in Chicago, in an elegant suite of the Ritz-Carlton Hotel, overlooking the lake. She said it never ceased to amaze her how comfortable he seemed in her company, that he had never had a steady relationship before. 'He's a very strange, complicated, and honest person,' she said. 'I've only been comfortable with three men in my life, and I married two of them.' Cher's children also seemed to like Simmons; Chastity called him 'Genie', and he taught Elijah to swim. For that matter, Chastity and her father maintained a close relationship, and Elijah called Bono 'Uncle Sonny'.

'People seem to think I sleep with the entire Mormon Tabernacle Choir,' Cher complained at one point. 'But in my entire life I have only been with these four men' (Bono, Geffen, Allman and Simmons). (She seems to have forgotten about a few earlier lovers, including the one-night stand with Warren Beatty.)

By the middle of 1980, Cher's romance with Simmons was over. There was no dramatic blow-up; it just fizzled out. Simmons became Diana Ross's lover after he was introduced to her by Cher. (Cher has said that Gene didn't know what to buy her as a gift and she suggested that he take her friend Ross with him, 'because I know that anything she picks out I will love'.) Ross and Simmons were attracted to each other, and their romance lasted a few years.

'Cher had three backup singers, six dancers, two female impersonators, two male strippers, a mechanical bull, a mammoth magenta slipper, a slide show, five people in her own band, the Greek Theatre Orchestra, and at least twelve (it was easy to lose count) Bob Mackie costumes for her return to the Greek Theatre in Los Angeles.

'Needless to say,' the review concluded, 'this was not an evening of understatement.'

The critic went on to note that Cher surprised the sceptics in the audience with an imaginative, energetic evening of entertainment. 'Cher may never win top awards in singing, dancing, or patter, but she certainly does know how to put on a show.'

The Cher nightclub act was always popular; she put on a superbly crafted, eye-opening production. She never had confidence in herself as a singer, so she surrounded herself with high-flash pop effects. Critics reflectively dismissed her show as Las Vegas fare. They called her 'plastic'. Said one: 'Cher does not perform, she wears clothes, and she wears them and wears them and wears them. . . .'

'She's no dummy,' said a dancer in her show. 'She knows that audiences, especially in Las Vegas, grow tired of the sameness of the greatest singers. So she throws a lot of opulence at the crowd so that they won't notice her inadequacies as a vocalist.'

'Diana Ross is no major vocal talent either, but because she sings all of her hits she can wear a body stocking with six jewels and be accepted,' noted Val Johns. 'Cher refuses to do any of her major records, so she needs more. But unlike Diana, what has made Cher a sensation is that the public has always been able to identify with her as a person. Despite the opulent furnishings, she has a "There but for the grace of God . . ." streak about her. She's an ordinary woman playing dress-up. That's what made her a star.'

In her act, Cher used two female impersonators to play the guest-starring roles of Diana Ross and Bette Midler. She, Ross and Midler had become close friends over the years. Privately, though,

Ross and Midler were both said to be very upset by Cher's blatant exploitation of their characters in her nightclub act.

Kenny Sacha, who portrayed Bette Midler, recalled that Diana (played by J C Gaynor) lip-synced 'I'm Coming Out', and he performed 'Boogie Woogie Bugle Boy'. At the end of the segment, the two characters were joined by Cher, who wore a different gown just to introduce each of them, and the three sang a campy version of 'Friends'.

'Bette saw the show at the Universal Amphitheatre in Los Angeles, and Diana saw it at Caesar's in Vegas,' Sacha recalled. 'Bette didn't come backstage to the party after the show because she was pissed off. She thought Cher was ripping her off. It was nothing but flattery as far as Cher was concerned.'

Sacha was an amazingly accurate Bette Midler, all nervous energy and robust humour, in full costume, floozy wig, and heavy make-up. As Diana Ross, Gaynor was a gushing wonder, long black mane of hair in place and silver gown that was almost identical to one of Ross's then-current stage outfits (which, it is said, was more upsetting to Ross than the impersonation itself).

(The odd thing is that Ross and Midler prerecorded a dialogue with Cher to use by way of introduction to each of their 'tributes'.)

'The major problem with the Cher show,' wrote a reporter in Las Vegas, 'is that it's not a show at all, it's a circus. It cost her eight thousand dollars to transport a mechanical bull she uses in her act all the way from Texas to Vegas via a horse trailer. She should have spent the money on new arrangements. . . .'

'Cher would get pissed off at reviews like that,' said Kenny Sacha. 'When people go to see Cher, they expect a real show, something extravagant, something special, and that's what she always gave. That was a lot of hard work. It used to kill her, and she hated it a lot . . . but she never did a show that wasn't a major spectacle.'

'Hollywood tends to get so pompous with itself,' added Val Johns. 'Underneath all of that so-called dignity, if you're not willing to make a fool of yourself like Cher did when she was playing Vegas, you're not going to please the general public.'

'Before we would go on, Cher would tell the troupe, "Go on out there and have fun,"' Sacha added. 'If you made a mistake, she'd say, "Fuck it!" (That was Cher; she loved to swear when she was nervous before a show.) Nothing matters if you can't have fun. She is not a selfish diva. Most performers would not give up the time she gave to singers and dancers in her act.'

In September 1980, Cher and Caesar's Palace were cited for what *Variety* called 'Cher Blare': The American Federation of Musicians filed a complaint with the State Department of Occupational Safety and Health charging that the Cher show violated the peak ninety-decibel safety sound level. In other words, as Princess Margaret would have said back in 1966 at the Hollywood Palladium concert, 'She's too *loud!*'

'Our people are suffering,' complained Irv Kluger, vice president of the union's Local 369. 'It's making our members go deaf. The sound level on Cher's show is 115 decibels. The famous transatlantic Concorde plane only hits a decibel level of less than 110.'

Someone else charged, 'Cher's whole thing is that if you make it loud enough, you'll convince the customers that it must be good, so pay attention.'

Cher and Caesar's were both fined $480, but the fine was reduced to $180 because Cher co-operated with the agency. (It wasn't Cher's first experience with this problem: back in 1974, there was 'Sonny and Cher Blare'. Audience member Edward Freed sued the Sahara Hotel and Sonny and Cher for $10,000 in November of that year, charging that loud music from their show had damaged his hearing.)

rock-and-roll mama

Les Dudek is a shy, gentle musician with shoulder-length brown hair and a thick moustache. To Cher's public, he looked as if he were cut from the Gregg Allman mould – 'all these long-haired rock singers look alike'. Dudek was a blues-rock guitarist for The Allman Brothers and Boz Scaggs before striking out on his own. Always a critical success – his *Ghost Town Parade* album was widely acclaimed by rock purists – he never found the popularity of Allman or Gene Simmons.

'Les is the person I have had more fun with than anybody,' Cher said to a reporter in November 1980 (and by this time most of her public took those kinds of statements by Cher with the proverbial grain of salt). 'He has a wonderful sense of humour, is really carefree, and is not very materialistic at all. We just have a good time doing nothing – riding motorcycles and stuff like that.' On their days off from concert touring, the two would retreat to Cher's wood-and-wicker Aspen hideaway.

Dudek encouraged Cher's fascination with rock-and-roll music and the two of them formed a band called Black Rose. The group was fronted anonymously by Cher, with Dudek, Ron Richotte (second guitar), Michael Finnigan (keyboards), Trey Thompson (bass), Gary Ferguson (drums), and Warren Hamm (back vocals). They would record one album, *Black Rose*, for Casablanca. Two members of Toto, Steve Porcaro and David Paich, played on sessions for the Black Rose project; Bernie Taupin wrote one of the songs.

'She delved into that project with a lot of gusto,' recalled Bob Esty. 'She wanted to completely erase her public persona, she wanted to be anonymous so that no one would know who she was when they saw the group perform. It was an odd thing for a performer to do.'

Black Rose, produced by Dudek, is not breakthrough rock. Most critics considered it a self-indulgent album of oblique music. Cher's performance is raucous, and even though she probably believed in the material, her delivery simply was not convincing. As the woman who not only defined but even set standards for Las Vegas bombast, Cher could never be perceived as a rock star.

Or, as one rock critic put it, 'This is probably the nadir of popular rock-and-roll music. . . .'

When the band appeared as guests on television programmes like 'The Merv Griffin Show', it wasn't because this was a sensation in contemporary music to which middle America could relate (when was the last time Merv kibitzed with Kiss?) but because its anonymous lead singer was anything but anonymous. She appeared on Griffin's show wearing a Chrissie Hynde shag wig and a ripped sweatshirt over Spandex.

Said a critic for the *Los Angeles Herald-Examiner*: 'When Cher talked, she mumbled incoherently, sort of like Patti Smith, but as if she had *paid* Patti Smith a huge weekly salary to teach her these mannerisms. The shirt was ripped, yeah, but somehow it looked like Bob Mackie ripped it for her.' (Mackie, incidentally, wasn't quite sure how to handle Cher's new image: 'I've been trying to figure this whole thing out,' he said at the time. 'It's just a phase. As soon as she gets into her new house, she'll go back to being an Egyptian princess.')

'I don't give a flying fuck what people do or say,' Cher countered. 'I've hurt my image so much, it's part of it to get into trouble.'

The group made its performing debut at a benefit for crippled children in Los Angeles. In an article for *Rolling Stone*, titled 'Cher Plays It Low Key With Black Rose', she told Jim Farber that it was almost impossible for her to generate enough support from the rock community for Black Rose even to appear as an opening attraction for a major act. Cher refused to allow the use of her name to help promote the group's concerts, and so promoters had no interest in the band.

'The people we wanted to go out with were terrified to be seen with us,' she said derisively. 'They said we'd get booed off the stage, that people would hate us.'

Elton John was a possibility, but even he passed at the last minute. 'I was really pissed off at him in the beginning, but then I thought, if I were him at this turning point in his career I wouldn't want to fuck around with a band I wasn't sure of.' (John was in between hit records and searching for a new image himself.)

Daryl Hall and John Oates finally agreed to use Black Rose as an opening act for six East Coast concert dates. *Time* magazine reported that the lead singer of the Hall and Oates supporting band was a major mystery. It was said that when Black Rose appeared onstage, most of the fans of Hall and Oates had no idea who it was they were watching and listening to (which is understandable, considering that Cher and Hall and Oates hardly had the same following). Though the rest of the band got introductions, Cher was not introduced, and she did not speak. She also didn't change costumes or wigs; she wore the regulation ragged punk haircut, T-shirt and Spandex.

'I saw Black Rose in Central Park on 30 August 1980,' said fan Brian Wilson. 'I'd have to say that it wasn't the second coming of Fleetwood Mac, but that's not important. This is a pivotal point in Cher's career because it's a perfect example of her independence as an artist. She has always done all of the things most female stars of her ilk have fantasized about doing and then she shows no remorse whatsoever for what she's done. She doesn't mind being tacky; she just doesn't mind it at all. Her forthrightness, flamboyance, and filthy mouth are *honest* elements of her personality that make her so appealing.'

Bob Esty agreed. 'To think that Cher even gave a second thought to how her public would react to Black Rose is silly. She sang rock and roll because she had a passion for it. To me, that's what art is all about, passion. Maybe it wasn't a smart move, but it was courageous art.'

'I'm going to stay with this for a long time,' Cher said with determination at the time. 'When I went to Casablanca, what I really wanted to do was rock and roll. Neil Bogart said that that wasn't my strongest thing. "Do *this* first ['Take Me Home'] and let me try to get you back in the music scene." I did it and it was successful, so I went along, but it wasn't what I wanted. This is.'

It has to be noted, though, that Cher's duplicitous nature some-how seemed to take the wind out of her sincerity; while 'struggling' as a rock band singer, she was also working in her time off as a Las Vegas star, making enough money to finance a whole fleet of rock bands. 'Las Vegas is my gig,' she would counter defensively when cornered. 'That's how I pay my rent and my kids' schooling.'

The *Black Rose* album failed to place on *Billboard*'s top 200. It was poorly promoted and not taken seriously – either by Cher's following or by rock and roll's.

the elephants' graveyard

When the Black Rose project failed, so did Cher's romance with Les Dudek. She never again talked about her passion for rock and roll in press interviews. Next in line was a lacklustre album called *I Paralyze*, produced by Olivia Newton-John's producer John Farrar and David Wolfert. It was very poorly received by Cher's fans and by the media.

Today, she looks back in frustration on her career as a recording artist. In terms of commercial success, she tends to underrate her achievements; in terms of personal fulfillment, she has only found any in the albums that were commercial disasters – *Stars*, *Two the Hard Way*, and *Black Rose*.

The final tally: twenty top-forty singles, ten as a solo artist and ten with Sonny Bono; three million-selling singles, one million-selling album with Sonny, and four million-selling albums as a solo artist.

'Historically, Cher has been underrated,' said rock historian Rick Wilson. 'Look at the facts: of all the girl singers who saw chart action in the Sixties, she, Diana Ross, Aretha Franklin, Dionne Warwick, and one or two others still have wide-ranging careers. Where's Dusty Springfield, Lulu, Mary Wells, Marianne Faithfull, Ronnie Spector, Dee Dee Sharp, Nancy Sinatra, Bobbie Gentry, and the rest of them? They're all in obscurity somewhere.

'After Black Rose, she just went back to Vegas to make a quarter of a million bucks a week. There were people who thought she should've been on the junk heap, an old broad who had her run. But she came back because there's always another commercial proposition when it comes to Cher.'

So Cher went back to living the life of a touring performer. Life on the road, though, was difficult for her. 'We were constantly invited to parties,' recalled Kenny Sacha, 'and she's not really a party person, but there are responsibilities, you know. She wouldn't go to a party unles the whole company was invited. She hates small talk with a passion. Most people don't know how introverted she really is, how when she's shooting off her mouth it's really because she's been backed into a corner. With the rest of the cast around her, she felt safe.

'But everything about her is dramatic, and that's the paradox with Cher. She puts on a real ranting and raving show when she's angry. Once I was robbed on the road and very upset about it, so I got drunk right before the show. I put my Bette Midler make-up on and Cher said I looked like Bette Davis in *Whatever Happened to Baby Jane?* "Here you are a part of my show and you are going to screw it up and make *me* look bad," she screamed. "How *dare* you?" That kind of stupidity pisses her off. . . .'

Sacha recalled one of Cher's famous shopping sprees; it took place while they were performing in Atlantic City, in the summer of 1981: 'Between shows, she wanted to go to a shoe store in the lobby, and she wanted to be incognito. Incognito to Cher is a very elaborate Japanese-style jacket, a full face of make-up, and a fabulous beaded wig. Before you knew it, as she was buying tons of shoes, the store got so mobbed with people clawing at her that they had to close the place down. It took an hour to get her out of there. She hates attention, but she craves it as well.'

Critics were charging that Cher had stopped growing as an entertainer, that she was just a high-flash fashion and prop show. But the people who paid to see Cher entertain did not want to see growth; they wanted to see Cher's expensive Bob Mackies and hear her wisecracks. Cher began to resent this line of work, and became embarrassed by it.

'Until you have to get in and out of twelve wigs and outfits every night for months on end, you'll never know what misery is,' she complained to some of her crew. 'It seems glamorous, but this is hard work. From the moment I become this Cher character until the moment I finish I'm uncomfortable.'

'One day she reached a point where I think her mind said, "I cannot do this any more, so I won't,"' said Kenny Sacha. '"I will never again be this uncomfortable, ever!"'

'Las Vegas was not the happiest period of my life,' Cher has concurred, 'because so many people were convinced that I couldn't do anything else. I am not satisfied when someone says, "You can't come and join us – you're not good enough," or "We don't want you; what makes you think you can do that?" So being in Las Vegas without any other outlet was terrible. I felt like I was in the elephants' graveyard.'

One evening, director Francis Ford Coppola, who used to play poker with Sonny Bono, went to see the Cher show at Caesar's Palace. After the show, he went backstage and met with her. Behind all the costumery and flash, Coppola believed, Cher had an intuitive flair for more serious drama. He felt that Cher was in a career trap, and she agreed. 'Then why aren't you doing films?' he asked. That question hit a raw nerve and she began to cry. She explained how wretchedly uncomfortable she'd become with her show, how she had tried to secure jobs as an actress, and how no one would give her a break. It all seemed to pour out at once. 'I *have* tried,' she moaned. 'I really have.'

'Bullshit,' Coppola decided. 'You haven't tried hard enough.'

Years had passed since she had embarrassed herself (in her own opinion, anyway) with *Good Times* and *Chastity*. She had a choice to make: either she could continue to work as a 'personality' and be one of those Las Vegas stalwarts like Lola Falana, someone who just *is* but never *does*, or she could give up her nightclub act and become an actress struggling for recognition.

The choice was an easy one.

part three

RECOGNITION

'It's ridiculous. People are too judgmental. I'm not any more serious now than I was before – when I was on TV or when I was modelling for Vogue. Now that people like my work, they say I'm a serious actress. . . .'

– Cher

jimmy dean: *one giant step . . .*

When Cher stepped out on to the stage of the Martin Beck Theatre on Broadway to play the role of Sissy in *Come Back to the Five and Dime, Jimmy Dean, Jimmy Dean*, it may have been one of the most paralyzing moments of her life. 'If only I had that thing called self-confidence,' she told friends. But she did have that and she also had something even more important – she had heart.

She was a beginner on a stage full of seasoned professionals. Without the excesses she'd become famous for, the costume changes – there wasn't a sequin or bead in her entire dressing room – the wigs, the glamour, it was as if she were standing naked to the world for the first time. 'This is it, folks, take it or leave it.'

After this night, she would think of herself in an entirely new way. She would look in the mirror and an *actress* would gaze back at her.

'She did what Richard Chamberlain did,' said one observer. 'Another of Jeff Corey's former students, he chucked it all at the height of his popularity to go really deep into the art of acting. Rather than accept the kinds of roles offered to him after "Dr Kildare", when he was considered just another pretty face in Hollywood, he went to England to study Shakespeare. *Jimmy Dean* is certainly not Shakespeare, but the motivation in Cher was the same. Hollywood is in the business of exploiting personalities. In Hollywood you don't see people go outside their own barriers – but in New York, they insist upon it. Cher was where she should've been . . . finally.'

In November 1982, Cher and a male secretary had come to Manhattan to check out possibilites, to see if the doors to a future in acting were still closed to her. She would try to enrol in some drama classes. 'I didn't come here to get parts,' she insisted to friends. 'I came here to learn how to *act*.' While in New York, she stayed at Gene Simmons's apartment (he was out of town on tour).

'When I saw Linda Ronstadt in *Pirates of Penzance*, I thought, "Jesus, if *she* can be on the stage, then what am I doing!" I finally decided to study with Lee Strasberg. He said, "You've got to stop all of this nonsense and get serious." I decided to finally prove to myself that I was an actress.'

Cher met with Joe Papp, the producer of *A Chorus Line*. What did he think of her chances? New York is a competitive city; people who want careers as actors and actresses walk the city looking for work. They're young; they have bright futures and no preconceived images to live down. And it's tough for them to make it. Papp told Cher, 'How can I tell you're talented? How do I know this? I certainly can't tell from that crap you did on television. I can't tell from anything you've ever done that you have any talent. . . .'

So now she knew what they meant when they said 'the truth hurts'. Cher prepared a scene from *I'm Getting My Act Together and Taking It Out on the Road* for Papp to see so that he could evaluate her worth as an actress. It wasn't a complex scene, anything that would indicate her ability to essay great emotion or depth, but Papp was impressed with it just the same. 'Unless he's a terrific liar, he seemed overwhelmed,' Cher recalled. 'He was genuinely surprised.'

She has always suspected that her life is somehow charmed, but now she knew it was true. When she came out of his office there was a message waiting for her. 'Call Bob Altman,' the note read. 'I'll never forget how excited I was,' she said in an interview with *Dramalogue*. 'I thought that this was really amazing – auditioning for Joe Papp, who was excited about my audition, and then getting a call from Robert Altman.'

Cher and Robert Altman are kindred personalities: both have overwhelming charismatic power, both are hotheaded, and both are controversial. Robert Altman, a talented movie director, has never forgotten or forgiven the movers and shakers he considers his enemies in Hollywood, 'people who hate me because I don't fit into their patterns,' as he puts it. 'Guys like Barry Diller [at the time, a chairman of Paramount Pictures]. I'd like to duke it out with him.' Altman has insisted that Diller jinxed *Popeye* (starring Robin Williams and Shelley Duvall) by leaking scandalous bits of gossip to the press before its release. 'I'd love to sue him for slander and libel and then get people on the witness stand to talk about what he did to me.'

Generally speaking a pattern has emerged when it comes to Altman's work: critics pummel his films, the public praises them. The two that were the most popular with general audiences, M*A*S*H and *Popeye*, received the worst reviews of Altman's career.

When his movies *Quintet*, *A Perfect Couple*, and *A Wedding* were commercial as well as critical disasters, he decided to take a sabbatical from film-making and begin directing small off-Broadway plays.

Altman had one prior connection to James Dean. Back in 1957, he produced a documentary about Dean's life to 'undo this God thing and find out the truth. I don't like the idea of superstars — they're an excuse for the masses not to think about their own problems.' Altman's work was scathing, but directly honest. Dean, one of the most popular cult figures of the Fifties, was the star of *Rebel Without a Cause* (with Natalie Wood) and *Giant* (with Rock Hudson and Elizabeth Taylor). Altman thought both movies were just mediocre.

As is usually the case in show business, Cher's connection to Altman is the result of someone knowing someone who knew someone else. In this case, her mother, Georgia, was a friend of Altman's wife Kathryn. Georgia has said that she was trying to find Cher in New York, and in calling her other daughter, Georgeanne, she accidentally called the Altman household. Just in passing, she happened to mention that Cher was in Manhattan and hoped to become an actress. Altman had 'a vague thought' and decided to track Cher down.

Come Back to the Five and Dime, Jimmy Dean, Jimmy Dean was written by Ed Graczyk, a forty-year-old director of a Columbus, Ohio, theatre whose previous two plays had only been performed regionally.

At first, Cher didn't want to read for the play. She had hoped to find something she'd feel comfortable with, a role that would make her shine. Most actresses want to shine, but few ever think they will as a transsexual, and this is the part Altman had in mind for her. It would be a pivotal role, one that would be important to the thrust of the play, but the concept was bizarre. Just for once, Cher decided not to walk that line between acceptability and controversy. Audiences would relate to Cher as a transsexual because it's an unusual role, and Cher is nothing if not unusual. But she wanted to be accepted on the merits of her acting, and hiding behind a gimmicky part wold be tantamount to walking onto that stage in full Cher drag – Bob Mackies and all.

She would keep an open mind, though, and read for the role. Altman thought she was fine, but when she read for the role of Sissy, he thought she was terrific. Sissy, a hip-swinging, tough-minded, but sensitive waitress, was Cher.

Cher's management told her that she didn't have the experience to make a strong impression on Broadway. The William Morris Agency agreed. In fact, before she informed the William Morris Agency that she'd been given the role, she asked one of the agents to investigate the possibilities for her. 'Oh, my dear, you couldn't *possibly* read for that. That's Broadway! That's Altman! Think in terms of a television commercial.'

'I already got the role, jerk,' Cher countered.

'It really pissed me off a lot,' she told writer Michael Kearns. 'I don't believe in advice too much. I believe in listening to advice and then doing exactly what you want to do. I'm very stubborn and manipulative and almost always get my way. This business is tough; people try to fuck with you every time you turn around. If you're a woman, I believe it's harder, because women aren't supposed to stand up for what they want. If you're nice, you'll get your ass walked all over; if you stand up for something, you're a bitch. . . .'

Graczyk's play concerns the reunion of five women, all former members of a Jimmy Dean fan club in the rural Texas town of McCarthy, not far from where *Giant* was filmed. The town is nearly deserted, all of its lifeblood sucked out by a long drought. The action takes place in a rundown Woolworth's five and dime store on 30 September 1975. The Disciples (the name of the fan club) are having their twentieth-anniversary reunion.

Juanita (Sudie Bond) is the proprietress of the store, and she employs Sissy (Cher) as a counter waitress. The first to arrive in town are Edna Louise (Kathy Bates), now a dowdy mother of six and pregnant again, driven in from Dallas by her bossy friend Stella Mae (Marta Heflin). When Mona (Sandy Dennis) shows up she begins to recount the glory days when she worked as an extra on the *Giant* set, and she confides that James Dean fathered her retarded child. Memories from all the women, mostly delusionary, are shared.

Sissy recalls the fun they had with Joe (Mark Patton in flashbacks) when the two of them would team up with Mona to lip-sync McGuire Sisters records (Joe in drag). Joe is remembered as a homosexual forced to leave town after a scandal, when he was beaten up by Juanita's husband and other townsfolk. Later an elegant woman blows into town to join them, and admits that she is Joe, now Joanne (Karen Black) after a sex-change operation. In time it becomes apparent that it was actually Joe who fathered Mona's son. There are verbal collisions galore, and at one point Sissy reveals that she has had a mastectomy, that her voluptuous figure is fake, and that this has ruined her marriage.

Emotionally drained by their lives, all five women are complex personalities, and the actresses breathed depth and sensitivity into their portrayals. The play sounded as if it shouldn't work, but somehow it did.

The three major characters, Cher, Dennis and Black, had never met before, let alone worked together. Black, thirty-nine at this time, had left the theatre circuit fifteen years earlier to make movies (among them, Altman's *Nashville*).

Cher became especially close to Sandy Dennis, despite the fact that Cher's boisterous personality is so opposite Dennis's reserved nature. She said that working with Dennis (whom she called her 'fuck-around buddy') was 'the thrill of a lifetime'.

It was said that Shelley Duvall, whom Altman had directed in *Popeye*, was originally considered for the role of Sissy, but that the chemistry wasn't right with the other two co-stars. 'I picked my leading ladies because I thought that just their names alone sounded interesting together,' Altman said rather vaguely. 'I don't pick one actress for one part and another for another part. I choose them by their chemistry together. . . .'

During the first day of rehearsal, Cher was so nervous she almost choked to death on a multivitamin. As she gasped for air, Altman performed the Heimlich manoeuvre on her. 'You might say I owe my new life and my old life to Bob,' she said later.

The reaction to Cher's casting was predictable. Most of the New York press felt certain that *Jimmy Dean* was really just a vehicle for a Las Vegas star hoping to become 'legitimate'. The rest of the casting was all but ignored. Cher was the main attraction. Altman tried to diffuse the attention: 'Cher is coming into this on the same terms as everyone else. With no limousines and she won't be wearing her snakeskin suit. She understands perfectly that this is strictly an ensemble project. No prima donnas. She's going to have to learn to take subways and hail cabs if she wants to be a New York actress. This isn't the Cher Show.'

Rehearsals for the play were intense, mostly because Cher was feeling the pressure of self-redemption. She knew that there were people involved with the play who felt she was just a frivolous person, people who never imagined that underneath that glossed exterior beat the heart of a sensitive woman.

'And if anything, Cher is probably one of the most sensitive people in show business,' said Sandy Dennis. 'She feels. That's what's important. And she lets it *out*. God, does she let it out. . . .'

Cher complained during the first few readings of the script that she wasn't sure of her 'motivation' (actors jargon for '*Why* do I have to say this?'). Altman would take her aside and coach her. 'Real people don't think about what they're feeling. They just act on it.'

'But in portraying a character, don't you have to pick a consistent feeling?'

'No,' he told her. 'Real people behave differently on different days.'

She wasn't satisfied with his answer. There must be a secret to this, she decided. And it's a secret that only *real* actors share with one another. Later, she would discover that Robert Altman's technique in working with actors was simply to allow them to react to written situations and not analyze or dissect those situations. She'd find that different directors worked in different ways, and she wouldn't always be happy with the way she was directed.

'I can't say I would've done this play if Bob weren't directing it,' she told friends. 'All I can say is thank God for him. He accepts all of us. We're okay, he's okay. He'll stop and listen to anything we have to say.'

Working on instincts had got Cher into trouble before, and this time would be no exception. Ed Graczyk, the play's author, and Cher came into immediate conflict when she wanted to change some of the lines he'd written for the Sissy character.

'This is not *you* talking, Cher,' he blew up. 'This is a character. If you want to act, you cannot change the script to suit yourself.'

'But if it's not *me*, it won't work. If I don't feel right about the words, it's nothing but a cartoon.'

Cher told Graczyk that she felt he had written the character with as much depth and purpose as he could have, but she believed she could take the role even further if he'd allow her more control over the dialogue. Coming from someone whose background included something called *Chastity*, Graczyk wasn't impressed with Cher's evaluation of his work. But after he gave her some room to stretch the role, he said that he was astonished. 'You have the instincts of a great actress,' he told her. 'Do whatever you like with the role . . . within reason.' She and the writer became great friends.

Sonny Bono married Susie Coehlo on New Year's Eve 1982, while Cher was rehearsing *Jimmy Dean*. 'The road to happiness took a detour, however, when Bono asked his fiancée to sign a prenuptial agreement. She refused and took off for Europe. He courted her again, won her back, and scrapped the idea.

Prior to this, Sonny appeared in a pilot for an NBC television 'whodunit' that teamed him with Lee Purcell, called 'Murder in Music City' (Bono conceived and co-wrote it). Bono starred as a successful composer who discovers a slain private eye in his bathtub. The show received fine notices, but was not picked up for a series.

Sonny also appeared in an episode of 'Fantasy Island' with Jenilee

Harrison, in Irwin Shaw's 'Top of the Hill', a syndicated mini-series; and in the motion picture *Airplane II*, as a mad bomber.

About fifty people attended Bono's candlelight ceremony in an Aspen nondenominational church. Bono, now bearded, was forty-seven; his bride twenty-eight. Chastity was a bridesmaid. At the end of the ceremony, the minister told the happy couple, 'I now pronounce you Sonny and Cher-ie.'

'*Who's Cher—ie?*' asked the horrified bride.

Sonny just mumbled 'Oh my God' to himself.

Once an image, always an image.

Later, Susie told Cher about the minister's blunder, 'and we just laughed ourselves sick,' said Cher. 'Susie is the best thing that ever happened to Sonny,' Cher noted. 'He's so nice since they've been together. Like when I first met him. . . .'

nothing to be ashamed of

The Martin Beck Theatre is a 1,300-seat Broadway house. On the stage was a large, colourful set conceived by Altman: two huge Woolworth signs, one gold and one red; a soda fountain; a Wurlitzer; photos of Jimmy Dean displayed in a shrinelike manner; Christmas decorations; red, white and blue Independence Day banners and streamers.

The opening-night crowd was an odd-looking pot-pourri of young people. One reporter noted that the audience 'was more tie-dyed than black-tied, more gold-chained than silver-haired'. This was a Hollywood gathering rather than a traditional Broadway group. Liza Minnelli sat close to the stage with her husband, Mark Gero. Halston sat nearby.

While the theatregoers took their seats, Cher was said to be backstage throwing up.

'She was sick before each and every show,' said one observer. 'Just like when she worked with Sonny.'

Not quite. Back then she was nervous about performing because she really did not want to. Now she was nervous because she wanted to so badly.

'I have been so nervous with this play, my entire body chemistry was thrown off,' Cher complained to Andy Warhol. 'I had to go to two doctors and they said my nerves have just totally fucked up my body.'

Warhol and Bob Colacello interviewed the new Broadway star for Warhol's *Interview* magazine. At the time, Cher was living in a duplex on top of the Mayflower Hotel on Central Park West and 61st Street, with her children, a nanny, a cook, a maid, and a secretary. 'After a few minutes, the star beckoned upstairs to her bedroom,' they wrote (Cher usually conducts interviews in her bedroom), 'with its spectacular view of midtown at her feet. Cher is wearing black jogging pants, a black T-shirt tied up above the waist, white cardigan, white running shoes, and purple headband. Her throat hurts, her skin's broken out, her nerves are racked. . . .'

Although she can hardly remember her first performance at the Martin Beck, it was a good effort – not her strongest (she'd get much better as she became more accustomed to working the script), but it was easy to see that Cher has a talent for resuscitation. The part of Sissy could have been a total caricature, an overwritten floozy who would never have come to life without the help of someone like Cher, someone who really understands the workings of emotion. Her best work was done with her back to the audience in a dramatic and important scene. It was difficult, then, for her to make as strong an impression as she might have if it had been staged differently. All of that would be rectified in the film version of *Jimmy Dean*, in which she would be totally uninhibited.

Later, Cher admitted that several of the other cast members were resentful of the way she drew so much attention to herself through her broad gesturing and mannerisms. A few of the women asked Altman to tone her down. One day he called her aside and said, 'Darling, child, you're a little bit too lively. *Calm down!'*

At the end of the performance, the audience cheered wildly and particularly, it seemed, for Cher, who somehow managed to outshine the rest of the cast. But, as is usually the case with Altman's work, the charm of the play was discovered by the audiences, not by the critics.

'Forget about whether or not Mayor Koch is going to run for governor. The *truly* momentous question of the month is: can Cher act?' wrote Frank Rich for the *New York Times* (9 February 1982). 'The answer, alas, is not to be found at the Martin Beck Theatre, where [Cher] made her Broadway debut last night. Cher does get to sling a few lowdown epithets, to shake her torso, and to drink a few Lone Star beers – all of which she does with great bonhomie. But act? Cher has but one speech of any duration, and the director, Altman, demands that she deliver most of it with her back to the audience.

'But let's count our blessings,' Rich concluded. 'Next to the rest of this dreary amateur night, Cher's cheery, ingratiating *nonperformance* is almost a tonic. *Come Back* could do with a lot more of Cher and a lot less of its other stars. . . .'

Of the play, Rich declared: 'At least two characters sob out the line "I am so ashamed", when they at last reveal their secrets to one and all. It's only the author, apparently, who is shameless.'

Variety said that the play was 'preposterous, undramatic, and silly. It won't make the grade.'

Another critic called the script a 'cosmic mess' and likened its premise to an episode of 'The Twilight Zone'. Still another said that 'this is the craziest plot since a Danish film-maker announced some years ago his intention of filming the sex life of Jesus Christ.'

Generally, most critics who panned the play praised Cher's performance and one observed that 'she disappears so thoroughly into her role that her debut here is nothing short of astonishing.'

The next day, Robert Altman held a press conference at the Backstage restaurant next door the Martin Beck to discuss the reaction to his work. Despite protests all around, Cher was a centrepiece to the production as far as Altman was concerned; he asked her to attend the press conference.

'It was the oddest thing I'd ever heard of,' said a reporter, 'a producer calling a press conference to talk about how unfair he felt it was that the media didn't like his play. But that's Robert Altman for you. . . .'

Cher knew that she had nothing to be ashamed of; the reaction to her work was mostly favourable, or at least not hostile, but she was crushed just the same that the play had garnered such poor notices. She realized that the only way it would have a respectable run would be by Altman investing his own money to keep the production alive. New York critics can either make or break a play, and in this case they did what they could to break it.

Most of the people connected with the effort felt that the New York media were prepared to criticize Altman's work before it even opened, that he was a Hollywood director for whom Broadway was off-limits, sacred turf. 'That's the way it happened for Martin Scorsese a few seasons back,' noted one observer at the press conference. 'When he brought in *The Act* with Liza Minnelli, the reviews were simply horrendous. Many people felt they were not justified. It's that New York theatre mentality that Hollywood personalities somehow don't have enough integrity for the Broadway stage.'

At the news conference, Cher wore a gold-threaded sweater, soft suede slacks, and a braided gilt headband. For the most part, she sat quietly, listening to Altman's commentary and the general buzz in the room. She said that she had no appetite when food was served.

'Did you read this Gannett review, Cher?' Robert Altman asked. He handed her a copy of a critique that would be distributed to twenty-five newspapers published by the Gannett Company, including the daily *USA Today*. Unlike the Manhattan reviews, this one was quite favourable, and the reporter called Cher's effort 'inspired'. As she read the article, her eyes brightened. She read it again and her appetite returned. While nibbling on some macaroni, she folded the copy in four and handed it back to Altman, wisecracking in a smoky voice loud enough for the assembled reporters to hear, 'Bob, this guy must have been on *drugs!*'

'Listen, Cher is an actress of the first order,' Altman said to the news crew. 'I heard of her when she was sixteen and taking a class out in Los Angeles [presumably Jeff Corey's]. This friend of mine said, "You ought to see this kid I've got – she's a pistol."'

'And that's when I met Sonny Bono . . .' Cher interrupted.

'Actually I felt off last night,' she added. 'I was so nervous that I was totally aware of the audience, which I knew was bad. All I could remember were Lee Strasberg's words to me: "If you get lost, just breathe and listen and you'll get it back." I got it back sometime in the second act.'

'I can't make the connection between the audience reaction and the critics,' Altman continued, determined to see that the critics would not have the last word on *Jimmy Dean*. 'Usually I can tell where the critic is coming from. I may not agree, but I can often see his point. But this situation is different. I heard those people in the audience last night and they didn't have a bad time. Doesn't that count for anything? Didn't the critics notice that at all? Or doesn't that matter?'

As the reporters filed out, Altman concluded, 'Well, what the hell . . . This hurts a lot, but it's an adventure, isn't it?'

The play ran for sixty performances before closing. Cher realizes that the play ran as long as it did because she was *Jimmy Dean*'s 'curiosity factor'. Fans who had never been to a Broadway show came to see this one, and many didn't know how to behave in a theatre like the Martin Beck. Cher said that people who came to the show were standing and cheering and yelling out in the middle of the character's monologues, having a terrific time. 'This gay club bought out the whole theatre one night and it was our *best* performance.'

By the time the play had finished its run, she realized that becoming a 'serious' actress meant digging deep into herself to interpret elements of the role that she could identify with and relate to. Other than to be her herself, there was no other way for her to prepare.

'One night all the girls were talking about what they do for preparation, and I didn't say anything,' Cher told William Wolf of *Cue* magazine. 'So Sandy Dennis came up to me – we had this great relationship where she was always busting my chops – and she said, "Well, what do *you* do?" I said, "I just put my make-up on. By the time I finish doing that, I'm late for my cue."

'When I get onstage, I just work. I don't know what the hell I'm doing and if I stop to think about it, I *really* won't know what I'm doing. Everyone was telling me, "Girl, if you fall flat on your face on Broadway, the whole world is going to know about it." I guess I was just too stupid to know how awful it would be for my career if I was terrible.'

Being in the Big Apple was an enlightening experience for Cher in every way. To her, the men were exciting, the shopping terrific, and the night life magic. There's a bluntness about New York living; New York is basic and honest. If you like confrontation, you'll find plenty in New York. 'I can never find honest opposition in Los Angeles,' Cher has said. 'People say one thing and do another. In New York, they think you're an ass, they let you know it. In Los Angeles they just gossip about it.'

New York cabbies are famous for their insolence. Cher told Andy Warhol about the time one cab driver met his match. 'The other day a cab driver marked my boots and it pissed me off, the stupid motherfucker. I was so angry. I had these beautiful boots and they were too expensive. My sister bought them for me for Christmas. We were on our way to Carly's [Simon] and I put my foot up like *that* to show my sister, and the driver thought I had it on the back of the seat. He came around with a pen and he said "*Don't. . . .*" And then he hit my foot and put a pen mark on it. I said, "I didn't even *touch* your seat. I just raised my leg." And he said, "You couldn't have raised your leg. . . ." I said, "*Bullshit*, you *asshole*," I got so angry!

'And then on the way back,' she continued, 'I was walking across the street and another cab stopped and the guy yelled out the window, "You go ahead across. I love you so much. You've given me so many hours of enjoyment. Go ahead." New York is black and white. If you're unhappy here you know it, and if you're happy here you know that too. In Los Angeles it never occurs to you *what* you are. It only occurs to you to decorate your house. . . .'

(While working in New York, Cher was remodelling her six-bedroom multimillion-dollar Beverly Hills home. She had already invested $4 million in the Egyptian-style estate, 'and every time I turn around, lumber's gone up forty thousand dollars,' she quipped. In August 1983, she put the house up for sale with an asking price of $6.4 million. *The National Enquirer*, however, reported that the house was haunted. So it didn't find a buyer for over five years, until December 1988.)

'I like the fact that in New York you can go around any kind of way and people will accept it,' Cher said. 'I really enjoy being able to look like hell. If I went into Beverly Hills looking the way I do in New York, everyone would stare and say, "Christ! Something must've happened to Cher. Did you see the way she *looked*?" But on the other hand,' she concluded. 'I will get dressed and become that other Cher if I like. I think that what I wear and how I look has nothing to do with whether or not I'm talented. Wearing brown tweed every day won't make me any more serious as an actress.'

Years earlier, Cher had approached director Mike Nichols about the possibility of a role in his movie *The Fortune*. He had told her that she was totally wrong for the part. What he was trying to say, in a tactful manner, was that he didn't believe Cher could cut it as an actress.

Yet Mike Nichols came to a matinee performance of *Jimmy Dean* and was astonished by Cher's performance. Ordinarily, Cher hated doing afternoon shows; it always meant that she'd have to do another that night. 'I've only got one good performance in me a day,' she complained. (In Vegas, Cher was one of only a few stars who got away with doing only one show a night.) But on this particular day, the afternoon effort was a good one. In fact, in her mind it was the best performance she'd given to date.

She has said that she didn't know Nichols was watching. ('Thank God, I would have been shit!') After the show, he came backstage and this time *he* had tears in his eyes.

'I should have listened to you. You *are* talented.'

Vindicated at last. Nichols had said the magic words. And then he offered her a role in an upcoming film he was to direct. Without even reading the script, Cher accepted the part. When he left the theatre that day, she didn't quite know what to make of his offer. People often say wonderful things and make generous overtures during the after-the-show bliss, she realized. But the next day, Nichols's office called her to offer her the role officially. The movie would star Meryl Streep and begin shooting in a few months.

While in New York, Cher dated hockey star Ron Duguay, but she told the press tht she'd fallen in love with 'the two most amazing men I have ever met in my whole life,' writer and vocalist John Loeffler and actor John Heard. She was confused because she wanted both men. Cher needs drama in her life; if things are running too smoothly, she goes into shock.

She has said tht she woke up one morning and thought she was having a nervous breakdown; she couldn't eat because she was so nervous about the play and excited about her new life in New York; she was existing on liquid vitamins. Sleep was impossible because she was so wired. In love with two men and getting ready to star with Meryl Streep – it seemed too much to bear. So she called everyone she knew on the phone and talked to them and cried for a couple of hours. Then she felt much better.

The relationships with Loeffler and with Heard never amounted to much. Cher claims that a point came when she was bored with single life and that one evening she spent the night with someone and decided that she'd had enough. On her way home, she vowed to get back into a serious relationship, and the next day she met Val Kilmer, a twenty-two-year-old actor, at a birthday party thrown for her by Meryl Streep at New York's 465 Café Central. She spent the next two years with Kilmer in spite of the fourteen-year age difference. (She told friends, 'You couldn't get an insurance policy on this relationship.')

Come Back to the Five and Dime, Jimmy Dean, Jimmy Dean closed on 4 April. Altman asked Cher if she would be interested in doing the movie version, and she said yes immediately. She felt comfortable with the role and felt that her portrayal of Sissy could only become more wide-ranging in front of the camera. After discussing the offer with friends, though, she began to have second thoughts. 'Why get involved with something that was a failure as a play?' everyone asked. 'Concentrate on the film with Meryl Streep.'

That made sense. So she told Altman that she would not be available. The disappointment registered on his face immediately. 'I can't do this movie without you, Cher. I just can't. . . .'

He had given her that first all-important break. How could she not do the film?

Goodson-Todman Productions, moguls in the television game show arena, financed the filming of *Come Back to the Five and Dime, Jimmy Dean, Jimmy Dean* with $800,000. Shooting began on 20 April 1982, on the Phoenix Sound Stage in New York City. Originally scheduled to be a twelve-day shoot, the picture took an extra week to complete. It was filmed in 16 mm and later blown up to 35 mm for cinema distribution. Altman's imaginative budgeting (he said the film was not low-budgeted, it was 'properly budgeted') demonstrates how to get the most out of a motion picture with a minimal investment.

Filming the movie was a bit more difficult for Cher than doing the play at the Martin Beck. Onstage, her actions and movements were instantaneous; any impulse was acceptable. But filming the movie was complicated by close-up shots, camera blockings and multiple takes.

'I cried a lot while we were making the movie,' Cher recalled. 'Bob took so little notice of me. I really didn't know what I was doing and I was sure the camera would pick that up in my eyes. But, apparently, I was all right. Afterward, Bob said, "I didn't have to talk to you. You were doing just fine."'

Cher's work in the film version of *Jimmy Dean* is memorable. It's a bravura performance revealing the humour, sentiment and emotion that are so central to Cher's personality. Her portrayal of Sissy, streetwise yet sensitive, invulnerable yet wounded, was more of an extension of herself than the play's author probably intended. The character (who wanted more than anything to keep her figure and someday join the Ice Capades, even though she'd never been on ice skates) was self-mocking and intensely likable. The emotion-packed revelation of her mastectomy was as touching as it was powerful. For a first-timer (who counts *Good Times* and *Chastity*?), Cher realized her role perfectly. Most of the film critics were taken by surprise.

'Where did all of *this* come from?' asked one reporter. 'Cher's performance is a towering achievement. Astonishing, if you will. Never before did we know that there was more to Cher than sequins and controversy.'

In July 1982, Cher was back at Caesar's Palace, fulfilling her contractual commitment. It would be her final performance in Vegas.

Now she was even turning down film offers. She had been mulling over the part of 'a rough girl who takes over a speedway' for Randal Kleiser's *Grandview USA*. The money was acceptable – $650,000 – and the work schedule light. But casting of the male lead was uncertain and the script seemed indefinite. 'I had the feeling all along that I shouldn't do it,' she said later. At the last moment, she decided against the movie and the part was given to Jamie Lee Curtis. As it turned out, her instincts were working for her; *Grandview USA* would not have meant much on Cher's résumé.

On 30 September 1982, *Come Back to the Five and Dime, Jimmy*

Dean, Jimmy Dean premiered at the Chicago Film Festival. It won the grand prize, the eighteenth gold Hugo award, and a ten-minute standing ovation. Altman quipped, 'We should quit while we're ahead.'

The movie, which opened in New York and Los Angeles and made its cable network debut in November on Showtime, never had a strong major distribution. It only played in small venues and as part of college film series. Altman, at odds with the Hollywood system, was said to have refused to release the film through a major studio because he feared it would be ignored the way his movie *Health* had been.

Considering Altman's terrible luck with critics, it's ironic that *Jimmy Dean* was one effort that gathered raves. The *Los Angeles Times* included it in its list of 1982's Ten Best Movies. Said film critic Sheila Benson: '[Altman] has extended the reach of performers in the past, but none so memorable as Cher and Karen Black in the fragile play-into-film film. . . . They have invested their characters with such wealths of intuition, tenderness, and truth that Ed Graczyk's overheated, preposterous play suddenly takes life and soars.'

silkwood

The life of Karen Silkwood, who died in a car crash at the age of twenty-eight on 13 October 1974, was the basis for the movie *Silkwood* (originally called *Chain Reaction*). The controversial movie told the story of Silkwood's determination to prove safety violations at the Cimarron nuclear plant at which she worked (in Crescent, twenty-three miles north of Oklahoma City). A week before her death, she and her apartment were found to be contaminated with the radioactive substance plutonium. She was apparently ready to provide documentation of dangerous activities taking place at the plant, and was on her way to a meeting with a union official and a *New York Times* reporter when she was killed. None of the evidence she said she had was found in the automobile.

Jane Fonda expressed interest in this property as early as 1975, and told the press that she planned to star in it herself. (It's been said that *The China Syndrome*, which starred Fonda, was inspired by the Silkwood tragedy.)

Meryl Streep had been actively involved in researching this story for years. When she was officially cast for the lead, she had not yet filmed *Sophie's Choice*. After Mike Nichols cast Cher, Kurt Russell was chosen to play opposite Streep as her boyfriend.

Karen Silkwood's boyfriend Drew Stephens told Meryl Streep that he and Silkwood had once attended a Cher concert in Oklahoma and had gone backstage after the show. He was fairly certain that the two of them had been introduced to Cher. 'When he told us, it really blew Cher away,' said Streep.

Mike Nichols, who would produce *Silkwood* with Michael Hausman for ABC Motion Pictures from a screenplay by Nora Ephron, was a successful comic and comedy writer in the 1950s (with partner Elaine May). As director of *Who's Afraid of Virginia Woolf?* starring

Elizabeth Taylor and Richard Burton for Warner Brothers in 1966, he received an Academy Award nomination. The next year, Nichols directed Dustin Hoffman and Anne Bancroft in *The Graduate*; again, he was nominated, and this time he won an Academy Award. He went on to direct such critical and commercial successes as *Catch-22* and *Carnal Knowledge*. *Silkwood* would be his first film since the ingenious comic documentary *Gilda* (starring Gilda Radner) in 1980 for Warner Brothers.

As Dolly Pelliker, *Silkwood*'s lesbian co-worker and housemate, Cher was extremely high-risk casting. *People* magazine put it this way: 'Cher and Streep could hardly embody more disparate cultural artifacts – Caesar's Palace and *Sophie's Choice*.'

At first, Nichols was apprehensive that Cher might turn down the role. Before sending her the script, he warned her that Pelliker was gay. Cher was still interested. First of all, this was a Meryl Streep movie; how could she turn it down? Secondly, she had decided that she would set her mind to playing whatever role came her way, as long as she had strong feelings about the script. After she read *Silkwood*, she knew that she could define the role of Dolly Pelliker, and bring the character to life.

She realized that her portrayal of a homosexual woman would have to be sensitively done; it could not be a stereotypical insult. She wouldn't play Pelliker as a tough, masculine type with a pack of Marlboros rolled up in her T-shirt sleeve. But she would cut her hair short, if Nichols thought that was important.

It would be too obvious, he decided. 'Let's not make a statement about Dolly with a butch cut. Though it may be harder for you to bring her across, let's not do it with something obvious,' he said. 'Let's have you *work* to get everything out of her without externals.' Cher agreed. The vital element in Dolly's personality would not be her sexual proclivity; it would be her confusion, her sadness, her warped sense of loyalty.

Silkwood was set to begin filming on 8 September 1982. The evening before she was to fly to Dallas, Cher decided that she 'just couldn't go through with it'. It was understandable. This would be a major film with strong distribution. It would star Meryl Streep, so chances were it would be a high-profile movie with a great deal of media coverage. She would have to be strong and convincing in a difficult role. Her sister, Georgeanne, reassured her. 'They've seen your work in *Jimmy Dean* and they know what you're capable of,' she insisted. 'You *can* do this. . . .'

On the first day of the three-and-a-half-month shooting schedule in Los Colinas, outside of Dallas, Nichols called a cast meeting to outline concepts and have the actors become familiar with one another. When Cher walked into the conference room she saw that fifty people were sitting around the table. She took her seat quietly, hoping not to draw too much attention to herself.

'Then I saw this bright apparition,' Cher recalled later. 'White hair, white eyebrows slanting upward. She was wearing a white dress, no make-up. It was Meryl. She got right up, came over to me, and gave me a big kiss. "I'm so *glad* to see that you're here," she told me. I was so scared, my armpits were sweating.'

Streep had completed *Sophie's Choice* in Yugoslavia three weeks prior to this meeting. She had her own recollections of the first encounter with Cher, and she shared them with Tom Burke of *Cosmopolitan* magazine: 'I felt so *intimidated* at the very thought of meeting Cher. I mean, in photos she always looks so wonderfully *thin*, and so beautiful and stylish. The first thing that struck me when we did meet was how different she is in private life from the public image of her. Cher seemed, well, like anyone else. Very real. Very honest.'

Cher and Meryl Streep became close friends, keeping each other company in the lonely town, working out Cher's anxiety attacks. 'Cher would hole up in her room a lot,' Meryl has said. 'She can get very sad and go into black moods. And she'd spend hours on the phone with the kids. She's a good mother and miserable without them. Val [Kilmer] came in to visit occasionally, but usually nights were long.'

Cher was amazed that Meryl wore plastic shoes; Meryl was astonished that Cher would call so much attention to herself by the way she dressed in public. Cher was stunned that Meryl did her own ironing. When Meryl told her that it was one of the ways she kept herself down to earth, Cher responded, 'I don't know what keeps me down to earth, but it sure isn't ironing. I send mine out.'

Cher has explained that Dolly Pelliker was orginally going to be costumed in jeans, a T-shirt and cowboy boots. When she put the outfit on she looked exactly like . . . Cher. It seemed that no matter what Ann Roth, the film's costume designer, chose for her to wear, when Cher tried the outfit on she looked like a high-class model, not a factory worker. She was asked to gain some weight, and she agreed that she would (she had lost too much, anyway, during the *Jimmy Dean* experience). She would also wear several pairs of men's polyester boxer shorts to bulk up her figure. Finally, she would wear size thirty-three pants loaned to her by two of Roth's male assistants (Cher is a twenty-seven). She'd wear a man's shirt, as well. As she tried on different clothing, she'd come out of the dressing room and everyone would exclaim, 'Oh my God! That looks terrible!' Then the outfit would be pencilled in for a scene. If the ensemble was flattering, it was trashed.

'We have to bring you *way* down for this role,' Mike Nichols explained to her.

'But can't I look good and be low key?'

'Cher, you are *never* low key. . . .'

Perhaps Cher would be able to adjust to the male wardrobe, but asking her not to wear any make-up was almost like demanding that she trade in her soul. She never for one moment imagined herself in front of a movie camera without all of the magic blusher, eyeliner and lipstick that had been the tools of her trade since she was seventeen, since she became Cher.

'But you're *not* Cher. You're Dolly Pelliker,' Nichols insisted.

'Well, Jesus Christ, didn't the woman ever wear make-up?'

'Maybe she did. But you won't. Just a touch of make-up and you turn into the Cher character.'

'Do you know what it is to face a camera without make-up on?' Cher asked a reporter. 'It is sheer hell. What I'd do every day was just take a shower, comb my hair through once, and then not comb it again for the whole day. And then just watch as the make-up people catered to everyone else's needs and ignored my presence.'

During the first few days of shooting, in between takes, Cher would sneak off to a corner and quickly dab on a little light rouge, maybe just a stroke of eyeliner to be on the safe side. When she'd return to the set, Nichols would examine her face and then make her wipe it all off.

On the first day of shooting, Cher was a major curiosity to the rest of the crew. She was a novelty attraction. Would she be able to act? How would she look? Cher must have felt the anticipation in the air as she put on her 'work clothes', ran her fingers through her hair and checked her appearance in the mirror. Later, she would recall wondering how she could allow anyone to see her looking like this.

She walked out onto the busy set. Kurt Russell took one look at her and his eyes started dancing. Before he knew it, he was doubled over laughing. 'What are *you* supposed to be?' he asked sarcastically. A couple of others snickered. (Russell didn't mean any harm by the remark; he and Cher went on to become good friends.)

Somehow, this wasn't what she expected. Whatever happened to decorum? She didn't like being laughed at, never had. She began to cry and ran off the set.

'This is a *movie*,' she complained to Nichols. 'I somehow always thought that when I did a major film like this, I would look *beautiful* on the screen. But here, I am so convincingly ugly. I want to be Audrey Hepburn, Mike.'

'If you want to be Audrey Hepburn, then go be Audrey Hepburn. But if you want to be Dolly Pelliker,' Nichols advised, 'then get out there, damn it, and *be* Dolly Pelliker.'

From that moment on, Cher resigned herself to Dolly's appearance with the same determination that brought her to Texas in the first place. She would play the role with riveting skill.

'Working at close range in a film you see everybody's tricks,' Meryl Streep said later. 'What they're able to do and what they simply finesse. What struck me about Cher is that she's completely guileless as an actress – instinctual and uncalculating. She is a *completely* natural actress and that's rare.'

Streep never dreamed that someone as consumed with artifice as Cher had been in the past would be able to dig underneath the surface of a role like the Pelliker character. Dolly Pelliker has many flaws, and the actress who played her had to be someone who could magnetize movie audiences; otherwise, the part would have been a complete turn-off. Cher played Dolly as a homely, wise-mouthed, sulking, and lonely soul. She is starving for attention and affection and so she tags along with Karen Silkwood and Drew Stephens, hoping somehow to bask in their shared warmth. She falls in love with Silkwood and, after a bitter argument, the movie's only sentimental moment comes when the two women make up: Dolly melts like butter into Karen's arms and lap, a waif who has finally found her emotional niche.

One of the characteristics that has always made Meryl Streep such an appealing actress is her eagerness to share openly with her supporting cast. Streep has never been a selfish actress. Her scenes in *Silkwood* with Cher were tenderhearted and *real* because both actresses were so giving to one another.

Writer Stephen Schiff said it best when he noted in his review of the film, 'Streep's scenes with Cher are little jewels of comic romance direction; they're love scenes, even though Karen remains a true-blue heterosexual (at least according to this film).' Schiff likened Cher's visualization of Dolly to 'Maynard G. Krebs poured into the sleeping body of a siren . . . she's splendid.'

Recognizing the great curiosity value of Cher on the screen with Meryl Streep, the studio made certain that she was integral to all of the film's advertising campaigns. A publicity photo of Streep cradling Cher in her arms appeared on the cover of the film industry's *Marquee* magazine. Other photos of the three main characters accompanied all press releases: Streep and Russell in a warm clutch. Cher looking sullen and leaning on Russell's right shoulder.

In truth, Cher's part in the movie was a small one. She was relegated to the sidelines, to watching, advising, wise-cracking, and maybe even plotting. (It was suggested at the end of the film that her character betrayed Silkwood by notifying the authorities of her plans to go public with what would have been damaging evidence.)

But the media seemed eager to welcome Cher back to Hollywood and give her fair recognition for her work in *Silkwood*. Peter Rainer of the *Herald Examiner* in Los Angeles noted that Cher's performance somehow seemed more natural than Streep's. 'Streep, in order to transform herself into a working-class Okie, pulls out every acting trick in the arsenal,' he observed. 'It's a prodigious makeover and yet it's oddly unconvincing. You can see the technique with every detail in place. Cher, by contrast, has the ability to just move into the role without any apparent artifice whatsoever. She *becomes* her character. The movie could use much more of her. . . .'

When the *New York Times* reviewed the film, the newspaper ran a photo of Cher, cropping *out* Streep and Russell. Wrote Vincent Canby of Cher: '. . . take away those wigs and gowns and there's an honest, complex screen presence underneath.'

The real Dolly Pelliker is Sherri Ellis, thirty years old when the movie was released. She is a slender blonde who looks nothing like the character Cher protrayed in the film. Because Dolly Pelliker has a sexual relationship with a female mortuary beautician, an affair that is purely fictional, Ellis refused to allow the film-makers to use her real name. She was paid $67,500 by the producers to allow them to use parts of her story. The fee was uncommonly high (the going rate for someone of her status is about $2,500). '[The money] gave them the right to defame my name . . . that's really all it did,' she told the *Los Angeles Times*.

She has never met Cher. When the script was finished, she asked that the Pelliker role be read to her over the phone. Fact and fiction collided in the script, and she has said that she was nauseated halfway through the reading. Later, after viewing the film, Ellis said that she enjoyed it, that it made her weep, but that the inaccuracies still 'hurt'.

Cher was nominated for a Golden Globe Award in the Supporting Actress category by the Foreign Press Club, and she was thrilled by this validation of her ability. But when she was nominated for an Academy Award as Best Supporting Actress, she was astonished.

The affluent, older, and very conservative 4,080 voting members of the Academy of Motion Picture Arts and Sciences, who make evaluations that can triple an actor's commercial prospects in Hollywood overnight, are not prone to acknowledging the Chers of this world. She had been a circus attraction for so many years in the eyes of old-line Hollywood that she felt it would take years to establish genuine credibility. Beyond that, she realized that her performance didn't really lend *support* to the other roles, or even to the plot, so much as it was just an artful job.

Competing against Cher were Linda Hunt, who played a male war photographer in *The Year of Living Dangerously*; Glenn Close, part of a strong ensemble in *The Big Chill*; and Alfre Woodard and Amy Irving for their roles in *Cross Creek* and *Yentl*, respectively.

The Hollywood community at large was stunned by Cher's nomination, even though most critics agreed that she had more involving presence as an actress than they had ever thought possible. Still, she *was* Cher.

In an article predicting Academy Award winners, Los Angeles writer Dale Pollock noted: 'Cher has certainly received the most publicity, but *People* magazine covers do not exert great influence on Academy voters. Her failure to appear at the recent formal luncheon for Oscar nominees is another strike against her.'

Cher won the Golden Globe, but Linda Hunt went home with the coveted Academy Award, because there was a feeling in Hollywood that Cher had had it 'too easy'. The way Sonny Bono protected, nurtured, and guided her through the formative years is now legendary. In her critics' eyes, Cher was handed her early success on a silver platter. When she finally did embark on a solo career, it was as a viable commercial property. On the surface, it doesn't appear that Cher has paid the proverbial 'dues', though in many ways she certainly has.

An actress is supposed to 'suffer' in Hollywood before she can expect great recognition, especially if she's moving from another field of entertainment into drama. (Diana Ross and Bette Midler, both Best Actress nominees in their careers, and both losers, can attest to this.) Cher makes matters worse for herself because she makes it clear in interviews and personal appearances that she's making it as an actress *despite* the system, that she's a box-office success doing it *her* way and not Hollywood's. By being a success as Cher – purple spiked hair, foul-mouthed, wisecracking and wonderful Cher – she's going against the grain of the system. The fight ahead will be a good one.

As far as she's concerned, her success in movies is encouraging but also long overdue. 'What's happening to me now reminds me of those old movies where the secretary trips and her glasses fall off, and the boss exclaims, "Why Miss Jones, you're breautiful."' On the piano in her living room is a framed photograph of Cher with Meryl Streep, with an accompanying note: 'You are a major actress and a great human being. Love, Mike [Nichols].'

Little things mean a lot. . . .

In *Mask* Cher combines the good-natured, heartfelt elements she brought to *Jimmy Dean*'s Sissy with that sullen, self-pitying confusion central to *Silkwood*'s Dolly. The result is a tough, modern-day heroine named Rusty Dennis. *Mask* is the true story of the emotionally complex relationship between Rusty Dennis, a streetwise biker, and her son, Rocky, a brave, physically deformed teenager.

Cher first received the script in December 1984, with an accompanying letter from producer Martin Starger explaining that he and Peter Bogdanovich were interested in having her play the lead. Cher began reading the script and was so drawn to the story, so impressed with its honesty and integrity, that she skipped through the manuscript, reading only related portions. She was hardly able to sit still long enough to deal with the emotional ending. After finishing the first read, she wept.

Later, Martin Starger called to ask Cher how she felt about what she'd read. He was greeted by a message on her answering machine: 'I've just read the most brilliant script in the world and I don't want to talk to anyone. . . .'

Starger (noted for his work as producer of the critically and commercially successful *Golden Pond* and *Sophie's Choice*) would produce *Mask*, with Peter Bogdanovich directing for Universal. Bogdanovich had just finished writing his book *The Killing of the Unicorn*, about his brief affair with Dorothy Stratten, the 1980 Playmate of the Year, and the events that led to her murder by husband Paul Snider in 1980. Stratten was featured in Bogdanovich's last movie, *They All Laughed*, for Twentieth Century-Fox; it was a commercial disaster. He had directed ten films prior to *Mask*, but because of the emotional trauma he underwent and the adverse publicity he received as a result of Stratten's tragic death, he had not worked in Hollywood for some time. Bogdanovich's *The Last Picture Show*, starring Cybil Shepherd, is considered one of his best works, but *Paper Moon*, which starred Ryan and Tatum O'Neal, is probably his most popular. (Tatum won an Academy Award as Best Supporting Actress for her role.) The unconditional loyalty portrayed so compellingly by the O'Neal characters is precisely the kind of screen magic Bogdanovich was hired to generate between Rocky and Rusty Dennis.

Also, Peter Bogdanovich was the first reporter ever to treat Sonny and Cher objectively and honestly, in his *Saturday Evening Post* article on the couple in 1966. His portrait of Cher as a young, spoiled 'daughter' to Sonny may have been confusing to their fans when the article was published, but it has taken on real significance with the passing of time and Cher's evolution.

Bogdanovich admitted that he had never seen Cher act, but he has said that he felt she would be perfect for the role in *Mask*. He said that Starger presented him with a list of 'basically every thirty-four- to forty-three-year-old woman in Hollywood,' with the producer's choice being Jane Fonda. Eventually, they agreed that Jane Fonda 'just wouldn't work as a biker', and so they settled on Cher. Eric Stoltz was cast as Rocky and Sam Elliott as Gar, Rusty's biker boyfriend.

It was the first screenplay for Anna Hamilton-Phelan, who was inspired by Cher's performance in the film version of *Jimmy Dean* and kept an eight-by-ten of her on the desk as she finished writing *Mask*. She says that she had a gut feeling that Cher would be ideal for the Dennis characterization (and, more than likely, Phelan is the one who started the corporate decision-making ball rolling in Cher's direction).

Phelan had met Rocky Dennis at UCLA's Centre for Genetic Research, where she was working on another story. She was so amazed at his determination and courage that she decided to write his story, with guidance from his mother. Phelan's screenplay and the real story are, with just a few changes, closely allied.

At fifteen years of age, Rocky Dennis could have been an ordinary American teenager living in Southern California, except that he suffers from a disfiguring congenital condition called craniodiaphyseal dysplasia, which causes calcium to be deposited at an abnormal rate throughout the skull and normally proves fatal by the age of eight. The child's head swells to twice its normal size; his eyes are pushed apart to the far perimeters of his face; he has no bridge to his nose. It's a ghastly sight that resembles a 'mask'.

His mother, Rusty Dennis, is a motorcycle mama, a boozing, fast-living but sensitive biker. She is told repeatedly and incorrectly that the child will die years before he actually does. She is also told that he should attend a school for the disabled, even though the child is obviously intelligent and well-adjusted. Devoted to her son, she is determined that he live his life as fully and as normally as possible. He will attend a normal school and relate to other children his age, even if some cannot relate to him. His mother tries to ignore his apprehension about the all-important first impression he'll make in school.

'I *am* different, Mom,' he says with exasperation.

'Yeah, you are just more beautiful on the inside than the rest of them,' she responds briskly.

Rusty Dennis is reunited with her lover Gar, who, like the other members of his motorcycle gang (The Turks) she hangs out with, treats the boy with affection, sensitivity and good humour. What's interesting is the way the youngster fits in with the gang. He doesn't have to dress in leather and rebel on two wheels; he's already a misfit.

Rocky seems stronger than his mother; he deals with his disfigurement sensibly, while Rusty is an addict because of it (she says she didn't use drugs until the crisis with Rocky). Drugs are the only sore spot in their relationship. After an argument with his mother over her refusal to help herself, Rocky agrees to work with blind children at a summer camp. There, he falls in love with a young girl who can't see him, but then again sees more than most. The puppy love affair is thwarted by her parents, who, unfortunately, cannot understand the relationship and won't allow their daughter to become attached to this boy. In the end, he has a pleasant reunion with her. Later, he dies peacefully in his sleep.

The most compelling moments in the film are the subtle ones.

When Rocky catches a glimpse of himself as he might have been in a crazy fun-house mirror, the moment has jarring emotional impact. Cher and Stoltz, who is excellent throughout, handle the scene beautifully, reacting naturally and refusing the temptation for melodrama.

The scene is pivotal. It's as much a reaffirmation of Rocky's disfigurement as a vision of what might have been. The moment is a cruel slap of reality in the face of their courage: Yes, no matter how you deal with it, the boy *is* doomed. The magnitude of his destiny registers in their eyes; Cher and Stoltz couldn't have done any less, and couldn't have been more effective.

Cher and Rusty Dennis share common streaks of determination and stubbornness. When the two met in Cher's Beverly Hills home, there was an instant rapport, a total sense of mutual understanding, acceptance and identification.

'She is tough, but she has an edge of softness about her,' Cher said of Dennis in an interview with *People* magazine (18 March 1985). 'She laughs a lot. She's soft-spoken and very warm, with a metaphysical side to her about finding her way through life. She is also quite beautiful, even though when she speaks you hear those biker expressions.'

'I wondered how she could be so crazy, yet be such a loving mother,' Cher said later (and she probably only had to look to herself for the answer). 'She's a strange, strange woman. She was wearing three religious symbols – an ankh, a cross and a Star of David. She met my son and gave him a hug. I walked in and she said, "Oh, what the hell," and she hugged me too.'

Cher and Dennis worked together on the manner of expression and attitude central to the Rusty Dennis character, and Dennis was Cher's shadow throughout production, which began on 1 May 1984. Cher was determined to be as true to the story as possible. As a result, the two-way supportive relationship that developed on the screen between Cher and Eric Stoltz is disarming in its honesty.

'I was one of the only people ever to see him without his make-up,' Cher said of Stoltz, 'and he and I became really good friends. He stayed at my house and we just spent a lot of our time together. So he was like two people to me. And one day, he said, "You know,

Ma" – he still calls me that – "you love Rocky more than you love me." And while we did this movie, it really was the truth.'

Cher has said that she never heard of Sam Elliott before working with him.

'Sam, what *happened* to you?' she asked. 'How come it took you so long to get going?'

He had the same question for her. 'We both started to laugh because we realized that it's a real pain in the ass what happens to some people in Hollywood.'

The problems between Cher and Peter Bogdanovich didn't surprise those who knew them well. Cher, independent at this stage of her career, unwilling to work within preset guidelines or restrictions, and Bogdanovich, used to enforcing his position as director, eager to make his own decisions about how characters in this movie would be developed, were bound to clash. There were plenty of tears – mostly Cher's.

Both have been vague about the details of their misunderstandings during production, but Cher has indicated that she never felt as if she were living up to her promise as an actress. There are scenes she would have played differently; she wanted more control.

She has said that working with Bogdanovich was like 'being in a blender with an alligator', that he reminded her of Sonny Bono because she could never 'read' him. In her mind, he always had an ulterior motive.

'The problem with Cher is that she doesn't trust men,' he said rather bluntly. 'She didn't trust me. I tried to help her, but I couldn't do it directly. I used every trick in the book, sometimes pretending to get angry. . . .'

'Nobody tells me anything. Nobody *dares* to tell me anything,' she has admitted. 'I want to be either successful or unsuccessful in reaching my goals or in whatever I do. It's like someone telling a painter, "I want you to paint a subject like this" or "Don't you use those colours." Then paint the fucking thing yourself and leave me alone! I want to do the work I want to do and if it's not successful then it's my decision or my fault or my choice. . . .'

The problem with that logic is that she closes herself off from worlds of possibilities. But Cher's no dummy. She's in transition, having been so manipulated in the past that now she refuses to allow *anyone* to dictate *anything* to her. A compromise must be made, and at one point she will probably find a happy medium between her visions and those of the people who will work with her.

But, for the time being, she closes doors behind her. She says she'll never work with Bogdanovich again. 'Let's just say it comes under the "life is too short" category.'

The film opened to favourable reviews in March 1985.

Said the *Village Voice*; 'The movie's saving performance comes from Cher, who apparently fought her director incessantly. The result is an angry, vulnerable, genuinely unstable Rusty. . . . The actress has radar for truth.'

A major rift between producer and studio developed when Universal decided to cut two scenes from the movie, and to use music by Bob Seger, rather than that by Bruce Springsteen, on the soundtrack. The scenes were cut because the studio felt that the film was too long. One edited moment had Cher and Stoltz singing 'Little Egypt' to a group of bikers. Bogdanovich felt that the cut scenes were crucial to the movie's plot development.

Universal was not able to come to terms with CBS Records and Springsteen over the use of his music for the film (although Bruce Springsteen seemed to be as flexible with his requests as possible and even offered to donate his fee to Rusty Dennis).

Bogdanovich maintained that Rocky Dennis didn't even know who Seger was, and that Springsteen's music was important to keeping the film honest. Supplanting 'The Boss' on the score was a breach of integrity in his eyes. He filed an $11-million lawsuit against Universal and Martin Starger and initiated a full-blown campaign against Universal, placing full-page ads in industry trade publications criticizing the studio's actions. The ads were signed by many of Hollywood's leading directors, including Martin Scorsese and Francis Ford Coppola.

Universal's counter-campaign included its own advertisements, apologizing publicly to Bob Seger, applauding his music, and criticizing Bogdanovich for irresponsible publicity.

Bogdanovich reportedly requested that Cher not promote the

movie until his disagreements with the studio were worked out. 'Some of my best work isn't on the screen, but do you trash the movie because you didn't get one hundred per cent? Do you say you're taking your marbles and going home? Not me,' she said.

Cher was surprisingly insensitive to Bogdanovich's dissatisfaction with the system's handling of his work. This time she sided with the system. 'The one scene he keeps talking about is my scene,' she told the Los Angeles Times. 'If I can live without it, he should be able to live without it. He was just amazed that the studio people were screwing with his work. Basically, what I said was, "You know you screwed with my work, now they're screwing with my work and I don't really give a damn." They really didn't hurt it as much as Peter hurt it in the beginning.'

When the film played at the Cannes Film Festival, two opposing camps promoted the effort: Bogdanovich in one corner, Cher and Martin Starger in the other. Cher's party called a press conference on 14 March 1985, to downplay Bogdanovich's criticisms of the final cut:

'It's like he has to fail in such magnitude that he destroys everything. Springsteen's music was all that Rocky played and it was all we played on the set. It's the music I heard when I saw a rough cut of the film. But I'm also a Bob Seger fan and when I heard his music with the film I didn't go home and jump in the bathtub to open up my wrists. . . .'

An hour later, Bogdanovich (who financed his own trip to Cannes) called his own press conference to explain his position: 'A director must fight to maintain the honesty and integrity of what it is he's doing. I am not trying to destroy anything. I'm trying to build something called truth.'

'It was a tough situation,' said an observer. 'Cher may have identified with what the director was going through, but by the time she finished working with him she was so angry she wouldn't allow herself to side with him. Plus, she was proud of her work as it was, even if it wasn't all there. And she thought Bogdanovich was going to take attention away from the honesty that she worked to achieve in her characterization and Stoltz worked to achieve in his, and for what? For music? For a couple of scenes?'

In the end Bogdanovich, who has been plagued by financial setbacks in recent years, dropped his lawsuit.

It's interesting to note the role drug addiction has played in Cher's life, and then on the screen in her most popular film role. As a child, she saw her father as a heroin addict. In the Sixties, she stood by Sonny Bono's attacks on drug abuse and participated in campaigns to discourage drug use in schools. Part of the reason Sonny and Cher's recording career ended was hard-rock influences, much of which were aligned with the drug culture. In the Seventies, there was the horrifying overdose in the Hollywood Hills and her saving of a man's life. There was also Gregg Allman.

Throughout it all, Cher has maintained a strong stance against drugs. She has said that if her children ever decide to experiment, she will vehemently oppose it. If they insist, she would prefer that they experiment with her, at home, so that she may supervise.

'I wish I could talk to every kid and say "Don't fuck with drugs, it's *dumb*." Telling them it's wrong is like telling them not to fuck because it's wrong – that has *never* worked,' she told *Cosmopolitan*'s Tom Burke.

Its because of her understanding of the drug culture and the anguish it causes both the addicted and their loved ones that Cher was able to portray Rusty Dennis in as compassionate a manner as she did.

Also interesting in the *Mask* experience is a scene in which Rusty tries to make herself presentable to her father, a man with whom she has obviously never had a heartwarming moment. Within minutes after his arrival, it's clear that the two of them will always be at philosophical and emotional odds. Again, the whole story could be read in Cher's eyes. It's a brief scene, but an ironic one.

'I have very negative feelings about my own father,' she has said. 'But my bad feelings are different from Rusty's because she had bad feelings that came from living with her father. My bad feelings came from *not* living with my father until I was eleven, and when I did, I didn't like him. He wasn't a nice person, and he didn't have the virtues that you'd want a father to have. Every now and then I would make an attempt to see him, but it just never worked out for us.'

Today, her son Elijah Blue deals with the same sense of deprivation. 'It amazes me, these fathers who just walk away and have no idea what becomes of their children,' Cher said. 'I once said to Gregg [Allman], "What if Elijah were sick? What if I were a terrible mother? You wouldn't even know!" The fact is, I'm a terrific mother. Elijah has everything – except a father.'

In comparing her three film roles, Cher feels that the Rusty Dennis character is closest to her personality. If she were in the same situation, Cher believes she would handle its complexities with the same kind of courage.

'Dolly was too uncomfortable with everything,' she has said. 'That's part of my personality, too, but she was uncomfortable with her body; she didn't want to be a girl and she didn't want to be a boy. Sissy is a little like me too, though. She's kind of wisecracking and full of bravado, but she keeps everyone at a distance.'

And in comparing her three directors, Cher sends out more of those famous mixed signals. She's really not sure what to expect from a director: 'Robert [Altman] leaves you totally alone. I mean totally. If you need something, you go to him. But he almost doesn't direct you. It's really *strange*. Mike, on the other hand, gives you a framework within which to work. But I don't really like being directed that much. Peter tells you exactly what to do, and you listen to him . . . and then you do exactly what you want to do.'

the witches of eastwick

Finding another property was not easy; there were a couple of misfires. When offered the lead in *Baby Boom*, Cher turned it down because it didn't 'feel right'; Diane Keaton took the role. Next, Cher turned down the femme fatale Theresa Russell role in *Black Widow*.

When the script for *The Witches of Eastwick*, very loosely adapted from John Updike's 1984 best-selling novel, was submitted to Cher, she wasn't particularly thrilled with it. But when she was told that Jack Nicholson would star, she immediately decided to do the movie; she'd always wanted to work with Nicholson, whom she had known for nineteen years. Produced by Jon Peters, Peter Guber and Neil Canton, the film would star Nicholson with Michelle Pfeiffer, Susan Sarandon and Cher. Bill Murray and Sting were both approached to play the Nicholson lead when he was undecided about it, but eventually Jack took the part.

In April 1986, Cher and some friends, including her boyfriend Val Kilmer, were celebrating her fortieth birthday at Heartbreak, a New York nightclub and discotheque. Cher wasn't having a very good time; a disturbed look played on her face the entire evening. Earlier that day she had heard the news, by telephone, that Jack Nicholson had decided he didn't want her in the movie – 'because she's not attractive enough'. It seemed like such a silly reason – and certainly didn't sound like the Jack Nicholson she knew – but it cut to the quick of her insecurities just the same. As her best friend, Paulette Betts, and daughter Chastity brought out the celebratory cake and sang 'Happy Birthday', Cher was weeping. What were thought to be tears of happiness really weren't.

That same night as she sat gloomily on the disco's sidelines, she spotted a young twenty-two-year-old man on the other side of the room. 'I thought he was *sooo* handsome, just beautiful and he kind of rocked my socks, you know?' Cher said later. 'I've never felt a physical impact like that, except maybe when my children were born.' Fixing him with an imperious look, she turned to Paulette and said jokingly, 'Have him stripped, washed and brought to my tent.' She added, quite seriously, 'He is the most beautiful man I have ever seen in my entire life.' Later Cher found out his name was Rob Camilletti, but she didn't speak to him, or flirt with him, that night.

Ironically, the movie in question that day in April 1986 is about the art of seduction and what happens when three lonely women – who are supposed to be witches, although the film never really makes that clear – conjure up 'Mr Right', who turns out to be the playfully diabolical Daryl Van Horne. Van Horne calls himself a 'horny little devil' and is played rather brilliantly by Nicholson.

It wasn't long before Cher discovered that it was the film's director George Miller, and not its star Nicholson, who was against casting her in *The Witches of Eastwick*. Warner Brothers forced him to use her, a dictate with which he was most unhappy. Before production had begun, the Australian-born director (noted for his *Mad Max* trilogy) laid down the law: 'I don't want Cher ruining my movie.' Every time he used her name, he would make quotation marks in the air. 'And I had to go through this every fucking day,' she said later.

Warner Brothers told Cher that she could have the sexy but confused role of Alexandra Medford, the man-loving sculptress, envisioned as the more central of the three small-town New England witch roles in the film. Cher says she didn't realize that the part had already been offered to Susan Sarandon. When they went into production, Sarandon gave Cher the cold shoulder, maintaining an icy reserve because she thought Cher had stolen her part. The two actresses didn't speak for weeks. Sarandon ended up playing the role of the sexually frustrated cellist.

Cher and Sarandon finally worked out their problems after deciding that they'd all been lied to by the studio, especially when Michelle Pfeiffer confessed that after she read for her role, she was asked to stick around and read for Cher's!

Filming the movie in the summer of 1986 in Boston, Massachusetts, wasn't a particularly rewarding experience for any of the women, or Nicholson for that matter. All of the actors got along famously and say they cared about each other's welfare – unusual in Hollywood movie-making, if it's true – but, according to Cher, 'we had a producer [Jon Peters] who saw none of us as human beings, not even Jack. Which really blew me away. And we had a director who was just totally unaware that we were there.'

'It really made me a different person,' says Susan Sarandon. 'It hardened me. I learned that a promise is not a promise, a person's word is not a person's word. There seems to be some advantage-taking of the other guy.'

There were rules; Cher hates rules. For instance, nobody was permitted to bring guests to the set. When Susan Sarandon brought her daughter Eva to work one day, Jon Peters ordered her off the set. But then when it was time to film an important scene, Peters allowed Barbra Streisand and a coterie of friends to watch. 'And what the hell is *this*?' Cher fumed. Later, Cher would admit that she felt the women on the movie were treated without respect because they were perceived by Warner Brothers as merely 'support' for Nicholson. She didn't stand up for herself as much as she feels she probably should have because she felt she wasn't really wanted in the film in the first place, and in the second place because it wasn't much of a part.

Anytime she needed anything and had a problem getting it, she had to ask Jack Nicholson – whom the female stars called 'Little Johnny' – to intervene for her. (Jack also had nicknames for all his co-stars with the exception of one. 'Anyone with the name Cher doesn't get a nickname,' he joked.)

For Cher, working with Nicholson was an amazing experience; he was bright, charming, sweet and she'd never known a man who gave so much of himself, and shared so much with his co-stars. Pffeifer, Sarandon and Cher spent hours fixated by Nicholson's stories of his youth and mixed-up childhood, his philosophies about life and sexuality, the fact that he grew up in a beauty parlour surrounded by women. He called his co-stars 'my witches' and would sit and watch as their make-up was applied; he'd bring them all lunch in their dressing rooms. 'He thinks women are smarter than men,' Cher observes. 'So that must be a point for him.'

One day when Cher was about to film an important scene, all of the problems with the producers, director and studio began to take their toll and she found herself caught in the tight grip of an anxiety attack. She couldn't remember her lines; in fact, she could hardly move. Shaking inside, she went to Jack's trailer and began to cry. 'I don't know what's wrong, I'm just so . . . so . . . *tired*, I guess.'

He put his arm around her. 'Look, it's free floating anxiety, nerves. You're all right,' he said very calmly. Jack wiped a tear from her cheek. 'I'll take care of you until it's over. Don't worry . . .'

Cher and Jon Peters argued about another scene that day and he turned to her and said, 'Look, you're angry with me. I'm upset. What do you want me to do? Can I buy you a dress? How about a bracelet?'

Feeling as if she was being patronized, as if she were the cranky child being heard out by the tolerant father-figure, Cher became indignant. 'What do I look like, a showgirl and you're Flo Ziegfeld?'

'The concept was out of my realm of possibility,' she admitted later. 'To be bought off with a bracelet. Unless, of course, it was some *unbelievable* fucking bracelet!'

The female stars were constantly treated in a manner that felt condescending during filming: Nicholson was referred to as 'Jack', while they were referred to as 'the girls' and every time Cher heard the tag, she had to grit her teeth. She felt a chill every time the phone rang; she knew it would be either Jon Peters or George Miller with another demand, insult or some other show of complete unconcern for her feelings. Cher wasn't used to having experiences in which she could find no value. In *Silkwood*, Mike Nichols had treated her as if she had Meryl Streep's ability and stardom, 'and I didn't know my ass from a hole in the ground then'. And, at the very least, her coldly contemptuous relationship with Peter Bogdanovich during production of *Mask* resulted in a film she was proud of.

The result of all of the turmoil during the summer of 1986 was, in Cher's opinion, 'just an okay piece of fluff'. In her other films, she loved the characters she played. In this one, she really didn't care (some critics say her lack of interest was noticeable on celluloid) but this was the first film for which she was – by Hollywood standards – paid well; she received $25,000 for *Silkwood* and *Mask* but nearly triple that for *Witches*.

The final straw came as the picture neared completion, when Jon Peters told the female stars: 'When the movie's over, we're going to show it to Jack and if you girls are good you might see it too.'

When the film was released in June 1987, Susan Sarandon went to Italy on holiday so that she wouldn't have to promote it – or say anything negative about the experience or Warner Brothers. (Cher and Pffeifer did all of the promotional interviews for *Witches*.)

Now Cher knew what it was like to have a totally unsatisfying movie-making experience. 'The work is good, but the business is shit,' she observed. From now on, she decided, the ideal of integrity would somehow have to be worked into her contracts with movie studios. Cher's last word about Warner Brothers and *The Witches of Eastwick* was: 'If I'd been fucked by my husband as much as I was fucked by Warner Brothers, I'd still be married today.'

moonstruck

She couldn't get him out of her mind.

Months had passed since Cher saw Robert Camilletti in that New York nightclub. Since that time, she and another boyfriend, Josh Donen, nine years her junior and a film studio executive, had broken up, this while she was still reeling over the fact that Val Kilmer, who came before Donen, had left her (and she wasn't at all used to men leaving *her* but, apparently, he wanted a more serious relationship and she didn't). After Val and Josh, what next? A moment to catch her breath, or another relationship?

While filming *Witches* in Los Angeles, Cher would call Robert in New York, cry about the problems she faced on the set and rehearse her many grievances before confronting Jon Peters or George Miller with them the next day. 'One night on *Witches* she had a tough time and we spoke for five hours,' Robert recalls. 'I knew then there was something happening to us.' Her phone calls to Rob did more than give her a soap box on which to relieve herself of her problems; they somehow offered her a temporary avenue of escape from *Witches*. She began to rely on him as an important figure in her emotional economy.

When she first laid eyes on Camilletti, he struck her as if he was an apparition: a tall, raven-haired, slim figure in tight jeans looking her way with deep, coal-black, sensitive Italian eyes; everyone else around him seemed to fade into star-filter. The last time anything like this happened to Cher was in 1962 when Sonny walked into a Hollywood coffee shop . . . and she was instantly his.

Rob was only twenty-two, about five years older than Chastity; Cher was forty, but she didn't care about the obvious generation gap. There was something thrilling about the immediate attraction she felt for this man and, as she puts it, 'all convention is forgotten because you only want this one thing, this one person, and you throw everything else out the window.'

Cher pursued Camilletti, and the two of them soon went out on their first date, set up by Cher's assistant Debbie Paull. Perhaps she felt she'd be more comfortable if surrounded by friends, so Cher had a double date arranged; she and Robert went with Sean Penn and Madonna to the theatre. Certainly, Camilletti must have been in a tail spin: out on a date with Cher, in the company of Sean and Madonna, but having to get home early enough to catch some sleep before having to warm the ovens at the bagel shop at dawn. It acts out like a twisted version of *Cinderella*. 'What the hell could she find interesting about a guy like me,' he wondered. 'I didn't admit to myself that I was attracted to her. We're from totally different worlds.'

Totally different worlds, indeed. She was a movie star. He was paying for acting classes and college by taking odd jobs, being a bartender at a Greenwich Village singles' spot and working in a bakery. If a career as an actor didn't materialize, he'd decided, he wanted to own his own bakery. Camilletti is the son of a construction supervisor for Con Edison, the New York utility company. He'd graduated five years earlier with a class of 586 students from Benjamin Cardozo High School in Queens. Cardozo is a state school that employs armed guards to patrol the playground and protect students against thugs and hoodlums. He lived in Forest Hills and would come into Manhattan a couple of nights a week with pals to pick up girls at nightclubs.

After spending the night at Cher's, Rob would leave at three in the morning to take the last train out of Manhattan to Great Neck, New York, in order to be at the bagel shop by four o'clock so he could light the ovens. 'I was rolling dough by five and out of there by noon,' he recalls.

'He's really a sweet boy,' she decided after the first date, 'and probably *not* a good thing to waste my time on.' Later, Cher would explain that she felt she was beginning to fall into a pattern of being with younger men, and that this was starting to worry her. She thought that perhaps her penchant for young guys was 'a fault or weakness, something detrimental in my character'. Older men rarely asked her out (the ones who did were always married) and she had to admit that she was glad they didn't! 'These younger men have been very loving and very supportive, and that's what's really important to me,' she said in an interview with *Playboy* in December 1988. 'I don't *need* a man to do anything else for me.'

There has always been a great deal of speculation as to why Cher prefers younger men. Press agent Bobby Zarem, a friend of hers for years, puts it this way: 'Who would you rather have? A twenty-three-year-old boy who can hold you all the time and give you all the passion and love you need, or a forty-seven-year-old old fart of a studio executive who leaves the house at 6 a.m., works till 10 p.m. and has nothing left for you at the end of the day?'

After giving it quite a bit of thought, she decided that she still didn't know whether or not her weakness for young men was a character flaw – but after spending the night with Rob Camilletti, she decided that she no longer cared.

Camilletti is a gentle, unassuming man who, by his own estimation, is not a complicated person. One has to wonder how he can even begin to understand Cher's private complexities – a personality that has evolved so dramatically over the last few decades. Cher began calling him 'Mookie' because he once told her he was 'just a mook from Queens' (a working-class borough of New York City). He began calling her Cherilyn, which she liked because the name cut to the core of who she really was beneath years of show business layering.

'She's a very smart woman,' Robert has said of Cher. 'I expected her to be so strong and so sure of herself, but she's not. She was a little awkward, as anyone would be when you first meet someone you're attracted to. There's the Cher that people see every day, but I also see a shy, wide-eyed little girl.' Camilletti insists that Cher possesses a natural lovableness most people never see; he says that she's the first woman with whom he's ever been in love.

Cher says that Robert knows her better than anyone else she's ever been with 'because I trust him more than anyone I've been with. He's trustworthy and his morals are just impeccable.' It upsets her when he's dismissed as a 'bagel-boy', 'because he was a great bagel-maker. I don't really care what he is,' she says decisively.

'Robert's not the best relationship I've ever had, but this one is the biggest Band-Aid. It's liniment, lotion, incredibly healing. I love his simplicity – he makes me feel peaceful.'

The great disparity in their ages is a subject that comes up only occasionally, and when it does it's rather jarring for Cher to consider that Rob was born the year Sonny and Cher's first record was released, and that he was a year old when 'I Got You Babe' was issued. Once, Rob was auditioning for a part in a movie that was set in 1955. 'Jeez, Rob, you were hardly even born yet, were you?' Cher said incredulously.

'What are you talking about, Cher?' he said with a grin. 'I wasn't born until 1964.'

She looked at him and suddenly remembered how young he really is. 'Oh shit! I was *nine* in nineteen fifty-five! God, you're young. And Jesus, I'm old.'

Another time when the age difference was being discussed, she said, 'Mookie, it's an awful big difference, you know? I look really good now, but if we're together, what's going to happen when I don't look as good?'

He thought about her question for a moment and responded, 'I thought that when you loved someone you weren't constantly looking at the way they look.'

'I'm serious,' she continued. 'I may start to get really wrinkly. How are you going to feel?'

Rob gently took her face in his hands and pushed her cheeks in toward her nose. 'Hmm, let's see how this looks,' he said very seriously.

'Okay,' he decided, 'I think I can stand it.'

Cher had been offered the role as a defence attorney in *Suspect*, a Tri-Star film directed by Peter Yates, and she decided to accept it. But while she was filming *Witches*, another script had been submitted to her that she couldn't seem to get out of her mind. Called *Moonstruck*, it was a sophisticated romantic comedy about the loves, jealousies and entanglements facing an eccentric Italian-American family from Brooklyn. In the story, daughter Loretta Castorini is thrown into emotional turmoil when she betrays her fiancé by having an affair with his brother. 'Each of our characters believes they're in control of their own lives,' screenwriter John Patrick Shanley explained to Cher, 'until a mischievous moon appears over New York and illuminates new passions within them.'

Cher turned down the role twice before finally accepting it (originally, the film was called *The Bride and the Wolf* and there were some who thought it was a horror movie). She just wasn't certain she was right for the film. 'As much as I liked it, it wasn't *Mask*, which I felt I just *had* to do,' Cher has recalled. 'I was a little frightened because there seemed to be all kinds of possibilities and all kinds of risks here.' But Cher could relate to the story, even if in a remote way. The quarrels, tears and family love she found in the script reminded her so much of Sonny's family. 'Everybody eating and talking and shouting, but having such good times,' she remembered.

Norman Jewison, the film's director and co-producer told her that it was fine with him if she didn't want the part, he had another actress in mind anyway. Proof of Cher's ascent into the small circle of bankable female stars was MGM/UA's ultimatum that either Cher star in *Moonstruck* or the company wouldn't finance the $11 million project at all. When the production of Tri-Star's *Suspect* was delayed, a six-week period opened up in Cher's schedule. She decided to take the role in *Moonstruck*, and one of the reasons she did so, she says, was simply because she was afraid to and she had to prove to herself that she could do it.

According to co-producer Patrick Palmer, MGM entered into an agreement with Tri-Star not to release *Moonstruck* until at least two months after *Suspect* came out; at the centre of all of this discussion was an actress very much in demand – a lady who, one day many years ago, said, 'I'd like to be an actress, but no one wants me to do it' – and her hectic scheduling; she had exactly one day off between *Witches of Eastwick* and rehearsals for *Moonstruck* and that was Thanksgiving Day, 1986. The entire script was rehearsed by the cast in a studio on lower Broadway as if it were a play. Filming would begin on Monday 1 December.

Cher had to admit privately that she was a bit intimidated by Norman Jewison's reputation as a brilliant producer (*Fiddler On The*

Roof, Jesus Christ Superstar, A Soldier's Story). As is typical of Cher, rather than admit to being frightened, she became defensive. The first time they met at Cher's Los Angeles home, she had just emerged from the shower, was still wet and wearing no make-up. 'I just want you to know something right off,' she told him. 'I'm really difficult.'

'Oh, yeah?' the director she later nicknamed 'the curmudgeon', challenged. 'What's that supposed to mean?' Studying her in her dripping wet condition, she certainly looked a lot more vulnerable to him than she did 'difficult'.

'Uh . . . I don't know,' Cher said thoughtfully. 'Because, I'm really *not.*'

Norman Jewison amused Cher because she'd never worked with a director who has so much fun during production; if she did a comical scene well, he actually laughed. Jewison is also used to yelling, but not used to being yelled at – so working with Cher was a refreshing change for him. He developed a relatively easygoing father-daughter relationship with his star. 'Cher thinks all directors are mad and crazy,' says Jewison. 'And if they weren't directors, they'd be revolutionaries. She's right, of course.' Throughout filming, Cher nagged her director for the identity of 'that other actress' he had considered for the role. She still doesn't have a name.

Filming the exterior scenes in New York for four weeks provided some interesting anecdotes. One day, while they were shooting in a delicatessen with the crew in place and security at the door, a native New Yorker barged into the shop. 'Hey! We're trying to make a movie here!' Norman Jewison protested.

'I don't care *what* you're trying to make here,' said the man. 'I came all the way from Wall Street and I *want my bread!*'

'You can't argue with a New Yorker,' Jewison said later. He turned to Cher and said with great resignation, 'All right, get the man his bread.'

Cher gave the man a loaf of Italian bread; he gave her $1.60 and walked out the door. Cher and Norman must have recognized an opportunity: by the end of the shoot that day, they had sold five more loaves and pulled in eight more dollars.

Cher's co-star Nicholas Cage (nephew of director Francis Ford Coppola) is about the same age as her boyfriend Camilletti. Originally, there was some discussion as to whether or not Cage should appear in the film; his character was so dopey and affected in his previous movie, *Peggy Sue Gets Married*, that Jewison wasn't at all sure he would be convincing as the complex character of Ronny. Cher held out for him because she believed he was perfect for the part, an intuition based entirely on his work in *Peggy Sue*. Like the character he was to play in *Moonstruck*, Cage struck Cher as being a tormented soul; 'He was – is just so real,' she said later. Cage, who had just completed two other films, *Raising Arizona* and *Gardens of Stone*, was cast at practically the last minute.

Though she was fascinated by him – especially by his heavy-lidded ice-blue eyes, the most beautiful, she's said, that she's ever seen – he wasn't easy to work with; he acts alone, says Cher, and she just got to work alongside of him.

'Sometimes he was a blast on the set,' Cher told the *Los Angeles Times*, 'and sometimes I'd get real peeved at him. But every time I got angry with him, I'd just look into his eyes; in fact, I don't think I saw any other part of Nicky.'

The plot of *Moonstruck* features Loretta Castorini, a thirty-seven-year-old widowed bookkeeper, who hopes to mend the bad blood between her uninteresting fiancé, a mama's boy named Johnny Cammareri (Danny Aiello) and his younger brother Ronny by personally inviting him to their wedding. But, under the spell of a full moon, she ends up falling hard and fast for Ronny, a brooding working-class dreamer, while Johnny is in Palermo at the bedside of his dying mother. This affair with Ronny stirs feelings within Loretta that she had not experienced since her first husband died after being run over by a bus; she unpins her prim hair-bun and falls into bed with him. The next day as she tries to pin the wild curls – and her life – back into place, Ronny professes his love to her. This can't be happening, she insists, 'This can't happen to me.' She fixes him with one of those impassive gazes that used to precede her television zingers to Sonny. She slaps him twice and retorts, '*Snap out of it!*'

'Her comic timing is natural and almost infallible,' observes director Jewison.

Loretta's dilemma mirrors that of her parents; her father Cosmo

(Vincent Gardenia) is trying to recover his lost youth by betraying her mother Rose (Olympia Dukakis) and having an affair with a floozy named Mona (Anita Gillette). Meanwhile, Rose flirts with a handsome, skirt-chasing professor (John Mahoney) from New York University.

There's a masterful make-over in a Brooklyn beauty shop and, in mid-story, Loretta Castorini is transformed into a radiant, beautiful woman ready for new life experiences. She and Ronny take in *La Bohème* at the Metropolitan Opera House and, on a freezing Brooklyn night, Ronny makes rhapsodic speeches about his all-consuming passion for her ('Love don't make things nice, it ruins everything, it breaks your heart, it makes things a mess').

Though the central themes of *Moonstruck* are betrayal and the reasons why men chase after women, at the core of the film is a strong, old-fashioned family structure. No matter how it seems to weaken as the plot progresses and the romance between Loretta and Ronny builds — loyalties and secrets collide over breakfast one morning at the Castorini table — in the end the family structure is as strong as ever.

'The people really loved each other and looked like they could be together for the rest of their lives,' Cher muses dreamily about the Castorinis. 'It's a little bit naive; a little bit simplistic.' The movie is low-budget, very subtle and European in tone. Julie Bovasso, who played Loretta's Aunt Rita Cappomaggi, was dialect coach on the film, with the responsibility of teaching the cast how to perfect the Brooklynese in their language. Cher and Olympia Dukakis were both nervous about how to approach the East Coast accent; for two weeks Bovasso could hardly get Cher to open her mouth. Eventually, though, Cher picked up the accent, says Bovasso, 'with a musician's ear'. (Bovasso performed similar duties for John Huston on *Prizzi's Honour*.)

The movie, which ends happily, was critically praised for its excellent ensemble cast performances and story line; writer John Patrick Shanley is a first generation Irish-American from the Bronx who has, obviously, an intimate knowledge of Italian-Americans. The film was wrapped in February, the day before Valentine's Day, on Friday the thirteenth, 1987. The moon was full. In a scene shot that night, eighty-two-year-old Feodor Chaliapin, who played Loretta's paternal grandfather, is asked by some elderly friends, 'Did you see the moon last night?'

Smiling, he replied simply, '*Si, la bella luna!* The moon brings the woman to the man.'

How ironic that *Newsweek*, in a cover story on Cher, said that *Moonstruck* 'may not be a brilliant career move'.

Cher had only five days off after completing *Moonstruck* before she was set to begin rehearsals for *Suspect*; filming in Washington, DC, began on Friday, 27 February 1987.

Her life had been such a whirlwind lately that one day she realized that Rob still hadn't seen her exotic home in Los Angeles. 'If we're ever gonna do that, we'd better do it now,' she decided. The two caught a plane from New York to the West Coast; they spent just four hours at the house and while there Rob presented her with a first-anniversary gift – an Akita puppy which probably set him back $2,500 . . . that's a lot of bagels. Then it was back to Manhattan for Rob, and on to Washington for Cher.

In *Suspect*, Cher as Kathleen Riley, a tough, no-nonsense and over-worked public defender, gets involved in a complex case that forces her to break the law and work with a juror (Dennis Quaid) outside the courtroom. The two uncover evidence on high government officials in order to defend a deaf, mute and homeless client on a murder charge.

Cher liked the script when she first read it, even though she was intimidated by the story line because she knew nothing about the law. She couldn't help but feel very distant – in terms of education and background – from the woman she was portraying in the film.

To prepare for the role, she spent time in the Public Defender's Office in Washington DC, where the movie takes place. She sat in on a murder trial and went to jail to spend time with convicts. Learning the complicated legal jargon in the script was particularly difficult for her because of her dyslexia. 'But she has a wonderful memory,' director Peter Yates told reporter Jan Hoffman. 'I'm dyslexic too, and I understand the enormous compensation that goes with it. When you play in a courtroom drama, you have very long scenes. When other actors blow it, they typically blame the lighting, their costume, whatever. When she blew it, she'd just scream, "Come on, Cher! What the hell do you think you're doing?"'

The film didn't turn out quite the way Cher had hoped it would – some of her best scenes ended up on the so-called cutting-room floor. Cher excised a sex scene herself because she didn't feel it was appropriate, especially after doing her research and meeting real female defence attorneys. 'I spent time with these women,' she told writer Harlan Jacobson, 'and learned that they don't have a life. They kill themselves doing this and I felt that [in the movie] we didn't show any of that.'

She and Yates disagreed over some aspects of the story line and about her character's background but, in all, she considers *Suspect* a valuable working experience. Cher says that co-star Dennis Quaid was fun to work with; she equates him to the younger brother 'you love but who's a pain in the ass'. He would come to her dressing trailer and boast, 'I've got Chinese food in my trailer – and you're not invited.' Her nickname for Quaid was 'Scum'. 'I don't know why,' she laughs. 'Because he's so charming and all the women were crazy about him. Maybe that's why . . . .'

The romance between Cher and Robert hasn't been a simple one; there has been strain and a certain amount of confusion, as should be expected when a young man who's accustomed to a normal private life suddenly finds himself on a 'worst dressed list', and when he becomes sneeringly known as 'Cher's bagel-boy lover' in virtually every media story. Cher's assistant and close friend, Paulette Bettes, describes Robert as 'a no-nonsense, Lord of Flatbush kind of guy. He's not a wuss.' Sometimes, when Robert needed moments away from the high-glitz life of Cher, he would put on his punky black leather jacket, skintight black pants and matching leather boots with spikes; he would then walk from the Morgan Hotel to the nearby subway station, and go back to the predominantly Italian section of Queens where he was raised, where he lived on a knife's edge in a tough neighbourhood. But he must know that his life has changed, that he's light years from Queens now – or, as a buddy once told him, 'Robby, baby, you're in *heaven* now!'

There have been times, though, when 'heaven' has resembled hell for Rob Camilletti as he clumsily navigated the right of passage into celebrity-hood. In July 1988, he was arrested after he allegedly tried to run over a freelance photographer from *Star* magazine who had been staking out Cher's Los Angeles home amid persistent rumours that the two were about to marry.

After ramming photographer Phil Brandt's parked Honda with Cher's $87,000 Ferrari, Rob jumped out of the Ferrari and charged towards Brandt shouting, 'I'm gonna kill you. I'm gonna kill you!' as he chased him down the street outside Cher's home.

'Rob Camilletti tried to run me down for taking a dumb snapshot,' said Brandt later. 'Then the first words out of his mouth were "I'm going to kill you!" I believed he was going to do me in. I was never so scared in my life. He turned into a maniac.' Brandt added, 'Sean Penn threw rocks at me, but no one has ever tried to really injure me.'

Unfortunately for Rob, an unmarked police car with a detective sheriff inside was patrolling the area. Brandt flagged down the officer. He was cuffing the fuming Camilletti when Cher came running out of her house in hysterics. 'What are you doing?' she screamed at the police officer. 'Where are you taking him?'

Then she turned to the photographer and shouted, 'You scum! You people will do anything for money!'

Rob was charged with assault with a deadly weapon; he was searched, photographed, fingerprinted and thrown into a cell full of Los Angeles gang members. Cher posted $2,000 to bail him out that same afternoon. Though she's used to having her privacy invaded, she was livid about what had happened in front of her home that morning. 'These people can scare my children,' she said of press photographers. 'They can say all the things that they say and then they can cause stuff like this to happen. I have people who are camped out at my house, who are going through my garbage, who are calling my telephone . . . I feel like we're in a bullfight being taunted. . . .'

'I tell you what I'd really like to do,' she said later. 'I'd like to be able to have the right, the legal right, to take a gun and *shoot* these journalists and photographers. I'm really a fine, loving person and a dedicated actress who wants to work hard and do good films. But, goddamn it, I also want to be able to step out of my house and not be tackled by some idiot creep with a camera. There's no escape from these sleazy people with their noses up our behinds all the time. It's hell living like this. . . .'

It was said that Cher and Robert disagreed on the way he handled the situation with the photographer. 'Why couldn't you just have ignored the guy?' Cher was said to have asked him at the police station. 'Since when are you such a hothead?' After the altercation, reporters started predicting a separation. 'Cher really thought Rob was cooler than that,' says a friend. 'He's never been one to go off like that, and what happened scared Cher. She wondered if she really knew him as much as she thought she did. He tried to explain that he was just sick of being pestered by the press, something she has just accepted as part of her life.'

The next day, Cher rented Rob a black $72,000 BMW 735 automobile that cost her $2,850 a month while the Ferrari was in the repair shop. It's said that for his Christmas present in 1988, Cher gave Rob a $135,000 Testarossa sports car.

After *Suspect*, Cher recorded her first album in five years for Geffen Records. 'It's so bizarre,' she said. 'I couldn't become an actress for five years because I was a singer. Now everyone is worried people aren't going to accept me as a singer because I'm an actress.' The album included a re-make of the Sonny and Cher classic, 'Bang Bang (My Baby Shot Me Down)', produced by Jon Bon Jovi (who Cher had met seven years earlier when she was recording an album at New York Power Station and he was a janitor there).

When he met Cher, Camilletti was studying acting with Stella Adler, a respected theatre coach in Manhattan. His ideas about acting and about his own career exhilarated Cher, and she wanted to do something to help him out. When she decided to use him in the video for 'I Found Someone' – the first she would ever direct – she met quite a deal of resistance from former boyfriend David

Geffen who owns the record company for which she records. Cher's concept was a strong one and there was much enthusiasm for the project from other executives at the label. But then one day Geffen called to tell her, 'Listen, you can't direct this thing, and your boyfriend can't be in it. That's that.'

'What? What are you talking about?' Cher answered, and now she was beginning to steam. She was sitting at her kitchen window, tears of anger streaming down her face. David didn't trust her directorial instincts and wanted her to work with a director she didn't like; that was one problem. But why pick on Rob when he could obviously see that she was trying to give him a break in show business? Was he jealous of the relationship?

'Because if you use Robert people will fixate on that and think you're not serious about your work,' Geffen tried to explain.

She argued that if the idea of using a live-in mate in a video didn't appeal to music fans, 'Billy Joel wouldn't have used Christie Brinkley and Belinda Carlisle wouldn't have used her boyfriend . . .' and, she recalled later, 'I started to name off a million people who used the people they live with.'

Geffen's mind was made up.

'It might work for everyone else,' he decided, 'but it won't work for you. We won't give you the $175,000 and you can't do the video. So make up your mind.'

He hung up.

'What a prick!' she decided.

Cher thought about the dilemma for a few hours and the more she went over it, the angrier she became. How ironic that David Geffen was once Cher's equal in ambition and one of the first people to encourage her to assert her independence years ago when she was trying to leave Sonny. And now he was proving to be a narrow-minded foe who didn't trust her or her wilful ideas. She decided on a strategy: she telephoned Don Wildman, one of the owners of the Health and Tennis club for whom she does spa commercials, with a proposition. If he would finance her video, she would, in return, allow him to use parts of it to advertise his spas. 'I can't promise you a hit record, but you'll have the most interesting commercial you ever had,' she said. Wildman bought the idea; and when the single was released, she shoved a hit record *and* a hit video down David Geffen's throat.

'Women have to harness their power – it's absolutely true,' she explained later to a *Cosmopolitan* magazine reporter. 'It's just learning not to take the first no. And if you can't go straight ahead, you go around the corner. That's what I would like women to get from me, nothing else.'

Cher lives in New York now – she and Robert had been staying in a rented eight-hundred-dollar-a-night, beautifully decorated two-level penthouse at the Morgan Hotel until Cher's new three-million-dollar Greenwich Village triplex home was remodelled to her precise specifications. Her neighbours at the condo include Rolling Stone Keith Richard. According to *The New York Times*, Cher's salary was a million dollars each for *Suspect* and *Moonstruck*, so she can well afford the glamour of the Italian top-of-the-line toilets she insists on in her homes.

In December 1988, Cher sold the seven-million-dollar Egyptian-style house in Los Angeles she had built eight years before – seven bedrooms and seven baths, ten fireplaces and fifteen thousand square feet of opulence on four acres – to actor Eddie Murphy.

The Witches of Eastwick and *Suspect* were both well-received by critics and ticket-buyers alike when they were released in June and October 1987 respectively, but *Moonstruck* (released the agreed two months after *Suspect*) became *the* holiday movie of the 1987–88 season; Cher was praised for her work and became a leading contender in the Oscar competition. After *Moonstruck*, she also became the subject of great scrutiny regarding the amount of cosmetic surgery she's had, and how much money she's spent in having it done. The truth is she's had a $4,200 nose job, and her breasts have been lifted three times – in 1969, 1979 and 1983, at a cost of $15,700. She also had a $2,000 chemical peel in 1981 to remove signs of acne after an allergic reaction to make-up while filming *Silkwood*. Her teeth have been filed and capped. There was a report that she had two of her ribs removed to make her waist smaller, which infuriated her because it's not true. Also, contrary to some reports, she's never had any surgery on her hips or buttocks.

As difficult as it is to believe, considering the memory of that little girl who used to toddle out with Sonny and Cher at the end of their programme, Chastity is now a twenty-year-old film student at New York University. A songwriter and singer, she recently performed with Sonny in a Palm Springs 'Oldies' concert with The Mamas and Papas and Donovan; they performed some of Sonny and Cher's hits. As to whether or not she will have a show business career, Chastity is understandably ambivalent considering what she's witnessed of her mother's; to her, the price of fame is too high. 'I'm scared to death of having everyone know what's going on in my life,' she says. '. . . of being really *known*.'

Chastity is now about the same age Cher was when 'SMB' was her personal catch phrase and the moon was made of Sonny Bono. But she seems infinitely more mature than Cher was at that age. Cher and Chastity couldn't have more different personalities; daughter has made it clear that she doesn't agree with many of mother's decisions. 'She has her life and I have mine. I've always accepted her the way she is, but we're different,' Chastity says, 'right down to the clothes we wear. She's extravagant, but I like to wear jeans and sweaters. I don't like to dress up. I'm not real showy.' Cher calls her 'Miss No Frills', but if all of the truth be told, Chastity does know the power of privilege even if she doesn't like to admit it. 'She wants our maid to come to her at NYU and wash her clothes and all that,' Cher has said. 'So she's got a lot to learn about the real deal.'

'Once in a while, their communications break down,' says Sonny of Chastity's relationship with her mother. 'I think it's tough on Chas, being the child of two celebrities, and extra tough on her being Cher's daughter because Cher is surrounded by so much glamour. If Chas doesn't feel a part of that world, it can be painful to her. Another thing that occurs between a mother and daughter is that, at a certain age, they become competitors. The daughter becomes a woman and they compete with each other. In some ways, I think that's going on between them.'

Twelve-year-old Elijah, a spitting image of his father Gregg Allman, attends a private boarding school on Long Island and returns home at weekends. His mother is tough on him, but she feels she has reason to be. Chastity always seemed to understand responsibility, almost as if by osmosis; she was always mature for her age – in fact, sometimes even more reasonable than her mother. But Elijah is a rebel who is, as far as Cher is concerned, just a little too much like his father for his own good. 'No homework, no guitar,' she tells him. 'And the deal with soda is two cans of sugar-free per week and that's take-it-or-leave-it. Next subject.'

'My son scares me because he's got two really, really strong sides to his personality,' she says, 'and one is as positive as the other is negative. He's as good as he is bad. I can do my best but, you know, he's his own person. I believe that you could sit home with your chidren twenty-four hours a day, and they could still go out and be the sniper in the bell tower at that school in Texas.'

If anything, the Cher of the Eighties has become a brilliant media manipulator. Perhaps she learned more from Sonny Bono than she realizes. In 1988, Cher was scheduled to appear on 'The David Letterman Show' to promote her movies and album. The first time she had appeared as his guest, Cher had called Letterman an asshole; the host likes confrontational television and, with Cher, you get what you ask for. Sonny was, at this time, running for mayor of Palm Springs, California. Though he seemed ill-prepared for the position he was, nonetheless, the odds-on favourite to win. Cher called to ask if he would like to appear on the programme with her, perhaps because she thought the appearance would boost his campaign, or maybe she just wanted to cause a sensation; whatever her motives, he accepted the invitation.

The show would mark the first time Cher had sung before a live audience in about six years. She performed a song from her latest album, in knee-high boots, open leather jacket and a lacy black G-string outfit, the back of which was cut away to reveal her back side with a flourish of multicoloured tattoos decorating it. As she sang her song facing the live audience, her posterior was facing Sonny Bono and David Letterman on the chat-panel. The symbolism – whether intended or not – seemed fairly obvious to some observers.

The reunion was a genuinely moving experience. Cher, obviously nervous and oddly still insecure in the presence of 'El Primo Bono', rattled on about the early days together, those years when their fans all thought they were so much in love. Sonny beamed, probably remembering a time when he would have done anything for her, when he was the little boy walking on a fence trying to impress the girl he loves. For the first time in over a decade, they sang 'I Got You Babe' together; his eyes were moist but hers weren't. She was determined that she would not cry.

It was just like it used to be – but then again, it wasn't. She had engineered this anxious heart-wrenching moment, this 'media event', by coaxing 'a man who represents a time when I had no power in my life' to appear on television with her once again . . . and who really knows why? Perhaps she felt a need to face him once and for all, but on her terms, and on her stage. Now, *she* was calling the shots. Certainly this bittersweet reunion must have signified to her a reaffirmation of what she's finally become: independent, in control, and her own woman, 'goddamn it!'

Later, Sonny would recall that, for the first time, he looked into Cher's eyes as they sang together, 'and I realized that I didn't know what she was thinking any more'.

Chastity, watching in the wings, squeezed the hand of a staff member and sobbed quietly as her parents buried once and for all this 'thing' her father had created called Sonny and Cher.

After the show, Cher ran in search of 'Mookie'. Robert had never met Sonny Bono before, though he had certainly heard quite a bit about him. With his arm around Cher's waist, he extended his hand out to Sonny who was with his fourth wife, the twenty-five-year-old Mary Whittaker. Camilletti towered over Bono. As Cher watched, the two men shook hands, studying each other carefully and probably wondering if this, too, was supposed to be some kind of a 'moment' engineered by the woman they had in common. Or was it just the awkward meeting of two perfect strangers – a fifty-two-year-old-man and a twenty-three-year-old 'whippersnapper' who really had nothing at all in common.

'He's sorta . . . nice,' Robert said of Sonny later.

'Yeah . . . I guess . . .' Cher responded absent-mindedly. She sighed wearily and, for a moment, leaned against her boyfriend with her eyes half-closed. Robert changed the subject, realizing that Cher was obviously not eager to discuss Sonny Bono.

Why get her started?

Cher and her handsome young man slipped into a waiting limousine and sped away towards home.

the academy award

Moonstruck was a much bigger success than anyone anticipated and when Cher was nominated for an Academy Award for her performance, no one was more shocked than she was. 'I can't believe this is happening,' she told her sister Georgeanne. 'I'm happy, you know, but I'm scared . . . what if I lose? How will I take it?'

'Listen,' her sister said, 'at least this time you're nominated!'

Everyone in Cher's family remembers only too well how hurt she was that she hadn't even been nominated for her work in *Mask*. Las Vegas bet-takers had had her neck and neck with Meryl Streep to win the award. 'If I don't get nominated, I'll just die,' she'd thought. But she wasn't nominated, and when that happened, the little girl in Cher surfaced as it usually does in times of crisis. 'Fuck them, then,' she decided. 'I'm not even going to the awards. I'll stay home and probably won't even watch them on TV. I'll lock myself in my bedroom. Who needs this?'

Georgia Holt had to admit that even she was surprised at her daughter's reaction, and she told her so. 'But I'm sick of it all,' Cher declared. 'I know all the talk: they don't like the way I dress, they don't like my choice in men, they think I'm too flamboyant, they don't think I'm serious,' she complained. 'And I am so goddamn sick of it all.'

Mask's producer Peter Bogdanovich surmises that the reason she was overlooked was because so much dirty linen about the film – and about his relationship with Cher – was aired in public. 'It had an adverse effect,' he explained, 'because the controversy became bigger than the film. I'm partly to blame, and Cher has to take the other part.'

Stanley Donen, the Academy Award ceremony's producer and father of Cher's boyfriend at the time, Josh, convinced her to attend the presentation: 'You have every right to be there. If you don't go, what will it prove? Nothing!'

At first, Cher was going to wear something simple and black, but, always a rebellious 'child' of the Sixties at heart, she decided to 'remind them what it was that they truly don't like about me'.

Cher's designer Bob Mackie recalls, 'She called me and said, "What can you put together for me to wear at the awards that will be so outrageous no one on this planet will believe it! I want it to be big, big, B-I-G!" My reaction was what it always is when Cher calls with such a request – which is quite often, I might add: "What time do you want to come in for the fitting and when do you need it finished?"'

Mackie's creation was an outrageous two-piece costume and headdress that *Cosmopolitan* called 'part outerspace and part Ziegfeld Follies'. It served to remind everyone of the cartoon Cher they hoped had disappeared long ago.

Josh Donen remembers: 'She had said to me, "Will it be okay with you whatever I wear?" And I never saw it until the moment to leave. She came out, and I thought, "What *is* this?" She was even wearing one brown contact lens and one blue one. The costume was all about protecting pain.'

'Of course, she didn't discuss her motivation with me,' Bob Mackie said. 'She didn't say "I want to stick it to 'em" and, to be honest, that never occurred to me. But if she wanted to make an impression, I'm happy to say she did. I think the photos of her and Don Ameche backstage are pretty hysterical!'

Geraldine Page, not Meryl Streep, won the Best Actress Oscar that year for her performance in *The Trip to Bountiful*. Cher had placed such a high price on that Oscar – which she soon realized had been unhealthy and unrealistic – that from that time on the award had less value for her.

Now she was nominated, and the competition was formidable: Glenn Close (*Fatal Attraction*), Holly Hunter (*Broadcast News*), Sally Kirkland (*Anna*) and her friend Meryl Street (with her seventh nomination out of fourteen movies, this one for *Ironweed*). She would say later that she never dreamed she would ever be competing with Meryl Streep. In all, *Moonstruck* garnered six nominations, including nominations for producer Norman Jewison, screenwriter John Patrick Shanley, and actors Olympia Dukakis and Vincent Gardenia in supporting categories.

She had won the Golden Globe award for Best Actress, but now that the Oscars were approaching she felt sure that she wouldn't win. Two days before the awards, Sonny telephoned her. She was surprised to hear from him and felt uncomfortable about it, almost as if she thought he could somehow jinx her chances just by calling.

'Cher, listen, you're *going* to win,' Sonny told her. 'I *want* you to win.'

She paused for a moment to let that sink in.

'You do, don't you, Son? You *want* me to win. I think you mean it, don't you?'

'I do, Cher. I really do,' Sonny answered sincerely.

'From your lips to God's ears,' Cher said.

'Don't be fooled by her "who gives a shit" attitude,' Sonny, the first on Cher's bandwagon to fame and fortune, would say later. 'Cher wanted that award badly. She knew that it would change her life and career – that it would make her an even bigger, more bankable star. I wanted her to win, I did. Listen, you have to respect Cher for what she's done; you gotta give her credit. I don't like all of the ways she went about it, but you gotta give her credit.'

As for Sonny, maybe Cher is beginning to work through some of that anger. 'I think that from the beginning, Sonny knew that he was the one who had to be the straight man through all of it, through everything,' she now says. 'And he never was deluded into thinking that he was the great singer or the great talent. But without him, I never would have walked out onto the stage. There would be no Cher without Sonny.' She could have added that without Cher there probably would not have been a Sonny.

'It's not always who wins or loses that causes the biggest commotion,' said *The Los Angeles Times*. 'Sometimes it's what Cher wears.' To the 1988 Academy Awards show, Cher wore a diaphanous Bob Mackie gown, with black sequins and beads draped down the front and back on see through net with a matching velvet cape. It was tasteful, but then again it wasn't. Jet black curls tumbled from a black beaded headdress. Robert was on one arm, Chastity on the other. Chastity took time away from her studies to be with her mother for the awards at the Shrine Auditorium in Los Angeles.

Never was the little girl in Cher any more visible than it was in her eyes when the list of nominees was read, her name was announced, and the camera panned to the longing expression on her face. It was, perhaps, the first time the world saw the real Cher – the Cher beneath layers of shooting-from-the-hip bravado, beneath the glitter and controversy, the child in Cher that is such a conspicuous feature of her character privately, but certainly not publicly. The stage was set for failure; if she didn't win, she would feel humiliated and choked with resentment, she knew that. In her humiliation, she also realized that she would have to work that indignant, leather-cutting tongue once again. Not caring, being completely unconcerned, not giving a damn, can be an exhausting business. That night, Cher felt that her life and career were on the line and, without realizing it, she revealed to the world a piece of herself she's always tried to hide. For that one moment, the look in her deep eyes registered a single, urgent thought: *'Please let it be me!'*

When Cher's name was announced as the winner, the huge audience of 6,000 stood and cheered her victory. The deafening sound of applause signified a moment of great recognition – and perhaps of sweet revenge and just desserts as well – that will no doubt change not only the public's perception of Cher, but also her perception of herself.

She stood before her peers and fans, before the world, and – as is typically Cher's style – first thanked her hairdresser and make-up person 'who had a lot to work with'. (Make no mistake about it, this is a woman who understands the importance of Hollywood illusion probably better than anyone in the audience that night.) She thanked Meryl Streep for teaching her so much about the art of acting. 'I knew nothing,' she admitted later to the press corps backstage.

'When I was little, my mother kept saying, "I want you to be something,"' Cher said carefully. 'And I guess [the award] represents 23 or 24 years of my work . . . and I never won anything from my peers before, so this means a great deal. I'm really, really happy.'

Olympia Dukakis and John Patrick Shanley also won Oscars that night. Later, backstage, Cher said to the press, 'I think that if I can win this statuette . . . anybody can do anything.' It was said that she felt guilty for becoming so nervous on stage and for forgetting to thank most of the people she'd planned to acknowledge. So that week, she purchased advertisements in the Hollywood trade publications to thank the members of the Motion Pictures Arts and Sciences for voting for her ('there are no words to express how grateful I am'). It's a game of sincere appreciation 'for letting me in' (or, as Sally Field would put it, 'You like me! You like me!') often played by Hollywood starlets. Cher, at least, has the good sense to be a team player, even though she surely must have some comments to make about the sport, privately. She also thanked some of the people from her past, including Robert Altman, Bob Mackie and 'Mike "I-picked-you-up-from-the-gutter" Nichols' (but, surprisingly – or maybe not so – not Sonny Bono), and then all of the cast of *Moonstruck* as well as Norman Jewison.

The next day, Sonny won the mayoral election in Palm Springs by a landslide. A week later, his wife gave birth to a son, Chesare Elan. He and Cher were as far apart in their lives now as they'd ever been. It seems sad – especially considering how charged the past is with poignant memories – yet somehow inevitable . . . and even a relief.

Cher has been one of the most famous, most admired and most trashed women in the world for the last twenty-five years. She has wrestled with life and done battle with herself – and with so many others – again and again, all of it under heavy public scrutiny. 'Failing in front of America is *so* hard,' she has complained. But now she is a creation of her own will. Certainly her Academy Award validates her as an actress, and as something much more than what Sonny Bono had intended for her. Her future in Hollywood is uncertain; the mecca of glamour and dreams promises nothing to any of its children. 'But Cher has . . . *something*,' her mother Georgia Holt insists. 'I don't know what it is. Maybe it's the ability to make people *feel*. And to do that, maybe you have to experience a lot of pain, like Cher has.' Holt believes that the reason Cher is so compelling on the screen is because of her sad side, the dark side. Perhaps that is also the reason for her specialness. 'I think it takes a lot of irritants to create a pearl,' Georgia concludes.

The night of the Oscars, as Cher stood on stage in Los Angeles holding her prize before her fans and peers – before those who have championed her life and career and those who have judged her harshly on both counts – she couldn't help but be moved. Indeed, she had come full circle, back to a time twenty-five years ago when it all didn't matter quite as much, when there wasn't so much exhausting urgency in her life, when 'failing in front of America' never even crossed her mind. When it was more fun.

Cher would later say that whatever happens in her life and career from this point on almost doesn't matter. 'I can breathe,' she says. 'I can finally take a deep breath.' Perhaps that's because the desperation that was so much a hallmark of her life was finally banished by that evening of victory; the days of proving herself are behind her. 'I don't think this means I am somebody,' she said of her award, tears welling up in her eyes. '. . . But, you know, I guess I'm on my way. . . .'

acknowledgements

Grateful acknowledgement is given to all of those who assisted me with this book in various tangible and intangible ways, including Harold Battiste, Snuff Garrett, Bob Esty, Freeman King, Kenny Sacha, Bob Mackie, Robert Altman, Joe Layton, Ted Wright, Stephen Bradford, Enda Wright, Darlene Love, 'The Fabulous Miss Velma', Mary Kay Robinson, Bob Johnston, Ronnie Spector, Val Johns and all of the other people who shared memories of their direct contact with Cher. Many others asked that they not be mentioned by name – for the first time in their careers, they've requested anonymity.

Nods to Art Fisher, Chris Bearde, Jeff Corey, Brian Stone, Charlie Greene and Joe deCarlo for keeping Sonny and Cher's motor running. Thanks to Rick Wilson for his amazing memory and loyalty to Cher; Jim Henkel for his help in obtaining rare Sonny and Cher tapes and records and for helping me sort out all of the statistical information regarding Cher's musical career; Steven Parish for supplying all of the video material so important to my research; Mayor Sonny Bono for his terrific sense of humour; Bono restaurant for the complimentary desserts; Gerald Gladney for my first big break with *Diana Ross*; and Carol Burnett and Mary Tyler Moore for the challenges.

Special thanks to the staff of the Academy of Motion Picture Arts and Sciences Library for their patience and understanding. Also, thanks to the staffs of the Lincoln Centre Library of the Performing Arts in New York, the American Film Institute, and the University of Southern California. Thanks also to all of the helpful clerical researchers at Los Angeles and Santa Monica Superior Court house for their assistance in sorting out many years of legal dramatics.

Thank you to the reviewers, journalists and reporters whose work about Cher provided other leads and dimensions, in particular: George Carpozi Jr, Vicki Pellegrino, Rowland Barber, Chris Hodenfield, Tom Burke, Brian Haugh, Leo Janos, Eugenie Ross-Leming, Bob Colacello, David Standish, Joseph Bell, James Bacon and Peter Bogdanovich.

For invaluable support, my gratitude to Al Kramer, Richard Tyler Jordan, Edward Jimenez, David Doolittle, George Solomon, André Pittmon, John Passantino, Linda DiStefano and Reginald Wilson.

Special thanks to James Perry, friend and manager, who secured the original contract for this book. And to my agent and friend Bart Andrews, who keeps me on the right track. Thanks for a job I'll never forget. And kudos to all of my new friends at Sidgwick & Jackson, including my editor, Karen Hurrell.

Thanks also to all of my family for support and encouragement: Rocco and Rose, Roslyn, Rocky, Rose Marie, Riddle and Rydell.

And to Cher: Give 'em hell, lady.

J. Randy Taraborrelli

June 1989

index